I used to be Irish

Also by Angeline Kearns Blain

Stealing Sunlight: Growing up in Irishtown
Tactical Textiles: A Genealogy of the Boise Peace Quilt Project

I used to be Irish

Leaving Ireland, becoming American

Angeline Kearns Blain

A. & A. Farmar

British Library Cataloguing in Publication Data
A CIP catalogue record for this book is available from the British Library

ISBN: 978-1-906353-05-6

First published in 2009
by
A. & A. Farmar Ltd
78 Ranelagh Village, Dublin 6, Ireland
Tel +353-1-496 3625 Fax +353-1-497 0107
Email afarmar@iol.ie

Printed and bound by GraphyCems
Typeset and designed by A. & A. Farmar
Cover designed by Kevin Gurry

Contents

Acknowledgements

I wish to offer my gratitude to Anna, Tony, and their daughter Katherine Farmar for editing my book with the greatest integrity, scholarship and friendship.

I want to express my deep appreciation to all of my friends who have supported and encouraged me in my work: Ariel and Ed McLuskie (who never turn a deaf ear to my stories), Lyn and Nick Lubamersky-Miller, Dick and Alicia Baker, Max and Katherine Pavesic, Gail Valentine, Mary Beth Connell, Judy and Martin Sheffer, Tony and Grace Walsh, my academic advisors (Professors Richard Baker, Sociology, and Todd Shallat and Phoebe Lundy, History) as well as valued colleagues and administrative staff at Boise State University, especially in the Department of Sociology.

A big thank you to my friends at the 'Women and Children's Association' Thrift Store, Boise, Idaho, who endeavour to make the world a better place to live.

Thanks to my husband, Michael Blain, for his solid advice and logistical support. I also want to acknowledge my son, Steve F. Lyon, for his support and Irish wit.

Angeline Kearns Blain
January 2009

To
The Beloved Mother
of Exiles —
The Statue of Liberty

Foreword

With earthy candour, Blain fearlessly explores the challenges of finding herself in a new land.

In search of the mythical American dream, which takes her across the USA, Blain tries on a variety of experiences, from working woman and new wife and mother, to university student and political activist.

She never shies away from confronting tough issues, such as segregation, expectations placed on women, loneliness and clinical depression.

Yet only when Blain confronts memories of her past of poverty in Dublin, and her true feelings about societal norms and the cultural upheavals in America in the 1960s and 1970s, can she define the future on her own terms.

With humour and honesty, Blain tells of her journey of discovery, both in America and within herself.

Dr Lisa McClain
Associate Professor of History and Director of Gender Studies
Boise State University.

Welcome to the United States of America

The four-engined Pan America clipper crammed with people leaving Ireland rumbled and bumbled down the runway like a drunken goose. Only God knew if the monster would be able to lift off and usher us up into the sky above. I clenched my eyes, crossed my legs, and hoped

*The kids on our balcony at George Reynolds House
who came to say goodbye before I left for the airport.*

not to wet my knickers like a nervous Nelly. The aircraft lifted off the ground and inched upwards as if pulled by a giant hand. I pried my eyes open to look out the window at the scene below and my heart missed a beat. I saw an exquisite landscape — verdant green fields crisscrossed with grey stone walls. I'd heard stories of a lovely Emerald Isle, but for all I'd seen of it the image below might as well have been China, Timbuktu or Down Mexico Way.

Had Da been leaning over my shoulder he would have commented, 'Titch, such beauty is wasted on the desert air.' Tears welled in my eyes at the thought that I came from such a beautiful land. I stifled my sniffles and thought, 'I don't care if I never see Ireland again.'

My urge to leave Ireland and emigrate to the United States began in the slums of Dublin in the 1940s. The Ireland of my childhood and young adulthood offered neither justice nor charity for families in need. For the first twelve years of my life, I didn't have the space of a frying pan to call my own.

Without Hollywood fairy tales life would have offered little in the horrible auld times. Westerns, referred to locally as 'bang-bangs', were shown week after week at the local picture houses. I collected discarded porter bottles along the gutters to sell for pennies at Ryan's pub to pay into the picture shows.

The *Home on the Range* films were about pioneering families moving west, jolly singing cowboys, showdowns between the US Cavalry and 'bloodthirsty Indians', and happy ranch wives who baked batches of biscuits.

I sighed deeply on seeing well-fed females stride along planked sidewalks carrying picnic baskets filled with chicken and fixings. I loved the parts that showed one drooling brown bear after another emerging from the backwoods, lured by the aroma of freshly-baked pies left on a window ledge to cool by a trusting housewife.

Going to see films about the American West became an addiction, but when a bang-bang ended, dirty Dublin reclaimed me, hunger and all.

In the 1940s and 1950s when I came of age, oppressive 'Brits' had long departed from Ireland. The English colonialists were replaced with Irish nationalists led by President Eamon de Valera and his gold-tasselled princes of the Roman Catholic Church who had contempt for the poor. While watching Roy Rogers on Trigger riding the plains,

I vowed to exit Ireland when I grew up and find a way to get to America. I kept such ideas to myself, not wanting to upset my mother who loved me dearly.

In 1950, when I was twelve, the slums in O'Brien's Place where I lived with my family, were condemned as being unfit for human habitation. We were relocated to one of the new blocks of flats, George Reynolds House, in Irishtown, a penny toss away from Sandymount Strand.

Our new home had indoor plumbing, hot and cold running water, a gas cooking stove, and — best of all — I didn't have to sleep with five other people farting and snoring not to mention having my sleep interrupted by one of my brothers calling out in the night, 'Buckle yr long legs — ye nearly kicked me in the balls again!'

We loved our new digs and had Da been employed, or either of my two older brothers been able to find work, we'd have swung on a star.

I quit school after Confirmation at age thirteen to work on the Irishtown dump collecting slivers of coke (used coal) to sell for a shilling a gunnysack to other poor people who used coke as fuel for the fire. The little bit of money I earned got our family through some bad times. At age fourteen I got a job as a factory girl in a knitwear factory in Upper Baggot Street that paid fourteen shillings a week. Factory girls were constantly laid off because factory owners never wanted to increase our wages. Instead the greedy-guts tossed us out without a second thought.

I worked at one job or another in factories across Dublin until at age fifteen I applied for a job as an ice-cream girl at the Regent Cinema in Blackrock. The job paid 19s 2d per week. I hawked ice-cream, candy, popcorn and cigarettes from a heavy tray carried over my shoulder inside a dark cinema from 2 p.m. until 10.30 p.m. six days a week. I stayed at the Regent until after my sixteenth birthday when I could no longer put up with the manager's sexual advances, his 'Okey-dokey' pawing all over me. The pointy-headed bastard thought he had me at his mercy until the afternoon I told him, in no uncertain terms, to singe the hair off his balls.

I got word that they were hiring ice-cream girls at the Theatre Royal in Dean Street, just off O'Connell Street in the city centre. I got the same pay as I earned at the Regent — minus the manhandling. I wondered if anything in Ireland would ever improve for working-class girls and their families. I dreaded the thought of selling ice-cream inside a picture house for the rest of my life. I began to hear the chatter of local people emigrating to other parts of the world to find a better life. The Irish government continued to ignore mass unemployment, forcing more and more people to emigrate. Their implicit message was 'Shut up or ship out.'

My feet got itchier and itchier to walk away from the land of my birth. I had dismal educational qualifications and no money in the

Myself and Noel, the assistant film projectionist, on the roof of the Regent Cinema, in Blackrock, Co. Dublin, 1956.

bank, but I had 'a way with me', as they say. At eighteen years old I began to realize girlhood lasted a short time. I needed to take a chance while dew moistened the bud.

Carmel, my best friend at work, and I took turns to look in the mirror to arrange ourselves for another day of selling inside the dark cinema.

'Been working inside for too long,' Carmel remarked, pinching her cheeks for a rosier look.

'We're Dublin ghosts,' I cracked back.

She passed me a tube of red lipstick and told me to rub some on my pale cheeks or sales would go down.

'Time for us to march up and down the aisles for another eight hours. I hate this feckin' job. It's like being in a coal cellar,' I raged, not caring if we were overheard by our supervisor.

Carmel and I began to talk seriously of leaving Ireland. For damn sure we would never go to Trinity College, or Oxford or Cambridge, or even get a look inside an office. We preferred to emigrate to the United States over anywhere else, hopefully to Beverly Hills in California, where the sun always shone and oranges hung low from fragrant boughs. We had no desire to get married in Ireland. Who could relish life against the wall, having bushels of babies with little to feed them, and fading by age thirty into paper roses, like our mothers? We had had it up to our chins with the Catholic clergy's incessant condemnation of birth control and abortion. 'None of their beeswax,' we concluded.

The zillions of snippets from Hollywood films that I'd seen over the years began to take on a new meaning. Attractive young females in most of the films found it easier to catch a husband with a job than plainer types. As ice-cream girls we were aware of being somewhat attractive otherwise we would not have been hired. Because of her beauty, Carmel sold more ice-cream tubs, popcorn, Cadbury's chocolate bars, orangeade drinks, packs of Player's or Sweet Avon cigarettes, boxes of Black Magic chocolates than any of the other salesgirls, including myself.

'Let's be Yank chasers,' Carmel challenged.

More and more American men were strolling along O'Connell Street in the heart of Dublin, handsome GIs on leave from US military bases scattered around Europe. We got winks and smiles from some of the Yanks as we passed them on the street on our way to work. We did not stop to say hello to the Americans, being aware that young Irish women who flirted with foreign men were viewed with contempt. To be seen talking or walking with a Yank in uniform could get a girl a reputation as a flirt or a prostitute. The young woman would be seen as bringing shame to the good name of her family; even worse would be having neighbours talking about someone's daughter or someone's sister. I decided to risk the wrath of others to find a better life.

We heard accounts of young English, French, and German women who married Yanks by the boatload. Why could we not join the ranks? What had we to lose? As my father would say, 'Better to die in the sun than the shade.' I seldom took that drunkard's advice, but maybe there was something to it this time.

'I'll find an American GI first,' said Carmel.

'I hope we don't cut each other's throat over who finds a Yank first,' I replied.

'Race is on!' she cried.

We heard from a couple of streetwalkers that the GIs preferred Irish girls who were not as outspoken as the women back home in the States, who acted like men.

'It's auld blarney Yanks are interested in,' remarked seasoned chasers.

'If it's auld blarney they want, auld blarney they'll get,' said Carmel.

'Jaysus,' I said, 'we'll mimic Maureen O'Hara in *The Quiet Man*. But we won't be dragged through a sodden field the way the Yank dragged Maureen.' 'Like a sack of potatoes,' agreed Carmel. Pretending to be rustic innocents from a heather-scented hill would be a tough act for a pair of streetwise Dublin 'young wans' who knew their one-and-ones.

After finishing work, Carmel and I sauntered over in the direction of O'Connell Street, the most beautiful street in Dublin, to trawl.

'I'm hungry,' moaned Carmel as we strolled along.

'Me too,' I replied, hearing gurgles in my belly.

'No bleedin' tips today,' Carmel said.

'None here either. People don't like the picture this week. They take it out on us, not givin' us a feckin' penny for a tip,' I said. We both stretched out a hand to feel the drizzle of rain about to curtain the city. We began to sing an alternative version of 'Molly Malone'.

> *'In Dublin's Fair City*
> *Where the girls are so shitty*
> *I first laid me eyes on*
> *Sweet Molly Malone . . .'*

We stopped outside the Green Rooster, a fancy restaurant, to look in the window. A scrumptious golden-brown chicken lay in the middle of a silver tray surrounded by flowery green parsley and clumps of velvety purple grapes.

'It says "roasted chicken" right on the card in front of the tray,' said Carmel.

'I'd eat and swallow that whole thing in two bites,' I replied. 'What holds us back from smashing that pane of glass and grabbing and eating the chicken?'

'We're Catholics, that's why,' Carmel said. 'Let's get away from this window before I forget I'm a Catholic.'

We headed back down O'Connell Street in the direction of Trinity College, linking arms. Although hungry as bears, we liked being young Dubliners.

Carmel spotted the movie-handsome GI standing at the bus stop in

*Taken by a Yank in Dublin in
1956 who took me for an Irish
colleen. He sent me a copy of the
photo.*

D'Olier Street, apparently waiting for a bus. We crossed the street to
make his acquaintance.

'Nice night. Waiting for a bus. Lovely Irish night — misty and magical,' was how Carmel introduced us to the Yank.

He looked at us, bewildered, not knowing if we were whores, pick-
pockets or Irish villains. I knew Carmel fancied the Yank for herself
as she acted like a will o' the wisp swinging her long black curls from
shoulder to shoulder like sausages. The Yank had a look of pure con-
centration on his face while she yakked a mile a minute about the
complexities of Irish weather, like the forecaster on Radio Éireann. I
prayed to God she didn't plan on providing him with an account of
Ireland's livestock (also given to listeners on Radio Éireann). What if
she started saying a decade of the Rosary to hold his attention? He'd
hail a taxi. I rolled my eyes at Carmel hinting that she'd mouthed off
enough to the stranger for one night. From the look on his handsome
face, Carmel might as well have been yakking backwards.

She gave me our signal to 'buzz off' that very minute and leave
her alone with the American causing me to jump in and say, 'I could

take you up to Clery's where you could get your bus in less time than at this stop.' He smiled, still gripping the strap of his camera, 'I'm doing fine, ladies,' he said, sizing us up like halves of a broken saucer. 'Only trying to offer you an Irish welcome,' I said.

The American's eyes found mine. Bingo. I fell in love on the spot. Carmel, not blind to the encounter, drew up to my back and whispered in my ear, 'Buzz off this very minute.' It's a good thing machine guns were outlawed in Ireland. She came even closer and edged a sharp pointed elbow into the small of my back while saying into my ear, 'You feckin, feckin little bitch.' With that, she flattened back her ears like a lioness and redoubled her claim on the Yank. I stood my ground. I assured him once more that I would be more than glad to walk with him to Clery's to catch his bus.

'I assure you, ladies, I can take care of things,' he smiled sizing us up. His eyes again found mine and caused my heart to pitter pat like heavy rain on the gutter. I prayed the bus he waited for would blow a tyre or that the driver would get distracted in some pub in O'Connell Street. The American stepped to my side, and bid a good night to Carmel.

Carmel looked at us both before stomping off in her spiked high-heeled shoes leaving a trail of zigzag half-moons in her wake on the damp pavement. My heart ached on seeing her figure fade from sight knowing our friendship had ended over the stranger.

The pilot directed the plane towards the wide Atlantic Ocean, and honest to God, I thought we were headed into the foaming innards of some old king's head.

I turned my attention to the sounds and sights of the passengers on the aircraft arranging and rearranging themselves in their seats for the long journey. I found myself in the only single seat on the airplane. Being alone made my brain bounce back and forth like a ping-pong ball, pondering one event after another. As the evening light diminished outside, one tiny star after another filled the sky. The moon appeared full-faced. I felt bereft.

My mother and I had loved looking at the night sky over Irishtown. She believed the moon had been set in the sky by God for people to ponder. The sight of the same moon hundreds of miles from Irishtown caused me pain at the thought of having left my mother in tears.

I berated myself for being a selfish little bitch, putting my desires and dreams ahead of my family. My mother, worn down to a hang-

Leaving for America: with my family at Dublin airport 1957.
From left: my brother Bob, Ma, myself, Da, Frank and his wife Bridie;
in front, my brother Noely is holding Frank and Bridie's baby. The boy
on the left is from the flats—he begged to come with us to the airport.

nail, loved me like a treasure. Why couldn't I settle for being a girl from the gutter, undeserving of any opportunity? Why not accept life under de Valera and be willing to be ground to the dirt? Would 1957 be a banner year for 'young wans' like myself, getting out of Ireland one way or another?

A flight attendant came down the aisle passing out complimentary packs of American cigarettes and books of matches. I held out both hands. The Pall Malls, Camels and Lucky Strikes offered me a chance to smoke my way out of one existence and into another. While chain smoking, I thought about the story my mother had told me about members of her family who went to the United States due to want and woe or dodging bullets. They stopped writing back home for reasons unknown. Her family, the Kanes, from the Royal County of Meath, splintered long ago due to emigration. My leaving for the States stirred up Ma's recollections. I'd not heard before of any relative taking the boat to America, though my mother's brother, my uncle Robert O'Connor, had gone to England to find work. When she was fourteen years old, Ma's mother, Catherine Kane O'Connor, got the opportunity to emigrate with relatives to America, but she packed her bags to go to Dublin. She found a job as a servant girl for four shillings pay twice a month, plus room and board. If the young Catherine fell behind in her chores, her Catholic mistress belted her in the face.

'I might have been born in America,' my mother remarked. Her mother told her years later that she regretted not going to America. I asked Ma why she hadn't mentioned this history before now.

'Emigration is like dying, and I didn't want to put any ideas in your head that might lead you to leave Ireland.'

I avoided meeting her eyes.

'Angeline, it's hard for me letting ye go so far away, you me only girl.' I remained mute.

'Your daddy and me be split in two. If only we had a future to offer ye, but we have nothin.'

In order to move the conversation away from me leaving her, I asked how long it took long lost relatives to get to America.

'It took six weeks to sail from Cobh, in County Cork to New York harbour. Wimmin, your granny's cousins, made batches of "hard-tack" bread, some called them "sea biscuits", to take with them on the long sea journey. Hardtack didn't go mouldy the way shop-bought bread did.'

'It's 1957, Ma. Airplanes can fly from Shannon Airport to New York in ten to twelve hours, and they serve food to the passengers.'

'Still, it's not a bad thing to know about hardtack. Remember, love, there's many the slip between a cup and the lip.'

'I won't be gone with the wind, Ma. Soon as I set foot in New York, I'll wire home a telegraph letting ye know if Eddie showed up.'

'God forbid he'd not show up, don't talk like that,' she said, rubbing a tired hand across her forehead.

'He'll be there, Ma, sure as there's a God in heaven.'

'You're only eighteen and never set foot outside of Dublin.'

'The fat's in the fire, Ma. What else is there for me?' She nodded her head in agreement. To reassure her and myself, I repeated her lifelong advice to me:

'*Love many, trust few and always paddle your own canoe.* Ma I'm trying to paddle up a stream. I'll send you a fur coat from America, honest to God and hope to die.'

'I'd rather have yourself wrapped around me than any pelted coat from America.'

How can I leave my mother? What's up with me? How many sons and daughters unwillingly aimed the dagger of emigration into a parent's heart?

I finished the pack of Lucky Strikes and opened up the Pall Malls to puff while I continued to wool gather like a granny by her fireside instead of a young woman spinning future dreams. I went over in my mind all the bits and scraps of wisdom and advice injected into my skull over the years by Ma and Da.

My mind shifted gears in the direction of sex and how little my parents said on the matter. I had got the lowdown on the birds and the bees from older factory girls earlier on. My parents' advice good, bad or indifferent, translated into 'watch your step'.

Ma and Da liked and respected Eddie, my American soldier, believing God had led him into my path. Still, my mother wondered if I really knew my heart's desire at age eighteen.

'Are ye sure you love him? Only y'rself can know that.'

'I need to go, Ma. It's my one chance whether up or down . . . I love him and I'm fed up with de Valera's empty promises to make things better in Ireland.'

I found out later that my future husband had paid his visit to Ireland after reading a travel brochure on a bulletin board at the military base in West Germany.

'Who could resist an invitation to "Come to Ireland and meet a real Irish colleen"?' asked Eddie lovingly. Thank God the picture of the half-starved colleen along with the shaggy jackass was not the centre of attention on the brochure or Ed might have stayed in Germany and sent a care package to Ireland.

GIs had made it known to Carmel and me that they had not come to Ireland for the weather or to rediscover dead ancestors or study ancient chronicles or purchase bolts of hand-woven tweed, bumpy as boils, for a sports coat. Carmel and I got their drift and made it plain we were not 'flash girls' (prostitutes) but young women open to love and marriage with an American.

From childhood on, Irish daughters were warned to keep their hands on their little balls of yarn or suffer the consequences. 'Who wants to buy a cow if the milk is free?' echoed in the mind of daughters like a refrain. Auld ones who instilled the phrase in singsong voices had to be kidding if they thought you got free milk of any kind in de Valera's kingdom.

Ma blamed my desire to leave her and Ireland on my seeing too many Hollywood pictures. She arranged a small going-away party for me and invited everyone in George Reynolds flats. Friends and neighbours flooded my ears with farewell renditions of 'The Tennessee Waltz', 'Molly Malone' and the heart-blister 'Danny Boy', all ten versions of it. I blurted out after the last version that someone should make up a new version and call it 'Danny Girl'. From the looks on some of the faces you'd have thought that I'd said, 'Down with the Pope and up with the Queen'. Most of the hand-wringing about young people leaving the country related to the departure of young men and not young women. Young females who were leaving in droves would be lucky to get a wag of a snotrag as a goodbye gesture.

The film-star-lookalike stewardess strolled up and down the aisle telling passengers that our plane had entered turbulence over the North Atlantic, making the plane shake like a baby's rattle. 'Imagine you are flying through an ocean of clouds,' advised one of the stewardesses. Her attempt at reassurance did little to comfort Irish passengers ready to leap from the plane rather than be blown to smithereens. Expecting the plane to fall from the sky, I lit one Camel cigarette after another and, at one point smoked two together. I turned over a pack of cigarettes to read the advertising written on the back. Camel cigarettes were 'mild' and 'rich tasting' and 'never jangled the nerves'. I'd smoked the whole pack while waiting for the end to come.

I had heard sad tales of starving Irish emigrants who braved tumultuous seas in coffin ships only to end up drowning when some of the ships sank in the Atlantic. I knew airplanes could fall from the sky and fling passengers into a cold liquid grave at the bottom of the ocean. The rattle of Rosary beads got louder in the airplane, then the aircraft steadied itself out like a pencil resting on a school desk.

I noticed a number of Catholic nuns and priests on board our airplane and wondered why they were departing Ireland for what many of them viewed as the devil's playground. Some of the holy anointed had cast glances my way as they went to use the toilet close by. Such people would never expect a girl from my background to be on the way to marry an engineer — more likely, they would speculate I was on my way to America to unload my 'sin child' conceived outside marriage. Parish priests usually made such arrangements for young unmarried girls in their parish who fell from grace. Such men had a list of well-heeled Catholic families in the States who yearned for a 'wee one' out of Ireland rather than a 'wee one' ill conceived on American soil. We were aware that as soon as a sin child slid into the hands of foreigners, the mother would be sent back to Erin's green shore for further browbeating.

No matter the sweet temptation, my legs would remain nailed together until wedding bells had ceased chiming. I wondered why nuns and priests on the flight to America were interested in going there instead of emigrating to England, the 'bowels of hell', according to them. Surely rock'n roll didn't lure them to the US?

I loved rock 'n roll. Hopefully, the guy I intended to wed loved it too. It had never crossed my mind to discuss such things with him. I assumed all Yanks were happy-go-lucky and not like dunderheads who hated anything modern. I didn't discuss my musical tastes with Ed when he visited me in Dublin, assuming we shared our likes. Heaven forbid he would ever be stodgy.

It amazed me that Ed cared for me so much. His wanting me to be his wife was like a Lourdes miracle. I raised my hand in front of my face to admire the sapphire engagement ring he had lovingly put on my finger. He'd soon encircle the sapphire with a gold wedding band that would join us for life. In the meanwhile, it was time to rid myself of childhood fantasies of living in a mansion in Beverly Hills, being a Hollywood star, having four white-coiffed poodles tethered on red leather leashes yapping at my heels, and sleeping between pink silk sheets on a heart-shaped bed, while gentle breezes came into the room from French windows facing onto perfumed gardens of great delight.

'I'm from Puritan stock,' Ed had laughed while he was filling me in on his upbringing. Not knowing anything better, I haw-hawed back. He grew up in Aroostook County in the state of Maine which is as far north as one could get in Maine. His hometown of Presque Isle nestled close to the Saint John River Valley. My future mother-in-law's parents had emigrated from Scotland years ago to join a stern religious group in New Brunswick, Canada. Later, the family left Canada to live in Maine, across the border in the United States. Ed had a sober and studious way about him that I'd never encountered before, unlike my Da, the drunkard and storyteller. But in spite of having a serious nod towards life, Eddie courted as giddy as any merrymaker in a field of clover.

The airplane rocked and rolled under my feet on the way to the bathroom. It seemed ages before I could align my bum with the toilet. I'd no sooner made the connection than fierce suction attached itself to my naked bottom. I shouted out in fright, believing I'd be sucked arse-first into the bowels of the airplane and flushed down into the ocean below.

A hostess heard my shout for help and unlocked the bathroom door, 'Are you all right?'

'I'm stuck to the lav.'

'Wiggle back and forth. The suction will release.'

We were well into our journey when a stewardess announced to the passengers that the pilot had decided to make a refuelling stop at Gander Airport in Newfoundland, Canada, before heading on to New York City. The sudden announcement about landing in Canada drew lots of responses from nervous passengers:

'Tell the truth and shame the devil—something's wrong with the plane! It's a crash landing!'

'Have the engines run out?'

'The pilot forgot the map.'

My heart began to race as I wondered if the planeload of passengers, myself included, were at death's door. 'Angeline Brigid Kearns, you're about to meet your Maker.' I heard members of the clergy rattling their Rosary beads as our aircraft ducked in and out of pitch-black clouds like a needle in a haystack. After what seemed years the plane began to descend lower and lower in the heavens. The cabin crew continued to reassure the hysterical first-time Irish flyers. 'It's all routine.' We knew they were lying. I thought of my family in Irishtown while I waited for the explosion that would catapult me into God's hands. What if He fumbled? Could saying Hail Marys and Our Fathers at the speed of sound save me from the flames of hell? Would the swarms of voracious tiger sharks in the Atlantic eat my head off first or my legs?

We landed at Gander, Newfoundland, in drizzling rain. The cabin crew suggested that we all get off and go into the airport for refreshments until the plane had been refuelled. Gander airport seemed the same size as Shannon. The whole building was lit up with electric bulbs outside and in. After departing the plane, I followed the other passengers into the airport building. The majority placed a hand firmly on their backsides as they headed fast as they could to the nearest toilet. Myself, I headed to the lunch counter to buy a cup of tea.

I asked the waitress how much it cost for a cup of tea. She replied they only sold tea by the pot, and it cost 50 cents. I thanked her and smiled that I really didn't want tea after all. Having to pay 50 cents for a pot of tea would dip deeply into the two dollars that I'd earmarked to have when I arrived in America. Others around me didn't appear to share similar concerns; pots of tea were passed back and forth. I felt embarrassed that anyone might catch on that I hadn't the price of a pot of tea so I decided to go back outside. The soft drizzle of the rain felt cool and refreshing on my face.

Gasoline fumes filled the night air. Under the bright lights, I could see a swarm of people taking care of the plane on the ground. It would be an hour before passengers were allowed to go back on. I decided to take a walk to the farther side of the terminal to get away from the harsh lights and the overwhelming gasoline smell. An overarching sky above was ringed with green stars outlining a golden-faced moon. 'I'm alone in the world,' I thought to myself, 'in a completely strange setting in the wilds of Canada, and nobody knows where I am. My family in Dublin thinks I'm still in flight to New York, as does my husband to be. Instead, I'm alone in the universe separated from all kith and kin.' A great sense of freedom and a reckless sense of joy took hold of me. What if I strayed off by myself in the direction of Canada to discover the great unknown? I'd little fear of getting lost in Canada unlike the United States, a country that had gangsters and guns. I knew families in Irishtown who had a son or daughter emigrate to Canada and in letters home they only complained about the cold winters. But my sense of duty returned. While heading back to board the plane for New York, I felt regret at bidding goodbye to Gander, the bottle-green stars, and a languorous moon.

We were no sooner up in the air than breakfast appeared. I cleaned the plate and drank coffee by the cup. I rechecked to make sure my two dollar bills were safely balled in the bottom of my pocket. My two dollars were all the wealth I had which made me speculate what would happen if Eddie were not at the airport. What if he got cold feet? What if he had second thoughts about marrying a working-class girl from a Dublin public housing project, with little formal education, a Roman Catholic, a believer in omens and tea-leaves? To put such thoughts aside I repeated to myself: *Never worry worry till worry worries you, for if you worry worry you worry others too.* Thanks to my mother's teaching, repeating the silly billy rhyme restored my trust.

I fell into a blissful slumber until a stewardess wakened me.

'We're about to fly over New York City and I thought you'd want to see it.'

I looked out the window at the scene below, barely believing my own eyes. The plane began skimming and swaying over New York City. Down below, I could see piles of high buildings reaching up-wards like stiff fingers intent on poking out the eye of God. The plane felt as if it had stopped in its tracks as it coasted over the world's most famous landscape. I began to wonder if something had gone amiss, was it curtains for us all? The palms of my hands began to tingle, and my ears re-echoed the warning of Seán Cassidy. Cassidy disliked native-born girls linking up with Yanks instead of locals. He got wind of my going away to marry an American and halted me on the street so he could slag me off:

'If God intended people to fly He'd a stuck a fistful a feathers on their Irish arses, Miss Yankee Doodle Dandy.'

God forbid the plane would fall — and me without a feather.

The pilot's calm voice came over the intercom and invited the passengers to look down at the Statue of Liberty standing in New York Harbour. In order for us to get a better view, he dipped one side of the plane. Then he dipped the plane in the direction of the Empire State Building. Beads of sweat cascaded down my face; my innards hornpiped like a drunken sailor. Everything in front of my eyes be-gan to blur. I'd barely time to reach for the brown paper bag stashed in the back of the seat in front before I up-chucked breakfast. Up came the jelly doughnuts, orange juice, scrambled eggs and bacon, buttered bread, and countless cups of coffee.

When I raised my head once more to look out the window the airplane appeared to be heading for the crown on the Statue of Lib-erty like an arrow slung from a bow. I squeezed my eyes shut as the plane skimmed Liberty, and then, as if guided by God's hand, began its descent into the airport, shaking and spurting, inching up and dropping down until the wheels of the giant craft plunked onto the ground. 'Thanks be to God! I'll never set foot on another plane,' said a slew of passengers out loud. The enormous machine had delivered me to the New Land. 'I'm here! I'm here!' I said to no one in particu-lar. Due to the lack of sleep, smoking like a chimney, and all the rest, I knew I looked more like a banshee than a sweet young thing. At this point in the journey, who gave a toss? The stewardess opened the doors of the plane and the hottest blast of air I'd ever felt rushed in. As I exited the aircraft I didn't know whether to laugh, cry, step onto American soil, run or hide. Or head back home to my mother.

The area for new arrivals was completely sealed off from the visitors' section in the airport. We were told by the customs officials to follow them and have our passports in our hands. I collected my suitcase and headed towards the sign that read 'Customs Inspection' and waited in line. When my turn arrived, the customs officer gave me a quick eye-over and asked why I had come alone to the United States.

'I'm going to be married,' I explained.

He fingered my passport embossed with the golden Irish harp on the front cover. His eyes ran over my name, Angeline Brigid Catherine Kearns. He glanced back up and said,

'Welcome to the United States of America, Angie, glad to have ya. Hope ya enjoy your stay.'

I looked around to make sure it was me he was talking to. I'd never had such a warm embrace in Ireland of the Welcomes. I picked up my suitcase and headed for the visitors' section — but not before stopping to ponder my situation. A feeling of shyness and uncertainty fell over me. A customs official eyed my hesitancy; and that added extra jitters. Unless I calmed down, an imminent dose of diarrhoea might go off, and — God Almighty, where were the lavs? In order to calm myself, I re-checked the two dollar bills balled into the corners of my pockets. I scolded myself for acting like a gillygoose and a jackass. My lifelong dream was coming true. I was standing on American ground.

Noise cascaded from every corner of the visitors' section. People of every description were talking, calling out, haggling, gawking and waving their hands in the air like distressed sailors lost at sea. People from all over the Earth stood before my eyes. 'Jesus God in Heaven,' I muttered in a prayerful way, 'where am I?' I stopped in my tracks and stood still. A clear strong voice called out in my direction, 'Over here! Over here, angel!'

I turned in the direction of the voice and saw Ed waving a large bunch of red roses in the air to catch my eye. He rushed towards me and enfolded me like a Christmas present. 'Angel, honey, you're finally here!' I puckered my mouth to be kissed and the man nearly ate my face off. He took my hand in his and whirled me around. 'I can't wait for us to get married,' he sighed kissing me with even more force. I thought his show of love very charitable considering how I must look after the long journey, throwing up, and everything else. But as a song of the day exclaimed, 'Love is a Many Splendoured Thing'. Eddie picked up my suitcase and headed for the exit. I fell backwards from the blast of heat that hit my body. Eddie grasped my arm in time.

'Honey, I should have explained about how hot and humid it gets here during the summer.' Jesus, now he's telling me. 'You'll love it in New England during the fall and winter. I'll make you a snowman.'

'I hope I'll last till then.' The intense heat seemed to have no effect upon him, he looked as cool as water in a trickling stream.

'That's our automobile,' Ed excalimed in the parking lot. 'Kelly green — just your colour,' he said with pride. I should have admired the Kelly-green automobile more than I did, but the overhead blistering sun had reduced me to mush.

Ed arranged my suitcase in the trunk of the car. Sweat now ran down my legs like water. I hoped he would not mistake it for me peeing in my knickers. After arranging the suitcase here and there in the trunk of the car, making sure it fitted some assigned location, while I wanted to fire off 'Put the fucking thing anywhere, for Christ sake', Eddie said, 'I have a surprise for you. The car is air-conditioned.' I didn't understand what he meant but he turned on the engine and the air-conditioner and cool air filtered through the car. I lifted the bottom of my dress up to my knees and let the cool air drift up my timbers, thanking God for sending a bit of Irish-like breeze my way.

I asked Eddie if I could find a post office first thing as I needed to send a telegram right away to my parents who would be on pins and needles until receiving word that I had got to America safely. We found a post office and he sent the telegram off to Dublin, and we headed back on the highway.

'Where would you like to see first?'

Refreshed from the air conditioner, alert with excitement, and feeling adventurous, I replied without any hesitation:

'Manhattan, Broadway, Times Square, and the Statue of Liberty.' I carefully enunciated each well-known landmark.

'Honey, I don't think we should take a trip down to downtown New York. My close buddy parked his car in the city, and when he came back to the car the tyres, radio, and window wipers had been swiped.'

'Stolen,' I said, feeling disappointed. 'It's too hot, anyway,' I pointed out fanning my face.

'We'll get on the expressway and head for Connecticut, your new home.'

Ed had moved to Manchester, Connecticut, after graduating from a university in Maine with a degree in engineering. He got a job as an engineer in East Hartford, Connecticut, and rented a room in a rooming house in Manchester not too far from his workplace. Six months later he was drafted and sent overseas to a US military base in West Germany. After his time in the service, he resumed his job, moved out of the rented room in Manchester, and went to live in a rented house in Glastonbury, Connecticut, where he and I would live until we bought a home of our own. He had arranged with his former landlady for me to rent his old room until we got married.

Cars zoomed by on the expressway in both directions causing me to cover my eyes out of fear.

'It's fine, honey, automobiles are a large part of American life. Don't let it throw you for a loop.'

How could there be so many thousands of motorcars in the world, I wondered, and they must all be in America. Back in Dublin bicycles and buses outnumbered motorcars a hundred to one. I began to enjoy the speed of the car and the lovely breeze and coolness of the air conditioner, and especially the tunes coming from the car radio. Ed looked pleased at my settling down. We talked back and forth, kissed back and forth, while the car zoomed along the expressway until he ran a red light at a highway four way stop. 'Better pay more attention to my driving,' he said, obviously shaken.

'After a few days, I'm going to find a job,' I told him.

'No need for you to get a job, Angie.'

'I want to earn some money and send some home to help my family.'

He looked surprised. While visiting my family in Irishtown, he didn't catch on to all the scrimping going on under his nose. My mother made sure that he got the grub if he came to visit. Irish hospitality and Irish pride demanded no less for a visitor. Eddie asked if Da was still on the booze.

'Do ducks swim?' I said for an answer.

'Both my folks are teetotalers like me,' Eddie said. 'Most of my relatives abstain from booze. We're a clan of Methodists.'

'That must be a blessing,' I replied tentatively.

'Alcoholism is a serious disease, Angie. Is your dad aware of that?'

Da detested the word 'alcoholic', fuming that it had come into Irish use from America. The auld fella accepted being called a drunkard but not being called an alcoholic. I thought if Eddie had ever used Da's most hated word to his face, he and I would not be flying along in an automobile on an expressway bound for Manchester, Connecticut. Da would have told Eddie to pack his bags and leave his daughter be or else! 'More American hogwash!' he would have roared.

On a sweeter note, Ed asked about my mother.

'She keeps things going.'

'Your brothers, angel?'

'Frank married Bridie from Kilbride, Bob got a job on a coal boat, and Noely Joseph is making his Confirmation; soon after that he'll be looking for a factory job.'

'Your kid brother is too young to leave school!' exclaimed Ed.

'Most kids look for factory work after making their Confirmation. Families with money are able to send their kids to private secondary school. These kids get all the lily-white jobs where they never have to get a speck of dirt under a thumbnail. There's no work, no money, scarce food, lousy schools, and the whole island is overrun with priest and nuns poking their noses into everyone's business.'

'M'gosh, honey!' said Ed in disbelief.

'I wish a fairy godmother ruled Ireland instead of the curs in power who don't give a fiddler's fuck.'

'M' gosh, angel! I never heard you say such things before. Jumping catfish. Phooey! You must be upset from the long trip.'

His shocked reaction surprised me. Better to spout on about fairy talk, Celtic crosses, myths, legends and noble wolfhounds that never raise a hind-leg. I quickly reassured Ed that my crabby talk had to do with having had little sleep on the flight over from Shannon airport, a landing in Canada, and the excitement of being here at last in the greatest place on earth. Of course it's nicer to be in the company of a purring kitten than a mad heifer.

'I'd love a cup of tea, to clear my head,' I said.

'I'll pull off at the next Howard Johnson's exit, angel.'

'Jesus, he's so nice,' I said to myself.

'Is there something wrong, Angie? You're shifting in your seat quite a bit.'

'It's the smallpox vaccination. I need to shift my leg.'

Then I went into all the folderol I'd had to endure at the American embassy in Dublin before being issued a visa to enter the United States. Four cheeky buggers who interviewed me at the embassy asked me the most insulting questions, including:

'Have you ever worked as a prostitute? Ever been charged with a felony? Been in prison for a crime? Owned a gun now or ever owned a weapon? Have you now or ever been a member of an outlawed organization? Been a member of the Communist party? Do you intend to overthrow the elected government of the United States of America?'

I would have laughed, but they were dead serious, carefully writing down my replies.

'Sorry you had to go through so much to get here, angel,' remarked Eddie, 'but our government needs to be careful who they let into our country.'

'Funny! The government in Ireland do handstands in private when thousands leave the shore.'

'Neon lights ahead, honey, coming up to a Howard Johnson's.'

'You're nice to stop so than I can get a cup of tea. I can't wait to be your loving wife.'

'Fingers crossed,' I thought he said.

After stopping off for a break, we listened to the radio as we headed for Manchester. Patty Page sang 'Old Cape Cod' in that lovely way of hers. Her singing put me in a romantic mood. Suddenly, a highly excited voice interrupted the music with a flash warning about something the Soviet government had done or said, and how the United States had to defend the Free World. Alarmed by the announcer's tone, I asked Eddie what had happened to cause such a commotion. He asked if I knew of the threat of Communism, how the Soviet government wanted to take over the Free World. He went into scary detail until I said, 'They can take the hide and hair of the place I just left.' 'You don't understand the horrors of Communism, honey.' Feeling inferior, I nodded in agreement.

'We've only Catholics and a few Protestants in Ireland, no Communist in the bunch,' I answered as if knowing a thing or two. The music resumed on the radio, and Johnny Mathis sang 'The Twelfth of Never'. We tuned out the previous agitation and sang along.

I fell asleep and awoke to a soft tug on my arm and Ed's voice telling me we'd arrived at the boarding house in Manchester. Eddie half carried me to the front door of the house. He took out a key from the letterbox and opened the front door. Once inside, he turned on the light switch and we climbed up the stairs to my room on the top landing. The light spilled into my room and, instead of finding a silk and satin abode, my eyes were greeted by plain and sparse. I sat on the edge of the bed while Ed went back to get my suitcase out of the car. 'This isn't Hollywood. This isn't silk and satin,' I said to myself. I quickly bucked up, afraid my future husband might pick up on my disappointment. He showed me where the toilet and bathroom were located down the hallway, and the ins and outs of the plumbing. Overcome with emotion, I dug into my lip with my teeth to keep from crying. Eddie told me to have a good night's sleep and said he'd be over the next morning to visit me and to introduce me to my landlady, Mrs Anderson.

Being alone and far from Ireland and family made my heart ache like a stoned bird. This was the first time I'd ever slept alone in a bed. From the time of birth, I'd shared a bed with at least one other member of the family. In O'Brien's Place I shared the same bed with five others in the family until reaching the age of twelve. After we moved to the flats in Irishtown I shared a bed with my mother.

The next morning there was a sharp rap on my bedroom door and a voice telling me that I had a visitor. I looked at the face of the clock and read: 11.00 a.m. The woman's voice urged me to get out of bed at once.

'I'm getting right up,' I called through the door. 'A nice young man is waiting for you,' she called out. I headed for the bathroom, then put on my clean yellow dress with the white ribbons down the front. I went over to the mirror and dabbed my face with powder and brushed my lips with colour. I arranged my hair into a ponytail, shaped my brassiere into place and headed down the stairs.

Eddie stood at the bottom of the stairs smiling like the morning sun. He had on a white cotton shirt; khaki pants creased down the legs sharp as a knife, and burnished brown penny loafers. 'Mr America,' I said to myself with pride. 'Sleep well, honey?' he called out to me. I nodded, still half dazed from the long journey.

'Let's go meet your landlady, Mrs Anderson. She's in the living room. You two will get on fine. I know it.'

No person newly arrived from Holy Ireland would have anticipated the sight of Mrs Anderson as she came forward to meet me. She was decked out like a wood nymph from a stage pantomime: red shorts and a halter top, her neck lassoed with marble sized pearls, her big head crowned in blue ringlets. I'd never seen a half-naked granny. Out of shame, I cast my eyes downwards. She wound her long naked arms around my waist. I looked at her naked legs outlined in blue veins all the way down to her naked feet. When she gave me another squeeze, the front of her flimsy blouse separated down the middle showing her sandbag breasts. I could not look her in the eyes without thinking of our Saviour or the modest grannies back in Ireland who never showed any flesh other than their face and hands. 'She must be a pagan,' I thought, backing away from her out of fear for my life.

'Sit down, missy,' she ordered. 'Let me have a look see at you.'

I sat on the chair not knowing what to do with my eyes.

'You look as if you've seen a ghost,' she chuckled.

'She's had a long flight from Ireland to the States,' Ed said, giving me a funny look.

'Might be culture shock. Some get it right off the ship,' said the pagan, lighting up a cigarette.

'Here, drink this iced water,' she commanded.

I kept my eyes away from her naked skin by gazing up at her mop of curls like little Shirley Temple's. A hungry bunny might mistake her mop of ringlets for radishes and end up with hairballs stuck in its gullet. I sipped my glass of water, timid as a sparrow in front of a streetwise cat.

'This young man of yours is a wonderful American. Never late with rent, doesn't drink or smoke cigarettes, and attended church every Sunday while he roomed here.'

I nodded to the floor affirming Ed's qualities. The landlady turned to Eddie and told him in the most matter of fact voice: 'She's an it-bitty little thing. The Old Country written all over her face.'

I had the urge to tell her to shag off. I also had the urge to let her know that it was a good thing she did not live in Irishtown because any old woman who rigged herself out as she did would be carted off to the mad dogs' home. I wondered if there were any grannies in America.

The old bag of wind kept going on about me, 'Your brogue hasn't the guttural sound of some Irishmen I've heard.' 'Ah, go kiss me green Irish arse,' I whispered under my breath. She sat down opposite me and went into a long discussion about how her ancestors originally came from Sweden on the 'first load of bricks'. 'I can trace my ancestors back to King Olaf of Sweden,' she sighed.

Over a mug of freeze-dried coffee Mrs Anderson went over the rules of the house with me: ten dollars a week for rent with an occasional cup of instant coffee; no food or alcohol or men allowed in my room; her day began at sunrise. Next she beckoned me to follow her upstairs to instruct me in the use of the bathroom.

The spacious bathroom seemed as large as the room I had lived in for the first twelve years of my life. A huge bathtub stood in the middle, deep as a vat. The very thought of taking a bath in such a deep trench full of water made me shudder. The bathtub could hold myself, Maeve, Finn Mac Cool, Oisín, Cuchulain, and a wolfhound without any overflow.

'This is a canister of Bon Ami cleanser. Take this sponge in your hand like this and pour some of the powder from the canister onto the sponge and clean off the bath ring you left.'

'I'll do that,' I said. She shook her thatch of radishes in approval. 'Do you have indoor plumbing back in the Old Country?'

'Only what coal or turf heats up.'

'We all have hot and cold in the United States.'

She turned her attention to the closet hanging on the wall. I watched demurely as she opened the closet door. 'If you use anything out of this medicine cabinet mark it down and an extra dollar bill will be added to your rent.' The cabinet held an assortment of bottles, jars, small boxes and cans. 'Remember, write it down.' A feeling came over me that the landlady mistrusted me. I'd hardly turn myself into a robber over something from the closet on the bathroom wall. If I were to become a robber, it's the Crown Jewels of England I'd be nicking.

Downstairs, Eddie said, 'Angie, let's explore your new neighbourhood.' Wings couldn't lift me out of the old woman's sight fast enough. As we strolled around, Eddie asked what I thought of Mrs Anderson. I mumbled a reply not wishing to offend his good nature.

'She reminds me a heck of a lot of Mom. That independent spirit,' he said. I nearly fell over my feet.

I liked the old-fashioned Yankee neighbourhood composed of wood-built homes all painted black and white like penguins. Every house projected an American flag from some level of the façade like javelins at the ready. The red and blue colours waved and shimmered in the afternoon sunlight creating a festive look as if the circus was coming to town. Each house had a green lawn with grass cropped neat as sheared sheep. Large old trees stood tall along the sidewalk offering shade and beauty to the street. Ed, because of his love of the outdoors, noted the types of giants as we walked past them: ash, oak, chestnut, hickory and willow.

The New England neighbourhood brought to mind the Hollywood film *Little Women* that I'd seen over and over at the Regal in Ringsend. I expected to see Amy, Jo, Meg, little Beth, Marmee, Laurie and crotchety old Aunt Bess. I looked at Eddie beside me and thought him a ringer for Laurie, the young man Jo shifted off for a rumpled professor.

'You can see from the flags that Americans are a patriotic people.' As we continued our walk about the neighbourhood, the numbers of flags increased, their size ranging from handkerchief to bed sheet. The shifting patterns of red stripes on the flags fluttering in the gentle breeze reminded me of my upcoming date with Mother Nature and me without a rag or two safety pins to my name. I should have packed a few rags or a tea towel to use for my period, especially now, being in a new and unfamiliar place. I'd felt too embarrassed to share my pressing need with Eddie, having been reared in a country where such a topic would never be mentioned to a man, especially by an unmarried female. I'd been taught never to mention 'Eve's curse' in the presence of any male, young, old, blind, crippled or on the last leg.

Back in the house, I went up to my room and put on four pairs of cotton knickers one over another, and added one of the landlady's crochet doilies as extra protection, before heading back downstairs.

Manchester was more like a small town than a city. The main street had lots of shops, places to eat, and drugstores. That first day Eddie picked the nearest Moby Dick's as the place to eat lunch. He'd eaten there before. Moby Dick's had a reputation for serving the best clam chowder in New England along with tasty crab cakes. An aroma of simmering seafood greeted us inside. We were seated in one of the booths, and handed a menu by a young waitress. I ordered potato salad, coleslaw, New England baked beans, a bowl of New England chowder, and, for dessert, baked gingerbread topped with cream.

'Ever tasted iced tea, honey?' Ed asked?

'Never heard of it.'

'We have iced tea and hot tea in the USA,' he said.

'Like to try some with lemon?'

'I'll take the hot.'

The waitress returned with two steaming bowls and a basket of crusty oven-browned bread. 'Eat up,' she said. Yellow butter floated on top of the chowder like petals. I scooped my spoon into the thick chowder filled with chunks of smoked haddock, cod, and clams. 'Ready for the crab cakes?' asked the waitress. 'Yes, yes,' I mumbled, wondering if this could be all a dream. Eddie staved off the crab cakes saying the chowder and home-baked bread had been sufficient for him. What a glutton, Ed must have thought, watching me eat as if there was no tomorrow. 'Might as well be hung for a sheep as a lamb,' I told myself, scooping my finger into the mountain of cream topping the dessert, licking it off with bliss.

'Honey, I don't mean to be curious, but what do you weigh?'

'It says ninety-four pounds on my passport.'

His question surprised me. He had no idea how scarce food had been for families like mine who could not afford much. In 1957, in the Republic of Ireland, where food abounded, poor families in the hundreds went to bed hungry.

When Eddie went to Ireland on vacation, he did not notice such problems, seeing the abundance of food in all the shop windows. When he visited my family he got most of the food on hand. We would never tell him how bad things were. Irish people had too much pride. Even now in Moby Dick's, as he watched me polish off all the food, he would not realize he loved a hungry girl. Why did he concern himself with my weight? As for myself, better a roly poly than a brace of ribs. Better to die with a full belly than an empty one.

While finishing up my scrumptious meal I could not help wishing that I could send such food to feed Ma and Da back in Irishtown. My youngest brother Noely Joseph would have stuffed his gullet the same as I had he been there. Years earlier I had taken him with me to see a bang-bang and he had caused an uproar when he got out of his seat and ran up to the screen that showed people sitting down eating a fruit pie. 'I want `tum! I want `tum thing to eat!' he screamed.

Ed suggested that we take a ride over to look at our future home in Glastonbury, Connecticut. It became evident automobiles were the favourite way for people to travel in the States. Even old geezers, with a foot in the grave and the other on a banana peel, drove about in automobiles. 'Everyone owns a car. Driving is part of being an American,' Ed assured me as he sped along in his flying machine. 'You'll be driving soon, Angie. We'll get a second car after we get married.' He must be joking — me driving a car?

We drove through lovely country on our way to Glastonbury out in the hinterland of Connecticut. Ed noted that the hot humid summers in the area produced ideal conditions for growing tobacco. As we got further and further from civilization, twinges of apprehension set in. Now only an isolated farmhouse here and there dotted the landscape like sugar cubes sparkling in the hot sunlight. 'There, honey, that's the place I rented for us.' I looked around expecting to see a neighbourhood with streets and shops. 'That quaint farmhouse surrounded with those century-old trees in that field. That's going to be our love nest,' he said as if in a state of enchantment. How could he have thought a person born and bred in Dublin would take to such a void? 'It's wonderful, honey, just marvellous for the pair of us.' Ed parked the car, flung open the door on the driver's side and scooted over to let me out on the other side. We embraced and he held my hand as he threw the house keys in the air catching them with gusto as if they were the keys to paradise. Did he feel any limpness in my grip on his hand?

We walked along a cow path up to the front of the house. Ed unlocked the front door and pushed it. Inside I saw a rustic assemblage of lodge poles, twigs, roots, bulbous burls, branches, and chiselled tree trunks. Had I entered a grotto? Into a scene from the film, *The Song of Bernadette*? My eyes tried to adjust to the assemblage of tangled woods. 'Am I about to see a heavenly vision?' My mental bearings buckled.

'It's all Adirondack,' said a familiar voice. 'Adirondack everything: end tables, bookcases, a love seat, footstools, those hazel-seasoned rocking chairs, and our marriage bed.' My future mate mistook my dumb-foundedness for awe. He elbowed me into the bedroom where a four-poster bed on peeled logs stood sprouting from the floorboards with a headboard like a field hedge. 'I just knew you'd love rustic furnishings over modern any day,' he said. 'The Maine woods make up our love nest.' We fell down on the hard planked bed — good thing it had a fat horsehair mattress.

Young love swept away concerns about home furnishings for the rest of the afternoon. Although a firmly committed virgin until marriage, I had the passion of Scarlet O'Hara when it came to my future husband. Still, caution prevailed out of a lifetime of fear and bitter poverty. Having been told till the cows came home about the precious gift of virginity to a husband, the precious sliver of gristle remained intact. 'Don't dust yer eggs off with a hammer,' came to mind even in the depth of passion and desire. 'Spilled milk can never be put back in the bottle.' 'I know, that for Jeyes' Fluid sake.'

'Fiddlesticks, Angie, why wait until September to get married? Let's get married now!' Amid a tussle, I bumped my head on the back of the headboard, barely skimming the antlers. Tucking my blouse back inside my skirt, I headed to the kitchen to make some tea while feeling like an ungrateful bitch for handcuffing love's powerful urge.

'Where do you keep the tea things?' I called out, casting a disgruntled look around the rustic kitchen with its wood-stove. My young heart wanted factory-made everything not feckin' piles of brambles.

While we were away, Mrs Anderson had put a handkerchief-sized American flag on my bed. At first I thought it had fallen from heaven to be used in an emergency. I twisted the flag in my hand and thought about how some people loved their flags above all else. Da's love of the Irish tricolour mystified me, especially when his country did nothing for him or his family. He'd pledged his life to defend the flag — probably would have killed for it. Did he ever get into a scrimmage with the IRA? The outlawed army, in our old neck of the woods, got more respect than any Irish Free State soldier. If an IRA soldier died penniless they were not flung into a pauper's grave like a moulding cabbage, as my father would be on his death. Ma and Da's first-born son got buried in a pauper's ditch while Da soldiered in the Irish Free State Army. After years strung out, my mother still broke her heart over having had to bury her small son, with rosebud mouth, in a ditch.

While twirling the American flag, I vowed to send money home at the first chance for a gravesite for my family in Irishtown. Maybe it would not be so easy to toss away the flag of my birth without some regret? Maybe it would require serious reflection to replace one flag for another. Maybe it would be best to keep my hand on the latch for a while before exiting Ireland for citizenship in America.

I thanked my landlady for the flag when I saw her next day. She came to attention like a sergeant major and felt compelled to drill me in the rules of the flag:

'In these here United States of America, we respect our nation's flag. You must not let it touch the ground or let any flag fly above it,' she warned, waving the flag about like a meat cleaver. 'This is the flag of our freedom.'

I'd never in my eighteen years of life seen or heard such goings-on over a strip of cloth. When the Lord returns to reclaim the earth, He'd better hold in His hand the flag of the United States of America.

I went upstairs and into the bathroom to poke over all the stuff packed in the medicine cabinet. I discovered an assortment of concoctions unknown to Irish eyes.

There were tubes and bottles of shampoo for normal and dry hair (I thought there was only one kind of hair); bottles of mouthwash; toothpaste for real teeth and powder for false ones; foot powder and body powder; lotion for hands and cream for the face; cotton balls; headache powders; X-Lax; underarm deodorant; and a concoction called 'vaginal spray' meant to be squirted between a female's legs. I wondered what in the world it could be. After pondering the 'vagina' it dawned on me that the word meant the same thing as 'y'r little ball of yarn' or the more familiar 'cunt'. 'Vagina' had a sweet chime to it unlike the other names used. I wondered who had come up with such a perfect word for the thing beyond compare.

I examined the can of floral vaginal spray in the landlady's medicine chest. 'Keeps a woman Spring Fresh,' read the caption on the canister. The idea was to spray one's moss with flowering scent. I retained my ocean mild whiff. I went through the whole contents of the cabinet and could not believe the products meant to be rubbed or sprayed on every inch of the body. This Irish shamrock found it too bothersome to become a full-blown American rose.

A few days later, I noticed Mrs Anderson looking sadly out of the large window in the living room. She turned and asked if I wanted a cup of coffee. I nodded, yes. Mrs Anderson pointed to a coloured photograph perched on a cabinet and insisted I take a closer look at it. A tall thin young man in a military uniform looked out from the photograph as if the world were his oyster. In all earnestness I inquired, 'Is he a film star?'

'That's a picture of my son Harold. He got killed in the Korean War. Made his mother a "Gold Star" mother.'

How terrible that such a young and lovely looking man died in war. My heart went out to my landlady. Trying to be of some comfort, I told her about my grandfather Joseph O'Connor who served in the trenches during World War I, and how he barely made it back home to his family in Dublin. 'Half of one of his fingers is still in the trenches,' I told her. My mother, his daughter, told me that he had been gassed in the war and shivered like a leaf when he heard a noise. According to my mother, 'even the sound of a fly beating its wings sent him for cover under the bed.' My mother hated war. The landlady seemed interested in the war story.

'Are you one of those superstitious Irish people? The kind who can get in touch with those who passed on?'

'Are ye talking about dead people?'

'Well, are you?'

'Me mother says that only a veil separates the living from the dead and all ye have to do is draw back the veil and ye can knock heads again with the departed.'

She let out a thunderous laugh and blustered, 'You Irish are all alike — full of superstition.' You ungrateful auld whore, I wanted to scream, but I held it in. Instead I said, 'What I just told you about only a veil separating the living from the dead is no airy fairy nonsense, it's Gospel.' I felt like she'd slapped my mother in the face by her lack of respect for our ancient belief. Maybe the dead would be better off not being contacted by her, a half-naked know-it-all pagan imp.

'It's time for my favourite show on TV,' she said dismissively, turning on her heel. I looked into my cup of coffee trying to determine how much longer I'd be under the same roof with her.

I bounded up the stairs to my room, opened the window, and roared like hell into the chocolate coloured leaves of the maple outside the window.

Ed promised to bring a newspaper that listed job openings. I longed to find work so that I could send some money home to help my mother make ends meet. Although Eddie vouched he would pay all my expenses, I still wanted my own jingle in my pocket. While I waited, I could not help comparing him and Mrs Anderson to the people I knew in Dublin. These Americans talked in such plain language. They never went on excursions as people in Dublin did before getting to the point. Nor did either say 'me this' or 'me that' or 'this auld wan' or 'that auld wan'. Neither cracked a joke or, when annoyed with something, called out, 'ah, the fuck with it.' Seemingly, Americans were serious people and mainly laughed along with TV.

I heard the car drive up and stop. I went down to meet Ed and we sat in the garden beneath a draping willow tree. We went over the employment section in the paper. Ed seemed amused at my determination to find a job. He told me not to worry about finding a job as he could afford to take care of my needs out of his paycheck. I appreciated his generosity but I wanted to earn my own money. He let me know that he would rather I didn't work after we got married. He wasn't alone in his thinking; images of the contented housewife, surrounded by every modern convenience, appeared in the newspapers. This seemed so old fashioned, especially in America where men and women were supposed to be able to do as they wished. I felt an urgent need to find a job and earn money to send back home, to buy some clothes, and to help pay for a private burial plot in the Grange, if, God forbid, either Ma or Da were to die.

My eyes pored over the employment ads in the *Hartford Courant*. I spotted the advertisements put in by the Traveler's Insurance Company in Hartford, seeking truck drivers and a 'mail girl'. Although I'd little formal education, I'd worked as a factory girl and an ice-cream seller without being fired. Hopefully, I could get the job as a mail girl. I underlined the ad, and showed it to Ed. 'Apply for the job if you like, Angie. I want you to know that I earn enough to take care of us both. But, go ahead; my bet is you will be hired.'

Eddie always acted as if I had a head on my shoulders and never appeared upset by my lack of formal education. But when he asked me if I could type and take dictation, it threw me off. I felt ashamed of having left school at age thirteen to work as a scavenger on the Ringsend landfill collecting cinders to sell for a shilling a gunnysack. Because of such work, children like me were shunned by better-off families who viewed us as the scum of the earth instead of children of God. So, no, I had no experience of office work and Eddie seemed surprised that I couldn't type fifty words a minute. All the same, he offered to take me to the personnel department in the Traveler's Insurance Company to apply for the mail-girl job, after the big Fourth of July holiday.

The Fourth of July arrived. The big event marked my third day in America. So far, I'd kept homesickness at bay. Ed picked me up at the boardinghouse in the afternoon to take me into Hartford to see the parade. The city seemed about the same size as Dublin, but not as spread out. Hartford had taller buildings, shops and streets were more crowded, and cars were everywhere. Crowds of people were out walking around. More people would be on the streets, Eddie noted, when it cooled off. He also said that there were areas in the city that were off limits to us. Black people and white lived in their own separate neighbourhoods. 'You're not familiar with the relationship between blacks and whites in the United States,' he explained. From the serious tone of his voice, I sensed that something was amiss in America. I didn't press him about the matter, but wondered about it.

By mid-morning more and more people were beginning to gather along both sides of Main Street to wait for the Fourth of July parade to begin. Black people gathered together and stayed in their location along the parade route, white people followed the same pattern.

Eddie and I found a place in front of the crowd which ensured we'd have a good view of the celebration. A feeling of excitement and celebration filled the air. Black and white people had children in tow; very small children were carried in the arms of their parents who put tiny American flags into small black and white hands. Older children held onto balloons in colours made for the occasion. Older people carried fold-up chairs which younger relatives unfolded for them to sit in before the parade got under way.

There were no exchanges of greetings between black and white people, although both were at the parade to celebrate the same national holiday. The muffled sounds of drums in the distance indicated that the parade was on the move. The crowd began to cheer at the approach. First came a group of people dressed in an old-fashioned style. Eddie said they were the 'fife and drum' marchers who represented those who fought in the colonial war against Great Britain. Two marchers were dressed as George and Martha Washington. Next came soldiers representing different military groups, all bearing flags. As the men passed by, people around us stood up and placed a hand over their hearts. A person next to me leaned over when the colours passed by and took my hand and placed it over my heart with an annoyed smile. Surprised, I looked at Eddie who whispered, 'It's a sign of respect for the flag of our nation,' then patted my hand over my breast. The military band began to play stirring sounds of a John Philip Sousa march. Ed told me Sousa became famous for composing the 'March King' and 'Stars and Stripes Forever'. Legions of soldiers passed along the parade route. I wondered why America had so many people in the military, unlike Ireland, where the military had to promise paradise in order to recruit new soldiers.

Big tanks and cannons followed the marching soldiers with their guns cocked. Then came several high school bands from different schools in the Hartford area. Next came an endless line of automobiles containing politicians, real estate brokers, and members of the Hartford Chamber of Commerce. People started to get antsy waiting for all the cars to go by. Then came the hit of the parade, announced with an earsplitting 'BOOM! BOOM! BOOM-BOOM-BOOM!' Eyes turned to see the Scottish Highland Pipers and drummers, dressed in whirling kilts, puffing on bagpipes and beating the drums. *The Campbells are coming! O-ho! O-ho! The Campbells are coming! O-ho! O-ho!*' the Highlanders sang out as they marched. Seeing Scottish Highlanders included in the American Fourth of July parade made me aware that people from all parts of the world were welcome to join in the celebration.

Eddie nearly leapt off the sidewalk when he spotted an oncoming group. 'Whoopee-do!' rang out other voices at the sight. 'It's the cheerleaders.' As the energetic group of beautiful young women came into view, I understood all the whoopee-dos. The beautiful young women were dressed in skimpy green satin outfits; they wore tall shiny helmets on their heads, and each had on white-tasselled, high-stepping cowboy boots that showed off their long tanned legs. Daddy Longlegs had nothing on these girls. They wore make-up galore plastered over their faces and they all had silver blonde hair shimmering like halos. The cheerleaders stopped in front of us, threw their batons up into the air, then jumped up after them, performing leg-splits a mile wide as they did so. Eddie whistled out loud with each split. My Irish eyes had never seen such goings on. The skimpy skirts on the girls fanned out to show off their starburst knickers, taut at the crotch, and seemingly ready to tear asunder without a minute's notice. Glory be! Had the gusset in the crotch of the starburst step-ins come apart, the Earth might have spun backwards. Wolf whistles resounded louder and louder with every leap; the cheerleaders continued to perform. I imagined that I heard the voice of Granny Legg calling from the grave 'COVER Y'R KNEES — Y'RE OVER SEVEN!' When they finished their gravity defying performance, the beauties began to trip-trot down the parade route, heads held high, hips a-swagger, and batons twirling.

The Fourth of July Parade ended with a rousing edition of 'Dixie', a song familiar to Irish people. I began to sing along with the rest of the people, '*I wish I was in the land of cotton, old times there are not forgotten, look away, look away Dixie Land . . .* ' Ed looked at his watch, noting three hours had flown by. My feet had swollen double from standing in one spot in my high heeled shoes. I began to inch from foot to foot. Eddie observed that high heels were great, but I needed some flat shoes to wear. He offered to buy me a pair the next day.

'When I find a job, I'll get them,' I replied.

'It's up to you, Angie.'

'OK! I guess I'll borrow the money from you to get a pair of flats.'

On the drive back to Manchester, Ed asked what I thought of the parade and how it compared to a Saint Patrick's Day parade in Ireland. The main Saint Patrick's Day parade held in Dublin seemed a mere tin whistle compared with the BOOM! BOOM! Independence Day parade.

'You liked the cheerleaders. I could tell by the look in your eyes. And you looked up their skirts too,' I said. He grinned .

'Why don't I take you to the Dairy Queen. Ever heard of the Dairy Queen?'

Is he kidding me? How many times had I tried and failed to enter some beauty contest or other for the prize of a few shillings to jangle in my pocket. Girls born and bred down in the country they wanted, not Dublin jackeens. Did he think Dublin females lacked glamour or a sense of fashion or never tried their luck in beauty pageants put on by the manufacturers of Irish butter, milk, and ice cream? Ed got an earful about the way beauty contests were conducted back in Ireland. I filled him in on how the promoters of the contests placed ads in the newspaper or posted the information on lamp-posts encouraging young females to sign up for 'only the fee of five shillings'. Who would not throw her hat in the ring for a chance to become the new Rose of Tralee or Katy from Killarney or Molly Malone? The winner would have her photograph put on a chocolate box, some new margarine spread, or a new set of pots and pans. I explained that judges, usually heavy drinkers, always selected some farmer's daughter as the winner, supposedly for their rosier complexion over Dubliners. Girls from housing projects like Ballyfermot or Bluebell or Irishtown never got a look in. There was an ongoing complaint among the losers: 'It's young wans from the bog they want.' Wans with mammys that come with the daughter on the train to Dublin to compete in the contest. Mammys who stash away egg money for such an expense thinking their daughter will win by a mile. Also, the mammy will offer a Novena if the daughter wins that a Hollywood agent will see the face of the beauty queen on the butter box. The agent will offer the daughter a film contract. The daughter and her mammy will get away from the miserable rainy Irish weather to Beverly Hills, California where the sun never sets, and oranges grow day and night. Boom boom — another Maureen O'Hara makes her mark.

'Gee, Angie that's some story. But honey, the Dairy Queen is not about beauty contests, it's a drive-in place famous for its ice-cream sodas and shakes.'

'I'm aware of that,' I lied, wanting to crouch down on the floor of the automobile for the weekend.

The Dairy Queen parking lot was packed with automobiles and young Americans. The aroma of sizzling burgers and fried onions drifted out of the restaurant and up my nose. Parked couples were ordering food from their car windows without a care in the world. It amazed me that teenagers were treated so regally in the USA. Back in Ireland factories were full of young people being worked to the quick for pennies, including girls and boys fourteen years old. I thought how lucky the young people in America were not to have to do such low-paying work. No wonder they called the United States the land of milk and honey.

'We're surrounded by teenagers,' noted my boyfriend. 'Let's go inside to eat.'

I followed him into the restaurant.

'What would you like to have, angel?'

I wished he wouldn't call me 'angel'. I didn't mind him giving me a nickname, as people did to those they liked back in Ireland. But 'angel' sounded too Goody Goody Two Shoes to me. I knew he meant the name in a loving way, but for Christ's sake, a girl from the gutter could never be an angel, except one with a dirty face.

While we waited for our food I rested my hot feet. I asked Ed if he had ever heard of the little pelican whose beak can hold more than its belly. 'Not until I met you.' In seriousness he asked, 'Angie, tell me honestly, how do you feel about coming to the United States?'

'It's like stepping out of a babbling brook and into a raging ocean.'

Before the evening ended, Ed told me how much he had enjoyed having me with him to share in the Fourth of July celebrations. He said that I should consider the day when I too became an American citizen. Becoming an American would be a big thing. BOOM! BOOM! BOOM!

'It's not a shoo-in to go from "yerra" and "begorrah" to "I'm a Yankee Doodle Dandy",' I replied.

'I love you,' he said.

I still could not believe such a superior human being loved every bone in my body. I edged over towards him as we drove back to my boarding house, and said, 'If you get a big boil on the back of your neck I'll burst it for you.' When we got back to Mrs Anderson's, Ed and I kissed each other's faces off. My landlady came into the hall-way and handed me a letter she said came from the Old Country. I held the green and yellow edged envelope in my hand as if it were the Holy Grail. Ed wished me good night, and I headed upstairs to read my letter from home. I could tell by the large writing on the front of the envelope that it came from the person I loved most in the world. It came from my Ma.

Her letter read.

My darling, I am happy you and Eddie are getting married. I know that he is the best in the world to you and he loves you very much. I feel happy for you and him. I feel very lonely for you but I can't help that. When I think how good you were to me in every way. You lent me everything you had and I left you with nothing. I never forget the Christmas you gave all the money you had in your box to me. God Bless my little girl. I love you so much that Eddie is getting my heart and soul with you. God Bless him too. I am glad and sorry over losing you. You will have everything with Eddie. I don't want you to feel lonely anymore. You will be in my thoughts the very time you are getting married. Tell me the time and I will go over to John Dwyer's and I will get a highball and drink your health and Eddie's even if I have to go by myself. This is all for the present so good bye my love for now. Your own mammy.

I read the letter over and over, hearing her voice in every word she had laboured over. I put my mother's letter under my pillow.

The following morning over coffee, Eddie explained to me that the Travelers Insurance company made Hartford the insurance capital of the United States, and that if I got a job with the Travelers it would be a real scoop. I told him that I planned to inquire about a job at the company. I felt like a chancer in a business office because I lacked any formal education. Working-class girls never applied for office jobs back home. We would not be allowed in the door. Such jobs were for middle-class girls. Before I went into the personnel office at the Travelers, I whispered a Hail Mary to myself for courage. I could not believe my boldness in applying for the job, but this was America and not Ireland where the lack of opportunity for the likes of me had been set in granite ten feet deep.

The woman in the personnel office sat behind a big metal desk and invited me to take a seat while she sorted out papers. I told her that I had come to apply for the job as a mail runner that had appeared in the newspaper. She handed me an application form and told me to fill it out. Then she gave me a set of written tests. I had 15 minutes to complete them. I stumbled over strange arithmetic questions that told stories instead of adding up numbers. The reading and writing questions were not too hard. I had no typing experience so that part remained blank. I took the exam back to the woman and she looked it over. I got the sums in the columns correct. I told her I could not make head or tail of the story sums. She said my ability to identify words and their meanings were good. Then she asked me a series of questions beginning with my place of birth. How much education I had. And did I plan to get married? I answered her questions as best I could. 'Are you from France?' she wanted to know. 'No, I'm from Ireland,' I replied a bit bewildered that she thought I came from France.

I explained that I'd recently come from Ireland to the United States. She said that the Traveler's usually employed only young high school graduates. 'How much formal education have you had?' I explained to her that I had quit school at thirteen and gone to work. 'Why so young?' I explained that I needed to earn some money to help out at home. 'Where did you work? Child labour is not allowed in our country,' she said. 'Ireland's different,' I told her, not wanting to go into the reasons that kids like myself quit public school: no money for books, no pennies for the African Missions, no money for school uniforms, and going to school hungry. As I thought about the reasons for having to leave school, I could feel my blood begin to boil and seeds of rebellion growing in my gut. 'Where did you get your first job?' the personnel woman continued. Shamefacedly I told her that I scavenged and collected cinders on the dumpsite in Irishtown, and that when I turned fourteen, the legal age to be hired in a factory, I went to work in a textile factory. 'How did you learn how to read and write and add up figures?'

She seemed surprised at what I told her. I let her know that although I might not have all the necessary requirements for the job as a mail runner, I learned quickly and by the grace of the Blessed Mother I'd be double-quick learning the ropes needed to be the mail girl. Then out of the blue she started to tell me that she had relatives on her father's side of the family who came from Ireland a long time ago with only the clothes on their backs. And that someone took a chance on them. She ended the interview by saying that if I were hired for the position as a mail runner, I'd be notified in the mail. I thanked her and said I'd keep my fingers crossed and my toes too. The interview had taken an hour. I found Eddie by his car reading the paper. He looked up when I came near and asked how it went. 'It made me real hungry,' I replied.

Over a plate of French fries and hotdogs, he asked me to describe the interview. He assured me that I would get the job. In the meanwhile, he suggested that we go and pick out a pair of flat-heeled shoes for me. He headed in the direction of the G. Fox department store in the middle of the city saying, 'Angie, you'll love G. Fox.'

The G. Fox department store took up a good chunk of the Main Street in Hartford. When we got inside, I saw mannequins all over the premises dressed in the latest women's fashions. The mannequins were as numerous as statues inside any parish church back home. And, like the religious statues, they beckoned onlookers up close to take in their heavenly appearance. I was suddenly overwhelmed with a need to own everything the mannequins were wearing. I wailed, 'I want everything on the mannequins.' For an instant, Ed looked stricken. 'Slow down, honey, everything you see is not going to fade away overnight. Let's find the shoe department.' After looking around three floors of fashions for women we found the shoe department. As soon as we walked into the section, a fashionable lady came over and asked, 'How may we help you?' Ed explained that I was looking for a

*Noely and myself on O'Connell Street, 1956. Noely
hoped I'd meet a Yank who would buy us ice-cream.
Taken by one of the street photographers.*

pair of comfortable flat-heeled shoes. He asked me if I had any colour
in mind? With a greedy squint I looked at the array of shoes. There
were shoes in every colour, style, and price. I loved the high heels, the
low heels, the buckled shoes, the laced shoes, and shoes made out of
animal skin only known by the likes of Tarzan. And, thank God, I did
not see any that looked like the charity brogues favoured by the Saint
Vincent de Paul back in Dublin.

The saleswoman asked my shoe size, which surprised me. Back
home a person tried on a pair of shoes until they found a fit. I figured
only people in Ireland and Africa were expected to stuff their feet

into anything. The sales lady fitted my foot onto a contraption, and then fetched a pair of black flat-heeled shoes. I asked her if they came in white. I got the white pair. As soon as I put them on my feet I wanted to rock 'n' roll with Eddie to the tune of 'I wanna be your teddy bear'. 'White shoes are hard to keep clean,' Ed reminded me.

'Did you see our summer collection of ladies' Capri pants?' The saleswoman inquired. Capri pants didn't ring a bell with me. Ed asked her to show me some. 'Just a sec, honey,' she said, 'I'll be right back.' She returned with an armload of Capri pants and matching blouses. 'Try 'em on,' she invited. Girls in Dublin did not wear trousers in public. One time I tried my friend Lulu's jeans on and went over to Coady's to buy something for my mother. Half way across the street a man in a lorry came to a screeching stop. He leaned out of the window and roared at me to take myself home, brazen thing that I was, and give my trousers back to my father so he could get out of bed. I could wear trousers in America and not get any lip from some old crab. 'Let your boyfriend see you in that outfit,' cooed the saleswoman as she shoved me back towards Ed. I felt awkward parading in front of him.

'She's a living doll in that outfit,' said the saleswoman to Ed.

'We'll take all of them.'

I nearly fainted at his generosity. What in the world had I ever done to deserve a man like him? On the drive back to Mrs Anderson's house, I asked Ed what the saleswoman meant when she referred to me as a doll? 'It means you're cute,' he replied.

'But I'm not a doll,' I responded; shamefacedly remembering how, as a child, I'd pretend to dress up the Lord Jesus Christ as if He were a paper doll.

I had asked my mother to buy me a game of paper dolls to play with but she never had enough money. During a novena at our parish church on Haddington Road I thought up the game of pretending to dress Him up on the Cross in order to keep from going to sleep as the parish priest droned on and on about the Mysteries of Faith. Going to the novenas gave me the chance to get out of our cramped smoky room and into the open space of our big church with its many jewel coloured stained glass windows. The large cross above the altar featured a realistic image of a deeply sad Jesus who seemed as broken as the people living in the hovels of O'Brien's Place. I asked Jesus on the crucifix if He'd play paper dolls. I answered for Him. Because of being nailed down, the Saviour couldn't go play Kick the Can.

Being confined to my rented room in the boarding-house made time drag. I watched for the postman, hoping to get a letter from home or a letter from the Traveler's Insurance Company. In the meanwhile, homesickness nibbled at me from head to toe. I ran down the stairs when I saw the postman put a handful of letters into the mailbox. I knew Mrs Anderson didn't like me galloping down the stairs because it would wear out the carpet on the stairs. She handed me a small, stuffed brown penny envelope earmarked with an Irish mark. I ran my eyes over Da's beautiful script. He wrote for both my mother and himself.

> *My own Darling Angeline, we received your very welcome letter. We hope you received ours. We are all delighted you are settling down, as we all want you to be happy. Then we will be happy. Our only concern is what you want to do. Write us big long letters and tell us all what's in your heart. We all love you so much. We didn't know how much until you were gone. The worse of all is your brother Bob. He is still crying. Write him a very special letter when you can. Your friend Rosaleen from the Royal came down to see us. She wants your address. . . . We want you to be happy whatever you decide to do. It's your life to do what you want with it. . . . Good night my wee 'Titch'. We miss you. Please yourself. It's your life. We will write to-morrow (D.V) from Ma, Da, Bob, Noel, Frank, Bridie and Wee Barney.*

I read and reread the letter; were it possible, I would have eaten it to feel whole again.

Working girl

The following morning, Mrs Anderson handed me a letter from the Travelers Insurance company. My hands shook with anticipation as I took the letter out of her hand. I ran up the stairs back to my room and tore the letter open. It informed me that I had got the job as a mail girl and to report for work the coming Monday at the supply department. My pay would be forty dollars every two weeks. The last paragraph instructed me to have my 'Green Card' in hand when I reported for work. I'd never heard of a Green Card. I phoned Eddie and told him about the letter and my need to have a Green Card. He explained that the US government had a law that required aliens to have a Green Card if they worked in the county. We could go down to the office and apply for an alien registration form, and obtain the card. The thought that I could not take a job without some card had never entered my mind. It amazed me that I could get a job with so little education, and I felt delighted and grateful for that. Ed suggested we go out and celebrate me getting a job. 'Let's go to the drive-in restaurant and get a hamburger with onion rings, French fries, and a thick chocolate milkshake,' I suggested. The voice on the phone groaned, 'I don't know where you put it away, honey.'

'I've a hollow leg.'

Over plates of scrumptious food, I told him that as soon as I got my first paycheck he'd get a bottle of the best Irish whiskey in Hartford, Connecticut. 'Thanks, Angel, but I don't drink liquor. My Methodist faith forbids it.'

'I'll buy wool and knit you a fisherman's pullover and a matching long fringed scarf should we ever get cold days in Connecticut.'

'It's a deal,' he smiled. The thought of knitting a heavy wool muffler, never mind a jumper, with the temperature in the eighties and the humidity in the nineties made the sweat break on my forehead. Who would believe that the Earth had hot places like Hartford where a rain shower fell on the arms and legs like sparks from a furnace then evaporated into thin air?

Mrs Anderson wasn't in the house when we got back. Thank God for the breather. I invited my love up to my room where we cuddled and kissed until the bed rolled to the other side of the room on its casters. My ability to keep a brake on desire began to wane the longer I spent in Eddie's company. The voice of Rome with its dictates on virginity before marriage continued to rise in my brain like a snake, as did Da's dictate to never dust my eggs off with a hammer until marriage vows were signed and sealed. Most of all though, I didn't want to get knocked-up and bring forth a babe without having a brack to provide for it. My virginity remained mint in the box. For all I knew and feared they might have places like the Magdalene Laundries back in Ireland where young women were sent for having relations with a man outside of marriage. The fear of such a thing happening to me either in Ireland or my adopted homeland kept the brakes on my sexual carousing. Ed, who did not know about life for girls back in Ireland, expressed admiration for me keeping my virginity intact until after marriage. Let's face it: what other gifts were mine to give?

As I waited for my Green Card to arrive in the mail, Ed filled my long days of idleness by picking me up after his work and taking me out to eat or spoon in the park. During the daytime, I took walks around the neighbourhood hoping to meet some people, but never saw anyone outside of their homes. Only the odd child played in front of their homes, not at all like back in Irishtown where kids hung from the rafters, and played in the streets. The silent neighbourhood made me long for the clutter and clatter of life on the Dublin streets.

The Green Card finally came in the mail. My innards jellied, as I got ready for my first day as a worker in America. I'd washed out all my underwear, pressed my yellow dress with the white ribbons down the front, polished my black spiked heel shoes until they glimmered, and combed my hair over and over. I had never had a job in an office before and did not know what to expect. While I waited for Eddie to pick me up and take me to work, I fiddled with the Green Card trying to understand what the word 'alien' implied. The United States Immigration and Naturalization Office described foreigners as aliens. I'd assumed aliens came from outer space, not from Ireland. I studied my face in the looking glass trying to determine if I looked anything like the bulbous shaped figures in Hollywood films. The sharp beep from Ed's car drew me down the stairs in a hurry. The landlady called out 'good luck' as I rushed out the front door. I made the Sign of the Cross to remind myself that being looked upon as an alien by the government didn't mean nuts. We listened to the car radio on the drive into Hartford. Once again, a panicked radio broadcaster accused the Soviet government of violating something and said that the Soviets were a threat to freedom. The frightening warnings about the Soviets began to concern me, especially knowing that no one in the flats at home in George Reynolds House had a clue about the goings on. Who ever met a Russian back in Ireland? Who ever encountered a Russian in America? Thank God, the US government kept an eye out for us or else we could be eaten like Spanish onions. I reminded myself to mention all the warnings about the Soviets in my next letter home. An invasion of Russians sounded worse than a return of the British, and by the dire tone of the radio announcers, more dreadful than the mad, bush-bearded Vikings. I'd also write a letter to Liam Larkin, who lived in the flats, to keep an eye out for the Russians. Liam had collected cinders on the dumpsite with me when we were children. For something to do, he collected used thread spools with holes in the middle and glued them together to make a telescope. He sat on the brick wall by the Pigeon House lighthouse and scanned the wet Irish skies for silver saucers, having seen *The Body Snatchers* at the local. He firmly believed that if aliens were to land on earth they'd ditch first in the dirt of Dublin. I'd write to him and suggest he squint an eye for any sight of the Red Army coming out of the sky above the Pigeon House. Eddie pulled the car up to the kerb outside Travelers Insurance, gave me a peck on the cheek and drove off.

I walked up the flight of stone steps to the entrance and arrived in the lobby where a guard in a brown uniform with a gun on his hip directed me towards a sliding-glass window marked 'Information'. A young woman pulled back the sliding window, and asked how she could help. I explained that I'd been hired to work as the new mail girl in the supply department. She told me to wait a sec while she called over the microphone for Miss Foley.

Within moments a perfectly groomed older woman came through the doorway and into the lobby where I stood. She greeted me with a big hello and directed me to follow her inside to the supply department. Miss Foley sat down at a large gray metal desk and indicated for me to sit in a chair on the opposite side. She informed me that she was the head of the clerical department and I'd be working under her supervision. With that, she drew out a folder from the top drawer of the desk, opened it up and told me it was my file that the personnel department had sent over. She flipped through the different forms, and asked me if I had a Green Card. Her eyes were drawn to a red-circled note on a loose sheet of paper that read: 'PS She just came from the Old Country and is cute as a bug.' Miss Foley closed the file and returned it to the desk. She asked if I would do a good job for the good of the department? 'With God's help, mam,' I answered, not knowing what else to say. She explained to me that her grandparents, the Foleys, had come from Ireland at the turn of the century. Her parents were both deceased. Her only brother had been killed in a plane crash on a trip back from California to Connecticut. She asked if I knew any Foleys back in Ireland. I thought about Bark-Bark Foley who used to live in O'Brien's Place. Bark-Bark managed to come back alive from the front where he'd served with the British Army in World War I. He never spoke human talk again. 'Bark, bark, bark' were the only words to come from his mouth. He was put in the mad house for a long rest. Seeing the eager look on Miss Foley's face and her high position, I replied that I knew Foleys whose son became a famous warrior. She smiled with the pride of an ardent Irish-American.

Her telling me about her brother getting killed in an airplane crash made me sad, and aware that misfortune flew on wings and settled down where it would. 'Let's go meet Madeline, who you are going to replace,' said the supervisor. Madeline had been promoted to a clerk typist in the department—up from the bottom rung of mail girl.

Madeline looked to be in her early twenties. 'Hi! I'm Madeline,' she smiled. 'Heard from Miss Foley you will be replacing me and that you're from Ireland.'

'Yes, that's me,' I answered, hoping she would not be disappointed. She walked me through the department filled with rows of young women typing at what seemed to be a mile a minute. Then she led me to where the men worked. 'These are the underwriters,' she informed me. 'They are the most important workers in the office.' All the men wore suits and ties, and were either talking on the telephone or scattering piles of forms on their desks. I'd never seen such busy people as in that office. Madeline then took me to her bench back by the wall, where she went through the mailbags and sorted out all the incoming mail and put them into pigeonholes that were labelled with different names. She pointed to the two large stuffed leather saddlebags on the workbench and said, 'Here we go.' She poured out all the mail from the two satchels and handed me a long dagger. 'That's a letter opener,' she said, picking up on my confusion. She ripped apart every envelope with the letter opener and smoothed the contents out flat with the palm of her hand, before sorting the forms into the pigeon holes. 'Most of these forms are requisitions,' she said, 'and they must be given to the right underwriter in the office.' When she'd sorted all the mail and put it in the right compartments, she reached back into the pigeonholes and collected the piles, which she carefully balanced on one arm holding the pile in place with the other arm. 'Follow me,' she ordered as she set out to deliver the piles to the right people. As we stopped at each desk, Madeline introduced me as the new mail girl. Some of the men looked up from their work; others ignored us both.

After all the deliveries were made, Madeline collected all the outgoing mail and told me to put it into the saddlebags. We took the saddlebags down to the shipping and receiving area, three floors down. Madeline handed over the bags to one of the men and he handed her two incoming sacks of mail. She gave him a smile and told him that I would be in charge of the mail now. She fitted one of the heavy bags over my shoulder and put the other heavy bag over hers, and we returned upstairs. The weight of the saddlebag almost caused me to buckle in the knees. Madeline stood head and shoulders taller than me, and she lifted the heavy mail as if handling a nest of feathers. The mail came in seven times a day and went out seven times a day, which meant that we were on our feet every moment except when we went to lunch. She handed me a letter opener and said, 'Let me watch how you open the mail and see if you get it into the right mailboxes while I read you the names on the envelopes out loud. Mr Machurek, Mr Lycklama, Mr Schaufelberger, Mr Scheirpeter, Mr Lumbermersky, Mr Charounlertdajkul . . .'

I listened to the gibberish and thought Madeline had suffered a sudden brain seizure that made her blather such unpronounceable words. I expected her to fall down dead on the floor. 'Anything the matter?' she asked, stopping in the string of jawbreakers.

'No.'

'Let's get on with it.'

'I don't have foreign languages, only a bits of Irish.'

'I'm not talking in a foreign language. These are the names of our underwriters; American names.'

'What about names like Murphy or Kelly or Flynn or O'Grady?' I asked. 'Are there any names like them?'

She replied, 'We have Miss Foley, our supervisor, Miss Noonan the head of her department in another part of the building, Miss Griffin, the head secretary to our vice-president and Miss Mary McGuire our company nurse upstairs.'

By the end of the week, no more Madeline: the job of mail girl resided in my hands, and they were sweaty. I made every effort to pronounce the names of the underwriters all the next week but some of them lacked hearing aids. 'I'm Mr Schaufelberger not Shovelburner,' scowled one. 'I'm Mr Lupinacci, not Mr Lupinachy,' another announced. And the handsome fella blurted, 'It's not Mr Luber Mercy. It's Lubermersky. It's one word. Got it? Store it.' Mr Charounlertdajkul, embarrassed by my plight, advised me to call him Mr C. The same underwriters were incensed when Miss Foley put me in charge of filing their requisitions in alphabetical order in between the incoming and outgoing bags of mail. The strain of alphabetizing the jawbreakers caused my right eye to blur, and it continued to blur scanning complicated and unfamiliar concoctions of letters.

The shipping and receiving area where I took the mail and picked up incoming mail was located in the basement. Most of the men who worked there were black. They unloaded the trucks at the loading dock, packed the boxes to be shipped out, checked the invoices, and took care of loading and unloading the mail. The men asked me my name. After I told them, they asked what part of the world I came from, then invited me to 'sit a bit'. Until now the only black person I had ever talked to was in a dancehall in Dublin. He'd invited me to dance and told me he was a student at Trinity College. He danced like Gene Kelly and had the bearing and manners of an African prince. The black American men in the shipping room were working men who toiled hard and sweated from the exertion. I sat down on a high stool offered by one of the men. The intense heat of the late afternoon soaked my hair and forehead as it did theirs.

'Where are you from?' one of the men asked.

'I'm from Ireland; I came over to get married.'

'How hot does it get back in the Old Country?'

'Never like this.'

'Are you marrying an American or an Irishman?'

'An American.'

'Uh hum,' said the younger one. 'How long you know this man?' he asked. 'He in the service?' One of the older men told the one asking the questions to hush.

'You look tuckered,' said the man who'd offered me the stool. 'Sit awhile, baby girl,' he invited as he pushed the leather mailbag aside. 'Here, let me get you some water to cool you down.'

'I'm not supposed to have a break yet,' I protested.

'Baby girl, you look about to fall on your face, isn't that so, Calvin?' I told whoever would listen that my smallpox vaccination caused me to feel faint. 'We got them shots when we shipped out for Korea,' said a man named Jackson.

'I should never have let the buggers talk me into getting a smallpox injection,' I said to all.

'It will be just fine; won't it be fine, Calvin?' The man named Calvin nodded his head, giving me a wary look. The men continued to work around me while I drank the water. I wanted to stay longer, but I had to get back upstairs with the mail. The men invited me to sit and have lunch with them in the company cafeteria and tell them about the Old Country. I promised that I would.

Back upstairs with the brightness of daylight filling the large office, I had to put on a happy face. The people upstairs expected me to feel lucky and grateful to be in their country. Any feelings of sadness or a longing for home would put them off. I'd already figured out that any thoughts of grief or despair were to be stifled amid American bliss. I found myself turning for comfort to Elvis and started to hum 'Love me tender'.

Next day Ed told me that we were invited to dinner at the home of his buddy and his wife. 'Bill and Lo can't wait to meet you. Lo's mother's family came from Italy a long time ago. They're Catholic. Bill's folks are from Germany. The dinner is semi-formal.' Bill worked with Ed in the research lab in East Hartford. Bill and Lo had been married a year, and had built a new home in Weathersfield, Connecticut. Al and Shirley Wilson and their baby, along with Nancy and Les Blair, were also invited. He told me in a sombre tone that the Wilsons' three-month-old baby had been born albino. He went on to say neither Al nor Shirley could figure out how Shirley had given birth to an albino infant. Al scratched his head constantly over the event. After Eddie and I finished our long conversation, I wondered what he meant by a 'semi-formal dinner'. I'd never heard of such a dinner. Nor did I understand what he meant by an albino baby. I thanked God my mother, when she had money for food, cooked sheep's brains, pig's trotters, pig's cheek, sheep's head, sausages, ox tail, and corned beef and never a semi-anything. Luckily, Ed went into more detail, explaining the meaning of albino or as sure as God is in Heaven, I would have guessed the word referred to the name of some dark horse that won the Derby horse race by a long shot.

Getting to meet some of Eddie's friends would be nice. I hoped to make a good impression. I hand-washed my blue dress in the bathroom sink for the occasion. Mrs Anderson charged two bits, added to the rent, for use of her washing machine and dryer. Not wanting to make her a millionaire, I kept the two bits for myself. She let me use the iron for free.

I'd met a few Italian people when I lived in O'Brien's Place, before we moved to George Reynolds flats. An Italian family ran a fish and chip shop in Bath Avenue not far from our neighbourhood. I went with my mother to Mass nearly every morning before we went to clean an office building in Upper Leeson Street. On the way home we would encounter one or two elderly Italian women on the way to Mass at Saint Mary's. The small Italian grandmothers wore only black clothing from head to toe. My mother would stop to say good morning to one or the other. They spoke a few words of English: 'It's cold. It's wet. No sun. Not Roma.' My mother nodded in sympathy. One of the old ladies gave me a three-penny-bit one morning after asking my mother if I belonged to her. My mother told me the old women were emigrants from Italy who'd come to Ireland to escape the war in their country. I wondered if Lo would be anything like the two perishing grandmothers from Italy who dressed in pitch-black clothes that matched the colour of their eyes.

We drove to Weatherfield, Connecticut on the Sunday afternoon. On the way, we drove past vast areas of green pastures, dotted here and there with dapple-gray and burnished brown horses munching in the fields. We also drove by wooded areas where pine trees lifted their branches to the sky like can-can dancers.

Bill and Lo wanted to raise their family in the suburbs. The couple had designed their new home from their own blueprint, according to Ed. After quite a drive, we came to a raw new clearing in what had been a wooded hillside. Newly-built homes and homes in different stages of development were being built in a thinned-out forest, now mainly consisting of raw tree stumps. Eddie slowed the car down to make a turn onto the newly opened, still unpaved road, then he turned into one of the drives that led up to a split-level house. He honked the horn, and a merry group trundled out the front door to greet us. The men were holding beer bottles. The young wives resembled an arrangement of freshly plucked flowers on the green grass. The smiling women came over with their husbands to greet Eddie and me. Before greeting them, Ed whispered in my ear that I looked lovely and that he loved me. Bill and Lo came up to us and gave Ed a hearty handshake and me a hug. Bill's wife looked like she was expecting a child from the way her belly bulged under her floral-print dress. The couple introduced me to the rest of the group standing on the lawn.

'This is Al. Shirley and the baby are sitting outside on the back porch trying to keep in the shade.' Al had a rumpled look about him as if he punched his way, one day at a time, through his life. He wore light tan pants, a blue shirt and a striped tie loosened at the neck. He had intense blue eyes deeply dug into a moon face surrounded with crinkle rusty-red hair. Bill was of German descent. He stood tall and lanky over the heads of the others, dressed in pale-coloured trousers, a white shirt and brown leather sandals that showed off long narrow feet with extremely pointed toes. When he smiled, his lips opened wide showing off every tooth in his head, each in perfect harmony. Everyone I knew back in George Reynolds would have given their right eye to have such teeth, especially the old age pensioners who were toothless and unable to chew on a crust of bread. The Irish State told such folks 'Gum your food to mush,' as a solution to their problems.

Les introduced himself to me and I could smell stale liquor on his breath. He asked me, 'Like a Highball? Martini with a twist? Scotch? Or maybe a beer?' Being a bit nervous and wanting to seem sophisticated I replied with a laugh, 'One of each, please.' Like a jack-knife, Eddie sliced through the group and told Les, 'She'd like a soft drink.' I felt miffed at his interfering. I had a job now, I was about to be married, I was not a child. 'Heck, honey, be serious,' said my intended. Snippily I reminded him, 'I'm in America, not Ireland, and I wasn't born yesterday.' I could tell Les might be a bit of a wayfarer; the kind of guy who wants what's on his own plate and yours, too. In the meanwhile, the bevy of tanned wives stood a little apart from each other and away from their husbands. Each bride rubbed one of her long, tanned legs against her other limb as if on cue, like crickets when they gather.

'This is Nancy, Les' wife,' said Lo. Nancy, burnt brown as a berry from the sun, offered me a slender hand with tapered fingernails polished to red points. She could have doubled for Doris Day. She even had the lilting laugh of Doris Day in *Pillow Talk*. Nancy asked me what part of Ireland I came from. How was I enjoying 'our wonderful country, the Land of Opportunity'? She taught at a public high school and said working there was a blast. 'Want my job?' I answered, 'Maybe some day.' 'I'm half Quaker,' she gushed. I thought Nancy was making a joke about being half–quacked, trying to be funny. I appreciated her making me laugh because the hot sun and the strain of trying to make a good impression, meeting so many new people, and trying to figure out American speech had begun to wither me.

Lo suggested that we go inside the air-conditioned house and see what the boys were up to. Merciful God, Lo's suggestion was a lifesaver. The inside of the house smelled of newly felled wood. The living room walls were painted white and the sofa and chairs were covered in aqua blue fabric. An array of tweedy wool rugs in colors of bright orange and avocado green were scattered over the highly polished wood floor. 'This is more like what I expected in America,' I said to myself, eyeing Eddie who favoured leafage instead of this. Lo explained how she and Bill preferred Danish Modern furniture to the overstuffed kind. The whole house had been furnished in Danish Modern, even to the three carved wood ducks in stages of flight arranged on the wall over the gray stone fireplace. Next, Lo showed me into her up-to-date kitchen, shiny and bright as a button.

Every shelf in the cabinets held cans of food: pears, peaches, plums, pineapple, tomatoes, corn, peas, carrots, mushrooms, spinach, and other goods unfamiliar to my Irish eyes. I looked at the supply of food stacked by size and could not believe that it was to feed only two people. My experience was of sharing a single can of beans or sardines with five other people. I was overcome by the abundance around me. Why had some people so much while others scrimped to live on half of nothing?

Lo beckoned for us to follow her down the hallway to see the new nursery she'd prepared for the baby. The nursery looked like a picture postcard of perfection. All the baby furniture had been hand-made. I couldn't get over the size of the crib meant for a tiny babe. The little mite might get lost in such a big crib. Hopefully the baby would have bellowing lungs to howl for a mammy or a daddy. I found myself thinking of times past. When my youngest brother, Noely was born, Granny Gale gave Ma a wooden orange crate to use as a cradle. 'Sweet oranges from Brazil' read the label. On sunny mornings Noely got carted outside next to where Granny Martin sat on her three-legged stool. Instead of telling my mother how to live her life, Granny would turn to Noely and list off complaints about the world.

Lo's baby in the making would be born into a different world. I grew tired of looking at all of the modern wonders, and slipped out the patio door to find Shirley and her much talked about albino baby.

Shirley rocked back and forth in a white wicker chair holding her dumpling on her lap covered up in a blanket. She wore a summer frock as green as the canopy above her head. She'd a forlorn look to her. I sat down in a chair beside her and introduced myself. She appeared not to get the drift of my small talk. Back and forth she rocked, as she held the swaddled albino on her lap, the baby from nowhere. The albino never budged. I gritted my teeth in anticipation of a glimpse of the rare specimen. The babe began to move under its shroud, and wanted out into the sunlight. The mother ignored its every effort to break free. 'Did you meet Al, my husband?' Shirley inquired. 'Our baby looks more like him. His side of the family.'

Thank God, Ed had clued me in to the meaning of albino; otherwise my imagination could have run off with itself. Eddie explained to me that an albino is someone who 'lacks normal skin pigmentation'. The seriousness of his tone filled me with dread. 'It what?'

'It has to do with pigmentation,' he repeated. 'Let me break the word up for you, honey: pig-men-tation.'

'Pig what?'

'Pigmentation.'

'Shirley had a pig baby?'

'No! No! Angel, the child is perfectly normal in every way except for its abnormally pale white skin. It must be kept out of sunlight.'

I sat as quiet as Little Miss Muffet next to Shirley in a matching wicker rocker, keeping an eye peeled for a peep of the mystery bundled on her lap. As if able to read my mind, Shirley inquired if I would do her a favour by holding Cleo until she went to the potty. The potty? I thought. What's that? I took the baby and Shirley went into the house. I could feel the small human being wiggle and waggle beneath the covers, and thought what a good as gold baby it must be to have the patience to remain wrapped up like a dumpling in the light of day. Casually, I let my hand rest over its small heart, which tick, tick, ticked like a grandfather clock. Mindful of my charge, I kept a wary eye towards the sun overhead, knowing that if the baby were to get uncovered, the sun would turn it into a beetroot.

Cleo continued to sleep in the crook of my arm. Apparently, the others inside the house had forgotten us both. As the sun bent lower behind the tall pines, I hoped the baby would wake up so I could get a peek. When would the mother come back from the potty? Wouldn't you know it, curiosity got the best of me. I folded the edges of the blanket back to get a peep at the sleeping babe. The baby's skin was the colour of a little white egg. I strained my eyes to distinguish her hair from her egg-white scalp. When I blew on it, the baby's fine hair flew into a zillion curlicues crisscrossing her head. Her tiny ears lay like petals against her little head. Her eyelashes were too faint to see. My nosey parker curiosity upset the infant's sleep. Hurriedly, I rearranged the folds of the blanket around her, but she forced her head from under the covers and looked up at me with sombre lily-pink eyes. The pink gaze from her eyes kicked my heart into double speed, never having seen such a wonder. The child puckered up her face and began to bawl with both lungs till the rafters rung. I took notice of the sun overhead and tried again to enclose Cleo among the folds of the blanket, but to no avail. Hercules himself couldn't have rewrapped the howling child intent on flinging herself skywards. Her roaring brought her mother rushing onto the patio to see what had happened. She scooped Cleo up in her arms, 'Sweetheart, sweetheart, mommy's here.' Cleo calmed down in her mother's embrace. I felt guilty about the child's distress vowing to make up for it as soon as possible.

Lo called through the open patio doors, 'Time to eat.' We went into the pale, cool dining room. The blond table had been covered with a mint-green lace tablecloth. A large vase of cut pink roses posed as the centrepiece. We were invited to find our place names and sit in front of them. Square white dinner plates were set in front of us. I'd never seen square dinner plates before, and wondered how to eat off them. After we were seated, Lo brought out a large tureen and placed it in the middle of the dining table. She looked at us all and said out loud, 'Gazpacho! Gazpacho!' 'God bless you, too,' I felt compelled to answer in return; Bill ladled out the mixture from the tureen into our soup bowls. At first taste I realized Lo had forgotten to turn the stove on under the soup, for it was cold as ice. Not knowing what to do, I blew into my bowl as if trying to cool it off. 'It's nice and hot.' Seven pairs of eyes searched my face. After the cold soup, Lo got up from the table and came back with a large platter she could hardly carry. 'Chicken Cacciatora', beamed the husband. Chickens cat what? I thought to myself. 'It's Italian,' said Lo, as if reading my mind. It was delicious. I wanted to be like Lois more than any other American woman I'd met.

Eddie and I were the only couple not enjoying glass after glass of deep red wine. Wanting to be on Ed's wavelength, I had ginger ale.

In between the mouthfuls of food, and the glasses of wine and water, snippets of conversation took place about wind tunnels, hi fi, Sarah Vaughan, burping plastic, a book written by Dr Spock, and something about the tenderness of Fisher's scone mix.

'Time for dessert and coffee.'

Al and Shirley left the party first. Before leaving, Shirley handed the baby to Al while she fiddled with her things. He held the infant at arm's length as if it were a ticking-bomb. Shirley promised to have me over for lunch.

I thanked Lo and Bill for a lovely time.

'Let's go, Angie,' Ed said.

'A minute.' I walked back to Lo and asked, 'Why are Al and Shirley's knickers in a knot over the baby?'

'She's so pale. So white.' Had they ever seen a red-haired freckle-faced Irish toddler, rosy as an apple?

I sat at my desk to eat lunch after a morning of hurrying and scurrying in the supply department. As I nibbled on one of Eddie's baloney and pickle sandwiches, Calvin from the shipping and receiving department came over to my desk. 'Care to join us for lunch at the cafeteria?'

On the way over to the company cafeteria, Calvin mentioned we would be joining Rufus and Jordan from receiving and Barbara, a friend from maintenance. 'Folks from Ireland like corn beef n' cabbage. That's what I've heard. You eat corn beef n' cabbage?' 'Like a horse,' I said.

The company cafeteria resembled a movie set. Crowds of people filled the huge place. Groups of people were seated around tables spaced close to each other. They were all eating, talking and laughing to their heart's content. Amid all the noise and bustle, Rufus and Jordan headed towards us followed by a young black woman dressed in a maid's outfit of white and gray. 'That's Barbara,' I thought, feeling a bit shy. 'This is the little Irish girl we were telling you of,' Calvin informed Barbara. She held out her hand and I grasped it. After shaking hands, she looked me up and down, still smiling, and stepped forward to give me a hug. 'Let's get in line before they sell out of that corn beef n' cabbage,' she said, moving me into a line of workers waiting to be served from chrome containers filled with meat, chicken, pork chops, all kinds of vegetables, potatoes, light and dark gravies, bread and rolls. The piled sliced roast drizzled with brown gravy made my mouth water, but I resisted, pointing to the corn beef. After we had piled our trays, Rufus nodded for me to follow along. Instead of sitting where all the white workers ate lunch, Rufus continued walking towards the end of the cafeteria with its dimmer light, and planked his tray on one of two tables set out. 'This is the Coloured area,' he said to me. After we sat down, Barbara told me that white workers didn't eat lunch with Negroes. I didn't know how to respond. Her words shocked me. Why would the white workers and black workers eat apart from each other? We all worked for the same employer, the Traveler's Insurance Company, which owned and operated the workers' cafeteria.

We looked at our overflowing plates crammed with delicious American food. Rufus, in between mouthfuls, invited me to talk about the Emerald Isle. 'Is it really as green as they say?' asked Barbara. Having sprouted from concrete in Dublin city, I'd had no idea of how green Ireland's mystical landscape could be until I was flying away from the place for America. But, as my mother would have it, 'Better to speak with a golden glow than thunderclaps', so I rambled on about fancies, fairies, leprechauns, saints and scholars and other artful lies. Aware of having attention as never before, I stretched out the blarney like a rubber band, including sighting of headless horsemen, Dublin banshees, ghosts, pointy-eared and dome-headed goblins, barking and talking foxes who mesmerized crows until the birds flew backwards. I ceased the yap when I noticed my lunch companions beginning to yawn and look at their watches. Jordan pointed with his fork to my cabbage and spuds getting cold on the plate.

Calvin asked me if I'd ever heard any jazz music back in Ireland. He said, 'Jazz music made by Blacks, not Whites.' I answered that we heard little or no mention of jazz on Radio Éireann, 'It'd get in the way of some auld farmer's weather prediction,' I added, also noting that the top-played song on the radio before I left Dublin went, 'Day-o, day-a-o, daylight come an' me wan' go home.' 'That's Harry Belafonte's tune,' Calvin informed me. 'It's called "The Banana Boat Song"', added Jordan. 'It's popular in America too.'

'Ever heard of segregation in Ireland?' Jordan asked me. I felt ashamed that I didn't know what the word meant, and told him so, saying, 'I went to work at age thirteen to help put bread and milk on the family table.' The revelation caused Calvin to remark: 'Little girl, we would not have guessed bad things like that about Ireland. You always are humming to yourself. Maybe it's a kind of keening.'

When we got back to the office building, the three men headed down to work in the basement and I went back to work with the white people.

When Ed picked me up after work, I didn't mention going to lunch with three handsome men who enjoyed having me along. The odd African student from Trinity College who showed up in a Dublin dancehall would get the cold shoulder and even worse if he spooned with an Irish lass whether she was a saint or a whore. Young hard-edged factory fellas would squint flint in the direction of a foreign man or a black-skinned man shimmering a Waltzing Matilda with some skinny-necked Irish swan. Until moving to America, the image of Black women who crossed my vision came from Hollywood. Dublin audiences were mad about the film, *Gone with the Wind*. It should have touched a raw nerve among the poor in Dublin who flocked to see it. Instead, their sympathy went to little Bonnie Blue, a child of rich parents, who fell off her pet pony and broke her neck and the comment I heard most went, 'If only they gave her a cat or a dog or a hen for her birthday, instead of that feckin' pony.'

Rufus, Calvin, Jordan and Barbara were waiting for me outside on the sidewalk. The three guys were engaged in a teasing conversation with Barbara as I came along. Barbara stood a head taller than the men. Because of it being a wet day out, she wore a light tan raincoat over her company uniform. She saw me coming towards them, and say out loud, 'Hi there.' Without any hesitation Barbara linked her arm in mine. I'd the urge to skip along with her down the sidewalk

*With a copy of Dominic Behan's 'Easter Monday
1916—Songs of the IRA'. Glastonbury,
Connecticut, 1958.*

in the rain, leaving the men in our wake. 'These guys been telling me about you. Don't pay attention to anything any one of them tells you.' Over lunch in the cafeteria, Calvin suggested I tell Barbara some leprechaun stories. 'A liar needs to have a good memory,' I joked as I went on about Irish traditions according to myself.

'Barbara wants to be in the movies,' said Calvin. I had no trouble imagining the lovely young women in a remake of the popular film, *The Bells of Saint Mary's* opposite Marlon Brando in the priestly role instead of Bing. 'Barbara would be a smash hit,' I said. She swivelled her head telling Calvin to 'hush you'. Calvin liked her. Barbara said that Calvin and her husband were old friends. Fred, her husband, worked as a mechanic in a gasoline station in Hartford. The couple had two small children, Selma and Freddie. They lived in a public housing high-rise apartment in Hartford and were saving up to buy their own home, outside of the city. 'Are you moving out to

Wethersfield? I know some people who moved there.'

'Wethersfield is not for Coloured,' she said.

'Why not?'

'Cause they don't want Coloured moving out there.'

'This is a free country,' I said. 'Isn't it?'

'Not if you are Coloured,' said Jordon, Calvin, and Rufus.

'No! No, honey, that's only for Whites,' said Barbara. 'Little girl, remember when I said about segregation in America?' asked Rufus. 'That's what this thing is about not wanting Coloured folk to move out to the suburbs.' Calvin looked at me and said: 'Have you wondered why we sit way back here in the cafeteria far away from Whites? Whites don't want to eat with us 'cause we're Negroes. It's segregation, same as in the South. This is the North. Call us Niggers behind our backs.'

Talk of segregation at work and in the cafeteria cast a gloomy shadow. Before getting up to return to her job, Barbara advised, 'Don't pay attention to what these men tell you about themselves. If you want the truth about them, talk to their wives.'

During another of our lunch hour get-togethers, Barbara told us that she had a problem in her apartment with cockroaches. She had filed a complaint with the manager of the public housing project who continued to ignore the problem. My ears pricked-up on hearing the word 'cockroaches' in Hartford, Connecticut above all things. Barbara described how the cockroaches were getting into everything in the apartment including her baby's cribs. I asked her if the cockroaches looked like crabs without the pincers? Surprised at my question, she said, 'Yes'.

'Same buggers, jointed legs and everything,' I told her how they scourged families who lived in the Dublin tenements where I once lived. 'Millions of the buggers scurried out of every nook and corner as if they were escaping from the *Titanic*. The whole floor heaved under a person's feet, the buggers were so thick. Need a shovel to scoop them up, honest to God.'

'Mercy me,' said Barbara.

Mrs Anderson reminded me that some of her girlfriends were planning to come to her house to play bridge and that it would be a good time for me to window shop for a wedding gown. While I gazed out of my bedroom the following afternoon, I watched a car park in front of the house. Four elderly women slowly got out of the car and stood together on the lawn dressed like the flowers of May in colourful floral dresses that barely reached their shins. Each wore a wide-brimmed hat perched on her curly hair. Some of the large straw hats were weighed down with bunches of make-believe cherries or posies of yellow daisies and variegated green ivy. The colourfully dressed old women on the lawn were a sharp contrast to the way older women were expected to dress back home: black drib and drabs. Maybe America was the real Tír na nÓg instead of Ireland? I might have believed that by the cut of the four women standing on the lawn, except that, on closer observation, the faces under the bonnets were crinkled like cornflakes.

I went downstairs on the pretence of picking up the morning newspaper. I longed to meet and greet the old ladies after they arrived in the house. The landlady gave me a sour glance. I ignored her and stared at the lovely glare of colour shuffling before my eyes. Whether out of annoyance or good manners Mrs Anderson introduced me to her girlfriends. 'This is Doris, Hilda, Marge and Florrie. This gal just arrived from the Old Country,' Mrs Anderson told her 'girlfriends'. 'Which old country is that?' inquired Flo.

'Ireland,' I said.

'Come over as a war bride?' asked Doris.

'I'd keep that war bride English accent. It'll work for you,' said Margaret.

'I'm Irish not English.'

Ed wanted us to drive up to Northern Maine to visit his parents so that I would get to know his family. We also had to make arrangements about our wedding. I let Miss Foley, my supervisor, know of the impending trip to Presque Isle, Maine. She agreed to me having a few days off from my job without pay. I got butterflies in the belly thinking about meeting Ed's parents. Would I measure up to their expectations for their son?

Eddie felt a need to fill me in on more details regarding his parents. He told me that when he had written and told his mother that he wanted to marry me, a Catholic, she got upset and went to discuss the matter with her minister who ended up writing Eddie a letter advising that he'd better pray about making such a solemn decision. His mom's biggest concern was that I would try to convert her son to

Roman Catholicism. The biggest obstacle for Eddie had been that we would not be buried in the same graveyard because of our mixed religion. I figured that us being young mattered more than burial rites. When Eddie began to dwell on where we would be buried, I'd shut his gob with a kiss.

My future in-laws might have fire and brimstone running through their veins being of English and Scotch ancestry. So, I anticipated some piss-and-vinegar oozing out at me being a Roman Catholic and marrying their son. I'd grown out of being a Popish slave earlier on, although I would not want our wedding to take place in a Protestant setting. Ma and Da back in Irishtown inquired in their letters where and when the wedding would be. They were getting anxious about the whole thing. Ma asked if we'd have a hooley after the wedding ceremony. Ed set the wedding date for September. But before the plans were finalised, we first had to meet with Ed's parents in Maine.

Whoever wrote the words, 'It's a long way to Tipperary' could have been describing the journey from Connecticut to Presque Isle on the lip of the Canadian border. Ed made and packed a half dozen tuna fish sandwiches, some apples, cartons of milk, and a few bottles of coke for the trip. After we got off the Massachusetts Turnpike we drove for the rest of the journey on a two-way road.

'Ever been on a 400-mile automobile trip, Angie?' asked Ed.

I said 'No.'

'My folks will love you, angel,' he assured me.

'Do they think I'm a war bride? Ireland stayed neutral in the war.'

'War bride? Where did that come from?' he asked.

'Some of Mrs Anderson's girlfriends thought you brought me to the USA as a war bride. They didn't seem pleased at the idea.' 'Some biddies,' Ed replied.

'You could say I'm a GI war bride 'cause growing up poor is like living in a war zone.'

'Tell Mrs Anderson's girlfriends next time they ask you such a question that a guy from Maine fell in love with an Irish colleen.'

His remarks made me recall my mother saying about him, 'Still water runs deep.' She meant that, in his thoughtful way, when he made up his mind to do something he'd considered it from every angle. I raised it one more time, 'I hope your parents like me. What if they don't?' He laughed and said, 'Oh honey, be serious.'

But I was serious; I'd taken a big chance coming over to America to marry him. If it all fell apart during the family reunion, would it be back to Ireland or go sell my wares on the street?

By afternoon, we'd left the busy motorway out of Bangor and headed onto a two-lane road, which divided the dense Maine woods in two. Eddie turned off the air conditioner in the car as we drove through the shady landscape of verdant green firs. The sun shimmered and splashed between the tall spiked fir trees as we drove along. A beautiful smell of pine trees filtered into the car's open windows, more intense and fragrant than any scent inside a church. At times, it felt as if we were sailing through an ocean of green waves that dipped and billowed around us. Here and there, I pointed to curls of black smoke coming from places within the forest like beckoning fingers of fog. 'The smoke is coming from a hunter's lodge or some lumberjack's camp.' Eddie knew a lot about the Maine woods and worried that more and more of the forest was being turned into tourist traps. With a yawn, I settled my head on the back of the seat and closed my eyes to consider how unlike Dublin city these surroundings were.

I must have dozed off; when I woke up we were still driving through the green vastness. The afternoon light began to dwindle. We drove across the landscape for hours without seeing a car from either direction. 'We'll pull over at the Loggers' Café up ahead for gas and for something to eat,' said Eddie. He veered the car off the two-way road and came to a stop outside a run-down looking restaurant. The neon sign read, 'Get Gas and Food at the Loggers' Café'. The smell of pine trees embraced me as I got out of the car, stiff as a board. The perfumed woods circled the café. The place looked like it had been there for a long time; the outside really needed the bang of a paintbrush. Ed gassed up the car, did some knee bends, and we headed through the narrow entrance one at a time. The man behind the counter gave us a nod to seat ourselves anywhere we wanted. The smell of pine, cut wood and homemade cooking filled the place. Rugged men dressed in rough gear were seated at small tables. Stuffed animal heads thronged the walls — moose, deer and elk heads, thickets of twisted horns, and large stuffed owls as dim as night. Pairs of amber glass eyes regarded us in an endless, unblinking stare. A big stuffed brown bear stood in the far corner, beside it a baby bear, the wee one the spitting image of the baby bear from Goldilocks and the Three Bears. It had a paw raised in the air as if bidding a hello or waving bye bye. I asked Ed who killed all the animals, and why. 'For sport,' he answered. 'The taxidermist preserves the likeness, as a trophy,' he added. The man behind the counter came to our table and wanted to know if we wanted 'chowdah or blueberry griddle cakes,' the specialties of the place.

'I'll have both please.'

'Just a bowl of chowder for me,' said Eddie. While we waited for our food, my eyes returned to the animals who should have been out playing in the wild woods, instead of being stuffed, dried, and studded with staring marble eyes inside this airless restaurant.

I'd become a food glutton since leaving Irishtown. The chowder and fresh popping blueberry griddle cakes were scrumptious and bottomless mugs of black coffee to wash the food down seemed out of this world. I ate my fill under the watching eyes of the stuffed and mangled zoo. Eddie's chowder and glass of buttermilk renewed his vitality, while I felt lazy and stuffed to the gills.

We got back in the car and continued our journey through the thick fir woods. I began to wonder if we would ever get to Ed's parents' home. Presque Isle had to be on the lip of some unknown universe. The long car ride continued through a dense forested landscape; evening began to arrive. We were both getting hungry and tired again and needed a break from the road. Ed pulled off the road and parked the car on a bank by the woods. We got out of the car and walked some distance into woods that looked undisturbed by humans.

Our footsteps made sprinkles of tiny pine needles pour down from the tree limbs and scatter at our feet. Then I heard a noise like little hammers off in the distance. 'Woodpeckers digging for bugs,' whispered Ed into my ear with a kiss. He set down the picnic basket on a spongy green area under a tall pine, which swayed like a feather duster over our heads when the wind blew. 'Hope you like tuna fish,' he said.

'First time for me to taste tuna fish.'

I tore away the paper and nearly keeled over from the fishy smell. He must have mixed the tuna with a can of sweet condensed milk. I never would have bitten into the soggy sandwich had I not loved the sandwich-maker. I would have buried it ten feet in the ground.

'Here's a bottle of coke,' he said. 'I know what you like, honey.'

He tore into his pile of tuna fish sandwiches as if he were just released from jail, and washed the lot down with bottles of root beer.

He asked me how I liked the sandwich. 'I never tasted the like,' I replied, hoping my bowels would hold until we got to Presque Isle. He teased that the fishy smell of the tuna might entice nearby bears. 'I'm only kidding,' he said, looking serious.

'That's not my idea of a joke,' I retorted, put off by such a thought and the lingering tang of the tuna.

'Let's continue on,' he said, picking up the empty bottles and paper. As we were about to get back inside the car, something big and white flew overhead and let out a strident scream scary enough to wake the dead. 'Jesus, Mother of God!' I called out. 'It's a ghost! It's banshees!' I grabbed Eddie's shoulder and began to whimper like a whippet. 'It's my fault for eating everything till I burst my belly. The banshees are in the woods. I want to go home to my mother!'

He put his arms around me and said, 'Gee! Angel, you are really scared. You take this banshee stuff seriously.' The strident screams got louder and louder and then ceased completely.

'Look, Angie. Look over there above in the tree. It's a pair of horned owls on the hunt.'

'I'm not looking at anything,' I said, my head digging deeper into his chest. 'I know the sound of the banshee. She must be in my wake.'

'We're in the Maine woods, honey, not Irishtown. That screeching is coming from that pair of large owls over there. See their beaks and talons?'

I unglued my face from his chest and followed his gaze in the direction of a giant pine tree. Two shapes appeared. The pair of owls, big as turkeys, sat on a large limb, peering into the distance. The pair expanded and ruffled their feathers, white as milk, against the dark green pine boughs. Had I not had complete trust in Eddie I'd have drenched myself in fright. I could make out the shape of four golden eyes when the birds swivelled their cat-like heads towards us. Suddenly the pair dived from the tree limb in unison, spreading out wings white as shrouds lifted by a breeze. It seemed the wild things had spotted something amid the narrow folds of the forest, beyond any human eye.

We got back in the car and I breathed a sigh of relief when we rolled down the road again. Would there ever be an end to the woods, I wondered, getting more and more anxious. After a long time, the pine trees began to get smaller, and we could see open space ahead. By now the sky overhead had turned to twilight and daisy petal stars were bunching out, and I had the urge to pluck the sickle moon from the sky and eat it.

We arrived at Ed's parents' home in Presque Isle at four in the morning. We had been driving for almost eighteen hours. I felt wiped out. I recall a woman in a long dressing gown with a pigtail swishing down her back leading me to a bedroom and pointing to the bed. 'I'll see you in the morning, dear. Sleep well in Ruth's bed.' My head dropped down on the pillow like a cement block and my numb brain brimmed with pictures of arrow-sheared fir forests still streaming by. I woke up late the following morning and wondered where I was. Surely not back in George Reynolds House in Irishtown with my family? Hoping to God that might be the case, I brushed sleep from my eyes and wiggled my toes before getting up. I found myself in a girl's pink-painted bedroom. The chest of drawers, desk, chair and a vanity table were all painted pink and highlighted with painted-on blue forget-me-nots. Had I still been a child the room would have suited me to perfection. The room belonged to Ruth, Ed's sister, who had left home years past to attend the University of Michigan; she stayed at the university for two years, moved on to Los Angeles, and met and married a man from Los Angeles. The pair now lived on Catalina Island where her husband Bud worked as a linesman for an electrical company.

I washed and dressed before going downstairs to meet Ed's parents and I braced myself for the fact that his mother was in her sixties, and his father in his foggy eighties. Ed had pointed out that his dad had married three times; his mom, Barbara, was third of the wives — the other two had died. I hoped my future father-in-law had no connection with the famous Blue Beard; of course, I kept such a thought under my hat as I headed down the long narrow wooden staircase. A now very familiar voice called out from another room. 'Is that you, angel? We're in the kitchen. Come in. We're waiting for you.'

Jesus. Here goes, I said to myself a knot forming in my belly. Eddie and his mother were standing in the middle of the kitchen. My future mother-in-law looked familiar although I had never seen her in person. She looked like the plain, strait-laced woman in the painting 'American Gothic'. The imagined canvas came alive as Eddie's mom stepped forward to hug me and ask how I had slept. 'This is Angie, the woman I love,' said the son, introducing me to his mom. Then he directed me to an old man sitting in a wheelchair. 'This is my dad.' His dad, he explained, had suffered several strokes. That explained the dribble coming from the old man's mouth and spilling onto his collar. 'He can't speak out loud anymore, but he understands what you say.'

'Poppa, this is Edward's sweetheart,' Ed's mom said to her husband. He gave no response. I wondered if the tufts of wool growing out of the elder's ears prevented him from hearing the spoken word? Ed drew me towards his aged father and placed my hand into the old man's claw, veined like liquorice, that clasped over mine tight as a clamshell. He squeezed my trembling hand holding it for what seemed like six months, before Eddie pried the claw open to release me. My future husband's parents were old enough to be my parents' mother and father. It would be odd referring to the ancient pair as Mom and Poppa.

Eddie's mom wore a homespun floral dress, rickrack at the collar and side pockets that draped to her ankles. She combed her reddish-gray hair into a tight bun at the back of her head; she wore thick eye-specs that magnified her pretty brown eyes making her appear sombre and serious. Old man Poppa snored in the wheelchair at times, like a tin-whistle or a whistling kettle. Ed went over to the wheelchair to prop up his dad and make him more comfortable. Mom put a pile of johnnycakes on a platter and placed them in the middle of the round table along with a glass dish that held her homemade blueberry compote. Although the knot still twisted my belly, I dug into the cakes and blueberry preserves, impressed by my future mother-in-law's cooking.

Mom asked questions about my family in Dublin, and asked me if I thought I could successfully adjust to a life in the United States. 'With the help of God, mam, sure anything is possible,' I replied. She gave me the eye over once more trying to determine if her new daughter-in-law were a fruit-bearing immigrant or a barren one. After breakfast, Eddie and I volunteered to do the dishes. Mom would have none of that. She had her own set pattern of arrangements for tidying up, she made it known. Ed reminded me we needed to make an appointment with the parish priest at the small Catholic church in Presque Isle to make our wedding arrangements. He wanted to be married in his home town among his large extended family. I agreed. The thought

St Luke's Catholic Church, Presque Isle, Maine

of getting married gave me a hiccup. I realized that three weeks had passed since I'd been around Irish people, and my heart pined. I longed to hear a voice from home, and to share a cigarette with Carmel. I'd give anything now to puff on a Lucky Strike. I wished Eddie smoked occasionally or uttered a curse. I vowed to buy cigarettes as soon as the coast was clear, and keep them up the leg of my knickers for easy access. I also wished I had a bottle of holy water to sip on like Da enjoyed. Had I the opportunity now, I'd not berate Da if he fell down drunk and rolled under the table. And I'd tell my mother over and over how much I loved her until she told me to 'Get up and make a pot of tea, for God's sake.'

We arrived at the red brick church at three o'clock. To my eyes, it looked run down, poor and plain. Ed knocked on the door of the rectory. A small, stocky, middle-aged man, dressed in jeans and a plaid shirt opened the door. Eddie asked him if the priest were in. 'You are looking at him.' The rumpled man was in need of a shave and a haircut and was dressed more like a lumberjack than a man of the cloth. He looked Eddie and me up and down with a critical eye as if wondering, 'Are they a couple of pole cats or a pair of sweethearts looking to tie the knot?' Ed gave our names to the priest. He introduced himself as Father Harris, stubbed out his cigarette, and with a sharp tone ordered us to follow him to his office. 'We came to make our wedding arrangements,' Eddie informed him. 'Angie and I would like you to marry us. She's Catholic and I'm a Methodist. She comes originally from Ireland and her folks expect her to be married by a priest.'

'You are asking me, the pair of you, to give my agreement and blessing to a mixed marriage?' Eddie and I both nodded.

'Holy Mother Church frowns on such arrangements and the Holy Father opposes such unions. Marriage between a Catholic and non-Catholic is to be denounced following Papal instruction.'

The priest paused to let his words sink in.

'My Methodist minister will marry us then if Angie agrees,' exclaimed Eddie. 'Would you go along with that, having been raised in Holy Mother Church?' challenged Father Harris.

'My mother'd feel crippled if a priest didn't marry me. She'd never be able to hold her head up in Irishtown.'

'I would be engaging in pastoral oversight if I performed a mixed marriage,' asserted Father Harris. Ed reached out to take my hand so we could both leave. I knew it wasn't likely I'd go along with having a Protestant marry me.

'I'll live in sin,' I said aloud. 'Sin.'

On the way out of the office, Father Harris called out for us to come back and 'talk some more'. We went back and sat down again, stiff as pokers in the armchairs.

'I'll perform the wedding vows but I will not allow you to have a wedding Mass or get married in front of the altar of God. The marriage will be here in this office.' Tears teased my eyeballs but I kept them at bay, not wanting to give Harris the satisfaction of seeing me cry from shame and disappointment. Ed stood up to leave expecting me to do likewise. Instead, I agreed to abide by the priest's punishment for loving and wanting to marry a Protestant man. Harris knew he had me by the short hairs. He turned to Eddie and noted that he would have to sign an agreement that any children born in the marriage would be raised in the Catholic faith. Moreover, the priest noted, it would be my duty as a Catholic to try and convert my husband into the Catholic religion. Father Harris also dictated that we have two Catholic witnesses to certify our wedding vows, and Ed would have to write out a cheque for one hundred dollars payable to Harris for his services. The priest excused Eddie from our threesome, as he wanted to talk to me alone. 'I'll be right outside, honey,' Eddie said to me. I reminded myself, 'I'm more than a poor Irish immigrant; I'm actually on American soil.' The power play commenced.

Are you with child? No. Are you marrying out of lust? No reply. Have you been naked together in bed? Rubbed naked bodies together? I didn't know whether to laugh or cry. When he kept repeating the same questions, I felt anger in my body. I remained cool as a cucumber, not wanting to throw a spanner into the works.

'Are you still a virgin. Have you let any man touch you down there?' I heard myself replying, 'I'm not up the pole. I'm a virgin.' 'Talk American so that you can be understood in this country,' he barked in my face. I thought to myself if that monkey continues with his line of questioning, I'm having a Protestant minister perform the ceremony and I'm joining the Methodist Church. The monkey sensed my agitation: by now both cheeks were elevated off the chair. 'I have ancestors who came from Ireland,' Harris said. I nearly lost my water. He expected me to comment as I stood up about to leave. The very idea of him to assume that I would be interested in hearing about his Irish ancestors. 'The nerve of that pigheaded . . .' I muttered on the way out, not caring if he heard or not.

Ed wanted to know if the priest had tried to talk me out of marrying him. 'He is dead set against mixed marriages, honey. What other kinds of questions did he ask you that he didn't want me to hear?'

'He asked if we ever rubbed our naked bellies together. And if we were marrying for lust.'

'Why that line of questioning? Is this a Catholic thing that I don't know about, Angie?'

'Apparently, even in the USA.'

Ed became sombre. 'I told the priest we only rubbed noses,' I joked.

The meeting with Harris had put a strain on our nerves and Eddie suggested that we take a drive around the countryside before going back to his parents. He reminded me that his home town of Presque Isle stood as far north as one could go before heading into Canada. 'All those green plants growing in the fields are potato plants,' he pointed out.

'Potato plants?' I repeated, surprised potatoes grew outside of Ireland.

'My three uncles grow potatoes in their fields and raise milk cows as well. They are getting ready for the potato harvest.'

'You mean all the plants in the fields all around us are potatoes?'

'You never heard of our famous Maine potatoes in Ireland? My relatives have farms in Forth, Fairfield, Easton, Mar's Hill, and Houlton, Maine but we won't stop to say 'hi' this time. Mom said they are completely snowed under.' I thought we would be well stocked with spuds from the relatives. Little did I know that thrifty Yankees could take two bites out of a cherry and carve a whirligig out of the pit.

For some reason when I rode with Eddie in the car, I became very romantic. In such a mood I said, 'I'm ready to live in sin. I don't care if I go to hell for all eternity.'

'Honey, where is that coming from?'

'I want to move in with you and live in sin.'

'What would your family think about me if I allowed such a thing?'

'They're back in Ireland and don't know what it's really like in America. Let me move in.'

'We'll go through with the wedding and have a wonderful life together.' Then in a serious voice he inquired, 'You're not going to try and convert me, are you, Angie?'

'Forget that fuckerhead back there at the parish.'

'Honey, you just used a four letter word!'

'Figurehead is not a four letter word. It means authority in the Catholic Church.'

'Oh, I must have misheard you.'

On the way back to town, I commented again on all the potato fields that stretched as far as the eye could see. Eddie told me that all the land planted for Maine potatoes had once belonged to various Indian tribes that used to inhabit the area. He named the Maliseet who lived in Presque Isle, and the Micmacs, Penobscots and Passamaquoddy who also lived in this part of the state. Eddie told me that after the Indian wars with the settlers, the remaining tribes were put on Indian reservations in remote areas of Maine. He said the Maine Indians now lived in poverty. During the Christmas season, he and some of his fraternity brothers visited some of the reservations to donate baskets of food and clothing.

'Want to stop for a bite to eat before heading back to the folks?' Eddie asked.

He pulled up outside a restaurant and we went inside. We sat down and waited for the waitress. I spotted a notice in block letters on the wall that read: 'NO INDIANS SERVED INSIDE.' I pointed the sign out to Ed, and asked him why Indians who'd been here forever could not eat in the restaurant and I, who'd so recently arrived in the country could? 'It's a long, complicated story,' he exclaimed. As we waited to be served, I imagined I heard the beat, beat, beat of war drums rolling through the restaurant and Red Men, half-blackened by smoke, rounding up all the palefaces.

Back in the car, Eddie reassured me we were going to have a wonderful life together and any reservations Father Harris had about our marriage, would not add up to a hill of beans. Harris had tried to use religion as a wedge to separate Eddie and me. I'd come half way around the world to marry my handsome American GI, but that didn't matter to old monkey-face. I thanked the Almighty every waking hour for my future husband, and his love for me. I had no Irish relatives to contact in America to take me in. I did not earn enough as a mail runner at Travelers Insurance to get by, and I did not have the means to purchase a ticket back to Ireland even if I wanted to. Ed's love had stood the test of devotion against Harris.

Ed's mom wanted to know how our appointment went with Rev. Harris. Eddie said, 'fine' and asked his mother if she knew any Catholics who might act as witnesses for our wedding. Mom shook her head in astonishment, replying that she had no acquaintance with Catholics. She turned to me and explained that Protestants and Catholics did not keep company. 'Maybe you can check with the ladies in your sewing circle and see if any one of them knows a Catholic couple?' I wished someone would give me a flagon of whiskey to knock me out of the world for a while. 'It's the same way in Ireland. Catholics and Protestants don't know each other. It's a good thing they are not cannibals.' She gave me an odd look.

'I'll inquire as you suggested, Edward, when our sewing circle meets again.' She turned in the direction of Poppa, strapped in his invalid's chair, and said, 'Edward's making plans for the upcoming wedding.' Poppa did not reply. The auld fella remained in the Land of Nod where hopefully things like being a Catholic or a Protestant, a black person or a white person, or an Indian or a cowboy didn't matter. Mom excused herself to make supper. I offered to help, but apparently she did not hear my numerous offers. Poppa continued to snore like a train off track. He had had three wives? Imagine. I wondered if he'd ever let a drop of drink pass between his stiff blue lips, or only words from the Bible?

'Time to wash up for dinner,' Ed said to me. I began fiddling with the buttons down the front of my blouse as I rushed up the stairs, thinking I had to take a bath in order to get a bite to eat. 'Washing before meals does not mean a bath, honey,' Ed laughed, noticing me undoing my buttons. 'Just the face and hands, Angie.' I liked being clean as much as anyone else but they overdid it in America, this constant concern with being spick and span. My skin had begun to resemble the dry skin of a codfish in a fishmonger's window from all the bathing required. I checked for odours under the pits and in the mouth daily, fearing the wrath of God. Granny Walsh, God rest her soul, had warned our mothers years ago in O'Brien's Place that too much soaping of a child's ears caused festering mastoids. I wondered if sticking all the cotton tipped sticks into my ears daily would have the same effect, and I'd end up with festering mastoids in both ears. It's a good thing Ed and Mom hadn't a clue how bad a case of child-hood scabies I'd gotten from the other kids in the tenements, along with ringworm and fleas. Knowing such things about me might have stopped them relishing their supper.

Mom appeared in the sitting room as fresh as a daisy and smell-ing of purple lavender. She asked us to follow her into the dining room. Eddie wheeled Poppa into dinner. Poppa, still propped up in his wheelchair, continued to sleep like a lamb.

The round table had been set for four people with plain white dishes and ordinary drinking glasses, and silverware, nothing fancy. A set of tureens covered with lids rested on the table. We sat down at the table, pulling Poppa's chair closer to us. Mom looked at Ed and nodded for him to say grace before the meal. He made the prayer short and sweet which made Mom jump in to ask forgiveness for any offence displeasing to the Saviour. I kept my head bowed until she finished, wondering if it were worth the effort to lift my noggin up again. After she finally finished, she looked at me and said, 'A Scotch blessing means a rough scolding.' I crossed my legs under the table and folded my hands on my lap and wondered what would happen should a little red devil hop on the tabletop and jig around the dishes? Poppa remained mute. Mom invited Ed to pass around the tureens. 'I prepared braised beef with root vegetables,' she said. I'd expected a more festive dinner for the occasion, like a leg of lamb or a nice roasted chicken, to say the least. The grey-looking meat sunk under common root vegetables looked like food for a funeral instead of food to celebrate an upcoming wedding — and getting me as a daughter in law. Ed praised his Mom's effort for cooking the dinner.

Suddenly, the woman got up from the table and went into the kitchen, returning with a glass jar of something. She told Ed to close his eyes and open his mouth. He obeyed her command. Mom unscrewed the jar and retrieved a slimy curled worm from the container and put it into her son's mouth. He began to chew on the green maggot. I held onto the arms of the chair in case I should faint at the sight. 'Fiddlehead,' she said into her son's ear. He remained silent. She spiked another fluorescent maggot out of the jar with the two-pronged fork and fed it into his beak. Again she repeated 'fiddlehead.' 'Jesus, Mary and Joseph,' I said to myself, 'Does anyone know in the beginning, what they are getting into?' Again she called him a fiddlehead. I could not believe the look on his face as he savoured the creature, contented as a tomcat with its head in a pail of cream. I kept silent through the whole scene, not wanting to get into a family squabble over name-calling; besides, the mother knew the son longer than I did. When he finally broke the silence, he told his mother that the fiddleheads he'd just sampled were the best she'd ever canned. The light began to clear for me about the fiddleheads when she explained how she got up at dawn to cut and collect the dandelion greens (fiddleheads) before the weeds spouted their yellow blossoms. She canned over a bushel, she told her son then sprayed the rest of the dandelions with weed killer.

The sight of the first raggedy dandelion forcing its way from under the broken sidewalk in O'Brien's Place meant the end of another cold and dreadful winter in our tenement. The young and old who had perished in the neighbourhood had been mourned and buried, thus the sight of any sign of new life shook the heart. Kids in the alleyway named the shaggy-headed dandelions Piss-in-the-Beds. 'Look at the Piss-in-the-Bed coming out of the cement,' a girl would scream, hand out to pluck the prize. 'I saw it first, it's mine,' Bridie would call out. 'No, it's not,' Franny would argue, 'cause it's nearer our hallway, not yours.' 'It's closer to our winda,' I'd insist, plucking the pot of gold with one swipe. 'Ah, there now, let me have the fresh dandelion to feed me sick budgie that barely survived the bitter winter,' would demand one granny or another in the alley. 'Me mammy told me finders keepers,' I'd say back.

The pair of Yanks in front of me continued to yak on about the consistency of the fiddleheads. I found it odd that anyone in their right mind would rave about eating weeds out of the garden when they had money to buy proper food like turnips, cabbage and potatoes. It's not as if they were poor Irish peasants forced to eat shamrocks to stay alive during the Great Irish Famine. 'Mom, you outdid yourself with preparing this batch of fiddleheads,' Ed exclaimed to the relish of his mother. As they gazed at each other over the dinner, the image of Bing Crosby crooning 'Galway Bay' to Barry Fitzgerald entered my mind's eye.

After supper I volunteered to help Mom clean up. I collected the scraps and bones left on the serving dish and asked Mom if there any stray dogs about in the neighbourhood that would like the leftover scraps. 'There are no stray dogs allowed in the neighbourhood and leftovers are saved to use for other dishes,' she said. 'Mom inherited penny-pinching Yankee ways,' chimed in Eddie. 'Folk in this part of the North Woods need to be thrifty and self-sufficient. A penny saved is a penny earned.' I put the leftovers in a container provided by Mom and stored in the refrigerator. Good thing dogs were able to wander wide and far, and hopefully any farmer in the vicinity didn't have to depend on free buckets of leftover slop for the pigpen.

We returned to the immaculate living room. Poppa had stayed asleep through the supper and still remained dead to the world. Ed invited his mother to play something on the piano but she didn't want Poppa disturbed. 'Mom usually plays an evening hymn,' Eddie said.

'Let me get my sewing basket out and get seated, then Ang-lin can tell me more about her family and the Old Country,' said Mom. She got the sewing basket and sat in her low rocking-chair made of willow. Ed told his mother that she had said my name incorrectly. 'It's not Ang-lin, it's Angeline.' His remark upset her. To lighten the air, I interjected, 'Just don't call me "Angela."'

I began to spin out happy fairytales about life back in Dublin City. Mom appeared to like the blarney. She began to crochet with her crochet hook and white silk thread. Her thin bony fingers worked frenziedly as she wielded the silver hook in and out of the silken thread.

I'd expected she'd work as calm as a spider weaving a lace web instead of like someone possessed. In retrospect, I understand that the woman's sewing frenzy reflected her fears of caring for her invalid husband, and feeling as if her head might fly off the spindle. Ed's mom probably ached for her daughter on the other side of the country, but she'd not let that show. Her daughter, like myself an only daughter, both of us leaving behind mothers who needed us. Ruth's mom tied down with a mute, invalid man incapable of even feeding himself; my mother back in Irishtown, with a husband determined to kill himself with drink.

Ed and I left the following morning to return to Hartford. His mother packed us a lunch for the long journey. We said our goodbyes and got into the car. As we drove out of Presque Isle the sun hadn't yet appeared in the sky. The morning air reeked with the lovely smell of pine trees coming from the Maine forest in the distance. As dawn broke, plumes of black smoke began to corkscrew into the sky above. Timber companies were already processing cut trees.

'That's the smell of Maine — pine pitch,' Eddie fondly noted. 'I love the smell of the pine trees too,' I told him. 'I hope no one ever cuts down the forest.'

Ed rolled down the car window and we both inhaled the pine-scented fresh air. Soon after I noticed tears rolling down this face. I wondered if he were crying about leaving his parents? Instead of commenting, I followed an adage told to me by my mother, 'A good cry clears a heavy heart,' and kept quiet. After some time, Eddie asked me to reach into his pocket for his handkerchief. He honked into the handkerchief with such force he could have unhinged his head off the shoulders. I wondered if his tears would ever stop. It's hard to see men cry.

The only time I saw my father cry was when he lost the last shilling on a horse, dropped a last cigarette into the blazing fireplace while trying to light it in his mouth, or shattered a bottle of porter from hitting the top off the bottle too hard with the poker, ending up with the precious porter spilled all over the floorboards where Minnie, our cat, lapped it up.

'It's hay fever, honey, that's causing my eyes to tear like this. I've got allergies.' I had never heard the word 'allergies' before or 'post nasal drip'. 'Is post-drip American lingo for snotty nose?'

By now his handsome face looked puckered. He swallowed a handful of hay fever pills washed down with some lemonade Mom had put in the thermos bottle. I planted a kiss on his cheek. We were hungry for lunch so Ed parked the car off the road by the edge of a field. While I set out the lunch prepared by Mom, he wrung out a handkerchief. My sandwich, made from the leftover braised beef from the previous day, tasted delicious, as did the cold lemonade and ginger cookies.

We pulled in to my boarding house as the dawn rose. While getting ready for bed, I noticed that my landlady had put a letter on the bedspread, a letter from home. Although exhausted, my heart bounded with joy on seeing the brown, penny envelope stamped with a John Redmond one shilling and three-pence stamp affixed in the corner. Da had addressed the letter in his scripted handwriting that I recognized clear as day.

The letter read:

My own Dear Little Titch, We received your letters and dollars and were delighted to know you are well. Your Ma said if you want to come home, you are not to send her any more money, but to save it for your fare home. She said that she would rather see you than have all the money in the world. You know if you don't want to get married don't do it! We would give anything in the world to have you here, and you wouldn't get away again. Your mammy and me have come to the conclusion that you are not to get married until you are over 19, and you know your mind better. We had a letter from Miss Foley, and she wants you to stay with her should you want to, but do what you want! You mean all the world to us. Love Da, Ma, Bob, Noel, Frank, Bridie, Barney, Darkie the dog, and the cat. Kisses, Kisses, Kisses.

I put the letter under my pillow and lapsed into foggy dew.

When I returned to my job at the supply department the next morning Miss Foley gave me a faint smile. I could not tell if she was pleased that I had returned or had a case of the gripe. Before heading down to the mailroom to bring up the morning mail, Miss Foley beckoned me to come to her desk. I thought she might be upset at me being a minute late for work, knowing she kept an eye out for such things. 'Sit down, dear,' she invited sliding over a chair. 'I have some serious things to discuss with your. Serious things brought to my attention by white workers in the building, especially the men.' 'Oh,' I replied, completely surprised. 'As you know, Angeline, you are not in Ireland anymore. There are some things that are not considered acceptable by a number of people over here. White people do not eat lunch with blacks or spend time in their company. That's the way it is here and in this company. You are not to eat with the Negroes in the shipping and receiving area. It's upsetting the white men workers. They know you don't understand the rules but they want me to set you straight about such behaviour. You are not to eat lunch with Negroes any more. If they ask you, you are to say no! I hope this is the end of such things. You are a bright girl.'

Talk about feeling Paddywacked! Miss Foley's words left me speechless. With that, she opened the desk drawer and handed me a long white envelope crested with a red umbrella and said, 'Your paycheck, dear.' I carried the two heavy mailbags down to the receiving and shipping room where the contents would be dispersed around the United States. As usual, Calvin, Jordan, and Rufus were all busy loading and unloading trucks.

'Hi, sugar,' called Jordan. 'Here for the incoming mail? How did you like Maine? Made all the wedding plans?'

'Hey, getting married isn't so terrible,' joked Calvin. I nodded and reached over to pull across the mailbags.

'Joining the gang for lunch? Barbara plans on being there.' I remained mute, not knowing what to say.

'Barbara wants to hear more blarney.' I avoided his eyes.

'Hey, anything the matter, missy? What's up, girl?' I remained mute.

'You are having lunch with us at the cafeteria?' I just looked at him.

'What's going on?' he asked. He called out, 'Hey, Rufus, something is wrong with the baby girl.' Rufus called out, 'Must be having to make all the marriage arrangements.'

'Don't think that's the problem. Think it's something else she doesn't want to tell us about.'

I felt shame and helplessness oozing from every bone in my body.

'Oh! Oh!' Jordan exclaimed. 'I get it. You were told not to talk or eat with the Niggers.'

'That's it,' affirmed Calvin and Rufus. Jordan stared into my face and said, 'The first thing newcomers learn in this country is to hate Negroes. Not your fault.'

A fog of pain and silence engulfed us. Calvin stepped aside, letting his chest heave in anger. He extracted a cigarette from a pack tucked in his shirt pocket, pondered the cigarette then placed it between his teeth biting down on it like a bullet.

Miss Foley beamed at the white male workers sitting around the lunch table with me sitting stiffly in a chair next to her. 'It's time you ate with your own kind,' said one of the men who earlier had told me that his relatives came from County Kildare at the turn of the century with rags for breeches and a determination to make it in America. I turned my head to look off in the distance where my friends were eating lunch. I despised myself for being a turncoat, a little bitch lacking backbone and gumption. Who, back home in Irishtown, would believe white workers in Hartford, Connecticut refused to eat with black workers? I would rather have sliced my heart in two with the bread-knife than plunge it into the maple bun. 'You need to eat more substantially, dear,' cooed Miss Foley. An older bushy-haired man at the end of the table called out to me that his grandparents came from Ireland. I nodded back at the geezer who looked like a wicked elf. Miss Foley said he held the job of supervisor in another area of the Traveler's Insurance Company. She signalled for me to accompany her back to our department after lunch. Much to my surprise, she told me that if I decided not to get married, she'd be willing to adopt me. I laughed out loud thinking she was making a joke. Then by the look on her face, I knew she meant it. If I decided not to get married, she informed me, I could move in with her and share the spacious private apartment she owned in West Hartford. She also let me know that if I wanted to pursue an education she would fund it out of her own pocket. I could be anything I wanted. I'd be the daughter or niece she always wanted. For some reason I began to feel woozy from her outburst of affection. Again I heard myself saying, 'You're kidding.'

'Angeline, dear, I mean every word.'

'Are you serious?' I repeated feeling nervous.

'Consider it,' she advised. Until now, I thought only small orphaned children were adopted, not grown people like myself who had parents still living in Dublin. I wondered why she said all the stuff about wanting to adopt me when she knew I would be getting married in the near future. Maybe she felt sorry for the poor guy who had pledged his love to me? What a baffler, what a headscratcher!

I needed to keep my mind on the job as the mail runner, keeping the incoming and outgoing mail running smoothly, especially getting the letters to the right people. Because of what had happened with Miss Foley earlier on, I felt in no mood to cope with cranky underwriters in the department yelling at me to 'Get it right, kid!' Would quitting time ever get here? I could hardly wait to see Eddie and fill him in on what had happened. That evening as we drove home together across the Hartford Bridge and onto the parkway, I told him about the day's events.

'It's terrible for her to tell me not to sit or eat with black people in the cafeteria. This is America and I'm supposed to have the right to eat with whoever I please, Goddamn it.' Eddie winced at my swearing. 'I'll lose the feckin' job if I eat lunch with the black people in the shipping department. I need the job to send money back home, especially to pay for a gravesite should Ma or Da die.'

'Someday our nation will solve this problem,' said Ed, sombre as a judge.

'That's not all that happened today,' I said. 'Miss Foley, my supervisor, wants to adopt me if I don't marry you.' Ed swerved the car.

'Whatever prompted her to say such things? Isn't she aware that our wedding will take place in October? That you are going to be my wife?

'She knows all that. Maybe she's soft in the head? Maybe she thinks like my brother Frank back home. He told me any man who married me must be fond of wedding cake.' He didn't appreciate the joke.

'You need to make it perfectly clear to Miss Foley that you have no interest in taking up any of her generous offers. Next time I pick you up, I'll go inside your department and introduce myself'

'I can tell her myself I'm not up for adoption, for God's sake.'

'Please be more reverent, honey.'

'Well, don't go poking into my lunch pail looking for worms.'

'Angie, I'm sorry. What a hectic day. An experiment we were doing in the wind tunnel didn't meet expectations.'

I reached over and linked his arm. 'I could make you liver and onions for dinner,' I offered. 'Thanks, Angie. Have you considered the kind of wedding gown you want?' I reminded him that the priest insisted that he would not marry us inside the church because of me being a Catholic and he a Protestant. 'Why bother with a wedding dress and veil if he'll only marry us in the church library out of sight of everyone?' Going to the expense and bother of selecting a bridal grown to be married in some dreary niche instead of at the high altar inside the church make little sense to me. Eddie thought otherwise. He intended to buy a whole new outfit for our wedding, and wanted the same for me. One of the girls at the office gave me the name of a bridal store in Hartford.

The following Saturday, Eddie and I went into the city to select our wedding outfits. He dropped me off a block away from where he intended to shop. I insisted the groom should never see the bride's wedding outfit until the big day. I intended to quickly select a bridal gown and veil, have it wrapped up, and that would be that. However, my mother's face came before me and I keenly felt her absence. I knew mother and daughter shopped together for the daughter's wedding gown. As I walked along in the direction of Church Street, I felt tangled amid a dream. I pinched my hand to make sure that indeed my dreams of finding an American husband and coming to live in America had come true. Yet the sense of being an exile from Ireland lingered. 'Buck up. Find a lovely wedding outfit to wear on the biggest day of your life.' The smiling face of Princess Grace dressed in tulle and lace emerged out of the blue. 'That's it—that's the way I want to look—just like her.'

Gloria Gay Gowns of Distinction, 18 Church Street, Hartford, Connecticut came into view. Wedding gowns of various styles were displayed in the store window like drifts of the whitest snow. I pushed the heavy oak door open and two saleswomen, dressed from head to toe in black, came over and inquired how they could be of assistance. I told the older one I needed to find a wedding dress. She asked me if I were alone. 'Yes,' I replied. She continued, 'Moms come with their daughters to pick out the wedding gown.'

'My mother would be here, only she lives in Ireland.' My eyes glistened. My mother and father had felt bad that they could not afford to buy me a wedding dress to take with me to America. Ma spent her last few shillings on a lovely Irish lace-trimmed handkerchief for me to slip up the sleeve of my wedding dress when the big day arrived in the States.

The saleswoman took me by the elbow and led me over to racks of bridal gowns that were slightly disturbed by a breeze from an open window. The puffy white garments looked like ghost gowns waiting to be inhabited. The array of gossamer veils that would cover the bride's head and face were sheer as cobwebs. Who would ever believe that I would be getting married in one of these lovely creations? The saleswoman slid her hand through the rack of gowns like a knife going through creampuffs, describing the gorgeous details of each one. The thought of trying on any one of the lovely ghost gowns made purple goose bumps appear on my arms. 'We have to find you the perfect grown. The dress is the most important part of the wedding. It's the only thing a bride remembers,' she told me. We walked back and forth looking at the stock. She asked if I'd a particular image of a bride in mind. I replied without any hesitation, 'Grace Kelly — Princess Grace of Monaco.' Wedding photographs of the princess and her husband were featured in all of the Irish newspapers when she got married. My mother, looking at a photo in the *Evening Herald*, said Grace Kelly was the most beautiful princess to inhabit the world. I settled on a long-sleeved, triple-tiered wedding dress billowing from the waist to ankle. The top part of the dress had lace cutout flowers over taffeta and a row of pearl buttons down the front. I picked out a gossamer shoulder-length veil topped with a small crown. The saleswoman handed me a pair of white satin shoes to complete the outfit. Then she led me to a floor-length gilt-edged mirror and told me to take a look at myself. The girl from the gutter been replaced by a princess — or someone who had been dunked headfirst into a bowl of sugar.

The girls in the office began to take more notice of my presence when word got around that Miss Foley took me to lunch at the company cafeteria. Betty, a married typist, Jonie, Norma, and Madelyn wanted to know if I would like to walk up town on our lunch hour. They wanted to do some window-shopping. Betty hoped to find a set of china that would go with the colours of her new kitchen. Delighted to be included, I accepted with a big thank you. The four women had worked in the supply department for a number of years and were chummy with each other. They came to work under Miss Foley after graduating from high school. Norma came after she finished secretarial training. Compared with the four, I felt backward because I hadn't even a junior high education. As we headed downtown the talk clicked as fast as the feet on the pavement — talk about boyfriends, deep kissing, heavy petting, and whether going for the cheaper plastic dishes would detract from the decor of Betty's in-progress family nook. The four stopped to look into every fashion window in every store. There was no mention about eating lunch until the last few minutes. Then they made a mad dash into a Woolworth's store and headed for the lunch counter to order chicken salad sandwiches and cherry cokes to go. I followed the leaders, and ordered the same, disappointed at having to pay so much for so little food compared to eating on the company premises. Once in a while one of them would ask what I thought about this or that. I never got to finish a sentence before they were all talking together about some other divine image in a shop window. Being out to lunch with the four made me feel back in touch with the world of young women interested in fashion, fucking, and scurrying round a cityscape, whether it be Hartford, Connecticut or the mean streets of Dublin City.

Miss Foley asked me how the lunch hour went with the girls. Panting from all the rushing around and gulping down of the soggy chicken on a bun and the too-sweet drink, I answered, 'I loved it. We're going again tomorrow. Betty is looking for a set of dishes for her family nook.' I went to the bathroom to wash my sticky hands before going back to work. Joni stood before the mirror in the bathroom piling her red hair on top of her head and keeping it in place with what she called 'bobby pins'. Her face seemed pale under the makeup but she looked as beautiful as a movie star. 'Got a Midol?' she asked.

'What's that?' I asked.

'What we take for cramps,' she said, rubbing her belly as if it burned inside.

'Are you taking about having the Charlie?' I asked. 'The monthlies? You know, what girls get?' We both stopped in our tracks to make sense out of what the other meant.

'I know what you mean,' Joni said. 'We're talking about the monthly curse.'

'Yes,' I replied, not knowing where further to step.

'Midol helps me a lot when I get cramps with my period,' she said while she took a small package from her purse. 'Got to put a new one on,' she smiled. 'A new what?' I asked. 'Kotex,' she replied. 'Have you never seen one of these before, a Kotex?' showing me the 'Kotex Sanitary Napkin' in her outstretched hand.

'No,' I answered reverently, as if being shown the miracle of miracles.

'What do you use?' she asked.

'Rags, odd socks, and whatever else comes to hand in an emergency.'

'Gad! Ugh! Gross. Why do you do that?'

'It's the kinds of things we use back in Ireland. We don't have them things in your hand. I never knew them things were in existence,' I told her. 'How do you keep the pad on?' 'There's a sanitary belt that goes with the napkins. I'll show you how it works.' With that she pulled down her skirt around her hips to show me a thin white belt fitted around her belly. 'The belt's got a loop on each end where you attach the long ends of the napkin. Easy as pie for anyone to figure.' Who could believe there would be any nation with the brains to come up with an invention of such magnitude? On our lunch hour next day Joni promised to take me to the drug store and show me where to buy a box of Kotex and the belt for attaching them. My mind could barely take in the information— I felt such intense relief from not having to worry any more about the issue of female protection or an itchy, scratchy crotch.

Miss Foley pronounced Ed to be a handsome, sober young man who would make a wonderful husband. She liked him a lot. And how fortunate I was to grow old with such a serious man. Apparently, she met few people from Maine. Maine people, she elaborated, were more likely to seek jobs in Florida or California than Connecticut. She made it sound as if Maine was somewhere beyond the pale, someplace few went to from other states. Ed seemed pleased that Miss Foley wanted to take him under her wing as she did me, and he found her fondness for me touching.

Eddie asked if I would like to cook some food at his place. 'Maybe eat in for once? We'll drive over to the supermarket. Ever been inside of a supermarket?'

'Hardly.' I said.

He told me that it was a good idea to make a list of what you wanted to buy at the store, and have it in hand when shopping. 'I'll made Dublin Coddle for dinner.' Up until now, I'd only shopped for food at Coady's shop on Bath Street across from George Reynolds House. Mr and Mrs Coady sold everything from a mousetrap to heads of lovely flowery green cabbages. Most of the goods in the shop were sold without packaging. The Coady family lived above the shop and any one of their six kids waited on the customers, dirty hands and all. In comparison with Coadys' shop, the supermarket seemed as big as a playing field. 'Got your list out, Angie? Let's get a shopping-cart.' I failed to answer, swept away by the immensity of the inside of the supermarket laid out like a maze before my eyes. I looked at the tiny grocery list and compared it with the tons of food stockpiled in the maze of aisles and felt completely disoriented. I hung onto the shopping cart as Eddie headed into one of the food tunnels constructed of canned goods of every kind.

'What's the first item on the list, honey?'

'Sausages.'

'The meat section is way over on the other side, near the frozen food section.' We pushed the cart it, seemed to me, for a half a mile before we came to the coldest place I'd ever felt — the frozen food section.

I poked my head into one of the upright coolers to find the contents covered with frost. 'Let's get a package of fish sticks,' said Eddie picking up a frozen square. I rubbed off the front of the frozen square and looked at the picture of skinny, square fish piled on a plate without tails, fins or heads. 'American fish,' I said to myself. I thought about my brother Bob, who'd fished a lifetime, reeling in a square fish out of the Irish Sea. I assumed God stocked America's harbours with fish to their liking, and let it go at that. We moved on to the meat section. There were meadows and fields of chopped-up cows, pigs, and sheep wrapped in cellophane bundles along one wall. The sight of tons of raw meat in pinks, purples and vivid reds made me feel queasy. I'd been used to scraps of this and that but never a mountain of flesh. Poor old Johnny Duggan who lived above us in O'Brien's Place had had a craving for flesh of any kind. Because of his poverty he snared pigeons that flew into the laneway looking for crumbs.

'See the sausages you need, honey? Let's go talk to one of the butchers,' said Eddie, blotting the image of the past from my mind. I told the burly man behind the glass case what kind of sausages I needed. 'I want thin sausages, not fat sausages.' 'Thin sausages, not fat sausages is what the little lady orders,' said the butcher. 'Hey Joe!' He shouted to another man working at the end of the meat counter.

'Joe, this little lady wants to know if we have thin sausages not fat sausages'?

'That so?' the man replied wiping his hands off and walking along to join us. He said to me for all to hear, 'What you want to buy thin sausages for when we have fat sausages?' Eddie began to cough while I felt confused.

'I'm making coddle for dinner. I only know how to make it with skinny sausages,' I exclaimed to both butchers.

'What's that? What's a coddle?' Ever heard of a coddle, Joe?'

'She probably means cuddle,' said the imbecile.

'I didn't say a cuddle. I'm making a Dublin coddle and I need thin sausages, a few small onions, Oxo soup cubes and four cups of water to make a coddle.'

'Let's go, honey,' Eddie said, tugging my sleeve.

'Oh, I know what the little lady wants. She wants some links. Joe, go bring us a pack of links for the little lady for her cuddle or coddle or whatever she's cooking for the boyfriend.' I realized the butchers were having a bit of fun at my expense.

Eddie suggested that we ask his mom to make our wedding cake, as a gesture of love. I asked if he expected more people at our wedding than his parents and us? I wondered if she'd make it bigger than a cup cake, but I didn't raise the question. 'Mom will do a heck of a job on the wedding cake.' I nodded in agreement.

Back in the office, the typists were constantly friendly towards me. One would say, 'I've Bayer aspirin for headaches in my desk drawer, if you need one.' Or Norma would exclaim when I passed by her location, 'If you are hungry let me know, I have all kinds of candy bars stashed in the drawer.' And Madeline and Betty kept an assortment of 'greeting cards' in their desks should I need one for a birthday, anniversary, or a sympathy card. Miss Foley took note of the budding friendships and seemed pleased. My friends in the receiving room, Rufus, Calvin and Jordan still offered me a cigarette if I wanted one. One Monday morning, I burst out crying in front of Jordan as I picked up the mailbag.

'What's up, baby?' he asked with concern in his voice.

'I feel terrible about being so far away from my family and I dare not tell anyone. They think I should be happy because I'm here in this country, but my heart feels broken at times, and I miss my mother so much. I miss the two of us having a cup of tea together and raking over our tea leaves to tell our fortunes, and hearing all the gossip, and finding out who's going to have another baby, and things like that.'

He nodded and patted my hand, and told me that he understood, his family originally came from the South, and they were heartsick about relocating for a long time.

On lunch hour the following week, Miss Foley gave me a crisp five dollar bill and asked if I would run an errand for her. She gave me directions where to take a pair of her shoes which needed new heels and to pick up a green banana on the way back. Her asking me to take her shoes to be mended gave me a chance to do something nice for her. It took me a while to figure out how to get to the cobbler's shop in spite of the directions given. I placed the shoes on the counter and told the man they needed new heels. 'Our motto is "Heels While You Wait",' he said. 'Take a seat.'

I enjoyed the smell of the leather as he cut it to circle the heels on Miss Foley's shoes. I examined the displays of shoelaces, buckles, and shoe polish on the countertop. I noticed a small stand that contained what I took to be doorknockers until I read the word 'taps' underneath. The silver metal doorknockers or taps went on dancing shoes. Taps for the bottom half of shoes cost two dollars. I examined the bottom of my white flat shoes that Eddie had bought me and wondered if they were solid enough for a pair of taps. The tapping sounds made by Gene Kelly in the film *Singing in the Rain* still echoed in my mind. The way he tap-tapped up and down the kerb and into the gutter filled with rainwater had been brilliant. I asked the guy working on the heel if taps could be put on ordinary shoes. 'Who'd want taps put on ordinary shoes?'

'Me.' I took off one of my shoes and he looked it over.

'Can't guarantee the taps will stay put,' he said.

'I don't need taps for the heels just for the bottoms.'

'Have a seat until I finish the heels on that fancy pair of alligators you brought in. Are they yours?'

'Those alligator shoes belong to my supervisor, Miss Foley. She asked me to take them for new heels.'

'Lady has expensive taste,' he added through a mouth of tacks. He charged three dollars to fix her heels. 'It'll be two bucks for half-taps on the soles.' I took out two dollar bills, which I'd earmarked to send home to Dublin, and gave them to the cobbler. 'It's your money, sweetheart,' he said, taking my shoes. I waited in bare feet while he nailed on the taps, excited as a rising star. 'Ready, little lady. Here, give them a try.' The shoes felt five times their original weight with the heavy metal soles on the bottom. I put the shoes back on and tested them like a galloping pony over the track. My tapping sounds were in joyous accord with the tap-dancing of Gene Kelly. I almost forgot Miss Foley's alligators sitting on the countertop as my feet quivered towards the front door and onto the sidewalk. I tap-banged, bang-tapped along the concrete pavement towards the store to get Miss Foley her under-ripe banana at the shop.

Although sweating like a mule from the heat and humidity, I continued to bang-tap my way up the hill to the supply department. I'd lost all sense of time and knew I would have to sign in on the late list when I got to the office. As I tapped on, I thought about having a job in a large insurance company that depended on accidental death, blazing fires, automobile crashes, airplane accidents and catastrophes of every description. Such grim reality stood in stark contrast with my concept of a happy, toe-tapping America. The sombre insurance capital of the world lacked any resemblance to Beverly Hills, Hollywood or the Wild West. I foot tapped up Church Street holding the green alligator shoes and the piece of fruit under my armpit. I wished Gene Kelly would hear the tapping of my white flat shoes and appear from under a tree and invite me to share his opened umbrella just as the scorching sky overhead turned to black clouds that would burst into rain showers. When I thought about it, sometimes Eddie's face became like Gene Kelly. They had similar smiles.

Miss Foley and everyone in the office were busy at work when I returned from lunch hour. The sound of my tap-shoes caused the supervisor to wheel round in her swivel chair. 'Whatever is that odd sound I hear?' she asked. 'My taps. I got taps on my shoes along with new heels on yours at the cobbler's shop.' Her Irish blue eyes opened a mile. 'Angeline, dear, why I never . . . ' she said, trailing off in mid sentence as I diddled with delight attempting to tap a la la la la on the floor by her desk, making heads around the office cant towards us. She thanked me for doing the errand, suggested I go about my work, and shoved the bag containing the green banana into the top drawer of her desk. I tap tapped all the way down to the receiving room, enjoying the sounds made by my shoes. Rufus, Calvin and Jordan clapped and smacked each other on the back when I showed them my shoes, and did a little two-step.

'The sound of my shoes makes me happy. I'd have loved to be a dancer with an umbrella.'

Eddie wanted to know if office workers in Ireland were allowed to wear dancing shoes to work. 'How would I know? People like myself only go into pawn offices, known in our vicinity as pawn shops,' I replied, peeved at his jab. I continued to wear my bang-taps to work and play. Mrs Anderson, my landlady, the descendant of King Olaf of Sweden, insisted I remove the shoes before walking on her plank floors — she'd charge extra should the boards need a re-surface.

I wondered if Eddie's Protestant family danced at weddings like the wild Catholic bunch I'd grown up with, remembering how they heeled it and toed it around the bride and groom until they passed out and fell on the floor from drinking too much black porter. My future father-in-law, old as Methuselah, would not be able to set foot on a dance floor or get out of his wheeled contraption without major assistance. My future mother-in-law didn't seem the kind who ever set her foot outside of her church, and any thought of her kicking her heels up in the air would be a stretch of the imagination. Eddie danced divinely and could sweep any girl off her feet, whether back in the Old Country or here in the New Country, but his religion did not allow him to dance on a Sunday. If our wedding took place on a Sunday, I'd be left hop-scotching around in a ring by myself. I did not expect to hear the sound of corkscrews drawing corks from bottles of beer on our wedding day or the pop of champagne corks. The thought of being toasted with glasses of milk instead of liquor seemed as alien as stuffing cabbage leaves instead of boiling the whole head in salt water as the Lord intended. There'd be a lot to learn about heeling and toeing it in America.

I started to get cold feet about the whole set of set of arrangements, expectations and marriage. I felt my head might crack like an eggshell. But I'd decided to keep such thoughts under the carpet.

The rush part of the working day turned out to be the lunch hour. If Miss Foley didn't want me to run an errand either to the shoemaker's shop or to get her a green banana, I went out shopping with Norma, Betty, Joni, and Madeline. Only Miss Foley shopped at G. Fox department store. Lerner's department store, Joni advised, had the best buys in Lanlon ladies' sweaters and fancy underwear. I had to be skimpy with my dollars due to paying rent, sending some home, and buying a few things like a new firm brassière that added extra curves under my new Lanlon pale blue short-sleeved sweater. Without meaning to, I splurged on a box of skinny little panties that came in different colours for different days of the week. Each little beauty had the day of the week embroidered on the front. Betty continued to search for the right shade of yellow dishes to no avail. We ate our lunch on the run, either a chicken salad sandwich with a bottle of coke or a Mars bar washed down with a bottle of coke. My back teeth began to ache from eating candy bars; luckily Joni kept aspirin in the desk drawer. Shopping for bargains with the office girls reminded me of the intense competition of shopping for Yanks in Dublin between myself and Carmel. Finding a good buy in a brassière, panties and sweaters in Lerner's department store didn't have quite the intensity of bagging a handsome American male.

Eddie told me that he had received a letter from Mom in Presque Isle reminding him that we needed to order wedding invitations and get them sent out, write a wedding announcement to place in the local paper in his hometown and select our silver service pattern.

'What's a silver service pattern? Never heard of such a thing.'

'It means serving flatware like knives, forks, spoons and other flatware pieces.'

'Is this a required condition to get married?'

'No, it's not a requirement. Selecting a silver pattern is something the couple agrees to and the desired pattern is made known to relatives and friends.'

'Who's going to need all the knives, forks and spoons and them other things you mentioned?'

'Dinner guests,' he replied.

'Silver goes dull and needs to be polished and shined,' I replied, hinting I didn't relish the job. Bad enough polishing my Blessed Mary medals around my neck with toothpaste.

'We need to get our wedding rings this weekend, honey. We will have the rings inscribed with our initials.' We picked out a pair of matching plain gold wedding bands and had them inscribed. My heart shook when I tried the ring on. The love in Eddie's eyes washed over me like a tidal wave. He didn't believe in cutting corners when it came to me. I wondered if he'd good eyesight or knew what he was doing. I'd be a perfect wife and show my love for him in every way, but I would not give up my job as the mail runner in the insurance company. I'd wait until the following weekend to let him know about my decision; not wanting to pack another thing, until then, into my sometimes unsettled skull. God! I could feel the increasing expectations being placed on my shoulders, expectations meant to chip away at the old me who used the same spoon for everything. Another letter arrived from Mom that included a long list of names of people who were to receive wedding invitations. If I was getting married back in

George Reynold's flats in Irishtown my mother would let the neighbours know that Angeline was getting married and everyone was welcome to the wedding. Mom up in Maine also wanted to know what kind of white flowers I wanted in my wedding bouquet. I had never thought about a bouquet. I had in mind a couple of flowers picked or pinched from someone's garden.

'Flaming red carnations are my favourite flowers.'

'Mom prefers a bouquet of white flowers.' I kept my lip buttoned, but wanted to say, 'I'm not a child making my First Holy Communion but a young bride picking her own favourite flowers for her wedding day.' Mom and Eddie might prefer that I carry angelic foliage but sooner or later they needed to see me as the person I was.

'Flaming red carnations are fine,' Ed said, obviously pleased by my insistence.

A lot of our wedding invitations were addressed to Protestant pastors scattered around small towns of Aroostook County in Northern Maine. 'There are quite a few ministers in our family,' Eddie smiled, adding, 'You will be the first Catholic in the flock.'

I sent wedding invitations to some of our closest neighbours in George Reynold's House. Ma and Da were astonished that Ed had the invitations printed as coming from them: '*Mr & Mrs Francis Kearns cordially invite you to a wedding reception in honour of the marriage of their daughter Angeline Bridget and Edward Walter Lyon on Saturday, the fifth of October . . .*' I took a handful of the invitations with me to work and passed them out to Miss Foley, some of the office girls, and my friends in the shipping department: Calvin, Rufus, Jordan and one for Barbara. Calvin joked that they might not be able to make it up to the Canadian border for the wedding. On a more serious note he said, 'If you have a change of heart and want to go home, I will take up a collection to pay your way.' I could feel my eyes fill with tears of shame at his kindness and consideration and despised myself for going along with Miss Foley.

My brother Bob wrote to tell me that he and other seamen had been laid off the coal boat due to the price of coal going down.

Dear Angeline, We got your letter and the post cards. Ma says that the ten dollars is a godsend. It arrives on the eight o'clock post every Monday morning. She goes into the American Express with it. She gets three pounds sixteen shillings for it instead of three pounds ten shillings when she exchanges it at Coady's. Da expects her to buy him a dozen bottles of stout out of it every Monday and she refuses. He is still the same. The minute she opens the letter, the faces he makes. Angeline if you want to send him anything, send it to him separate. He has me ma pestered looking for drink. Ma has to pay out the whole ten dollars you send to cover rent, electricity, and food. She does not have to pawn my suit now, thanks to you . . . Love Bob.

Joni looked over my wedding invitation at her desk. She caught my eye and gave a signal to meet her in the 'john'. I hoped Joni would share a cigarette with me. I found her leaning over the washbasin examining her face in the mirror. She opened the top part of the bathroom window and we both lit up our cigarettes. I gave her a dollar for three cigarettes and some matches that I slipped into my pocket.

'I'm having trouble with my boyfriend.'

'What's the matter?'

'I think he's skunking around with another girl behind my back. Mandy always had a crush on him. I'm sure it's her.' She quickly changed topics and asked: 'Have you and your boyfriend done it? Gone all the way?'

I expected young American women to be blunt about sexual matters, so her question did not surprise me. 'It's against my religion to do it before marriage,' I told her, feeling my face blush. 'Are you lying? ' She laughed. 'You come across as a cute little mouse but I think you're more like a tiger.' I knew other reasons existed that prevented me from going all the way besides Eddie believing that it was better for both of us to wait until our wedding. 'Well, if you haven't done it yet let me give you a warning: it's like trying to thread the eye of a needle with spaghetti.' Her imaginative description of the sex act remained with me for the rest of the workday.

The heat of summer finished at the end of August. The light of day dimmed and as the nights grew longer the trees turned into colours that I'd never seen before. The Glastonbury countryside looked painted over with colours of vibrant gold, red, amber, and pale yellow splashes. My wedding day grew closer. Miss Foley wanted to know if I intended to quit work after the wedding. 'Absolutely not,' I told her. 'Absolutely not.' She asked if Ed would go along with my decision to work. 'I intend to continue to work, Miss Foley, even if I have to shovel coal.' I'd discuss the matter with him after the honeymoon. Ed got a letter from his pastor inviting him to have our wedding reception at the Grant Memorial Church, in Presque Isle, Maine. 'Everything is set to go, honey,' he said.

'Thanks in great part to your mother,' I replied. 'She must have explained things to Mr Grant.'

My friend Rosaleen Byrne, who still sold ice cream in the Theatre Royal in Dean Street, sent me a long letter. Rosaleen lived at home with her parents and one sister in the Annamoe Park public housing estate in Cabra, Dublin. She began her letter,

> *My dearest Angeline, received your most welcome letter on Wednesday. I hope you will always remain happy. I'm delighted that you are getting married. Anne Byrne is coming home from West Germany to see her family before she goes to the States with her husband. They are going to live in Texas. How many ice-cream girls are marrying Yanks? I hope you will be coming to my wedding soon ha ha ha. The flu is going around in Dublin. I am just up for a few hours after a bad dose of the flu. I had the doctor every day. I am out of work for 2 weeks; no pay. Mammy is also laid up with the flu and had the doctor. If it should hit you over there, look after yourself because it's hitting some people bad. Leana Kelly is still working at the Royal. She expects to get engaged soon and fly away too. Kay O'Shea, the Chief Usherette, is getting married this month. We will lose them all. Carmel left the Royal for a job in Jacob's factory. She got fed up selling ice-cream tubs in the dark picture house. Don't forget and send me some of your wedding photographs. Your one and only best friend, Rosaleen. Kiss, kiss, and kiss.*

Rosaleen would have been my pick for a bridesmaid if things had been different. Her beautiful long blond hair, oval shaped face, black-blue eyes and curved body made passers-by stop and look twice. I hoped she'd find a Dublin fella with a steady job at the Hammond Lane Foundry or at the Boland's Mills and marry him. Hopefully she'd stay in Ireland where we belonged.

Eddie packed up the car for our wedding trip to Maine. He carefully hung up my bridal dress on a hook in the car along with his new suit

Wedding day: 5 October 1957

for the wedding. Father Harris would marry us at noon on Saturday in the library — not in the chapel because of it being a mixed marriage. I had a small suitcase packed to the brim with all the fancy, see-through dainties the girls at the office had bought for me to take on the honeymoon. I carried my Irish lace-trimmed handkerchief that my mother gave for the wedding. I had it and her recent letter in my purse.

> *Dear Love, If you want to marry Eddie you can. It's up to yourself. You should know his ways by now. If you love him that's everything in life and I know you will be very happy with him as he is very good to you. God Bless him. You tell me nothing in your letter only that you love me. I sit by the window waiting for you to come home. I say to the dog, 'Darkie get your leash, here is Angeline' and the dog looks all around for you. I have poor Darkie when everyone is out and she loves me. Are you going to*

get married in white? Your daddy and me will have to get a few
bottles that day. Your daddy went to Mass this Sunday for you;
he loves you. Patricia O'Brien is getting married on the 25 of the
month. Mrs Coady was asking for you. I love you my own little
titch. I love you. From her Mammy, Kisses, Kisses, Kisses. I love
you.

I could see her and the dog sitting by the window looking for the
number 2 or 3 bus to stop across from George Reynolds flats on the
Irishtown Road. She and Darkie kept their eye out for me getting off
the bus from work night or day. Da really showed his love for me by
going to Holy Mass after an absence of twenty years or more. In my
eighteen years of living with him, he never put a foot inside the door
of a church. When I pleaded with him to attend Mass he ignored me,
even when I warned him that the nuns said anyone who did not
attend Mass on a Sunday would burn in the fires of Hell for all eternity. The thought of him going to Mass for me made the bottom fall
out of my heart. I wondered now and then if Da had been a defrocked
priest, knowing all the Latin he did, and that's why he became a
drunkard. If true, how else could he not be a drunkard in unforgiv-
ing Ireland?

Eddie and I arrived in Presque Isle on the Thursday before the
wedding. Eddie's sister and her husband wrote that they could not
attend. Her decision not to attend our wedding made Eddie angry,
as he had flown to California for her wedding before he got drafted
into the army. Mom scurried about making last-minute preparations
for the wedding. She turned down my offers of help in an 'It's a pity'
tone of voice, adding, 'Brides need to be refreshed on their special
day.' Her standoffish tone put me off by a mile. The old father-in-law
continued to get his thoughts scrambled in his head. He couldn't tell
from one tick to the next if he or his son were heading to the altar or
if he still logged in the Maine forest, or had returned from a church
after a Bible lesson.

I began to question how I ever got into such a situation. Eddie
appeared out of nowhere and banished such thoughts. He kissed me
passionately, and told me that his half-sister, Gladys and her husband,
Stan, wanted to have a wedding dinner for us both at their farmhouse. An
evening reception would be held for us at the Methodist Church Hall, in
Presque Isle to accommodate the rest of the clan.

I could hardly wait to mingle among all the Protestants, never mind having to come face to face one more time with Harris, who would join us in Holy Matrimony. I knew Harris pleased himself by trying to see me as a sexual sinner instead of a star polisher. By now I longed to get away from all the preparations, and wondered if the town of Presque Isle had a pub or a beer joint. I needed a stiff shot of whiskey to calm my nerves. The reality of becoming part of a large Protestant outfit scared me and made me long to be reunited with the wearin' o' the green.

On the morning of the wedding I woke early. I could hear Ed talking downstairs with his mom, going over the loose ends. She had made arrangements for a married Catholic couple to stand up for us at the wedding. I don't know how she found the two Catholics amid all the Protestants.

Eddie left first for the library in the church. I'd told him that it was a custom for the groom not to see the bride attired in her wedding dress before the ceremony. He agreed to my wish. His mother and I followed in a taxi. The old man would remain home in the hands of a visiting nurse until we got back. He'd got a case of the runs, either as a result of preparations for the wedding or from eating too much apple sauce. My thoughts turned back home to my mother, Da, my brothers, Bridie and baby Barney. I knew they would have made a big do over me getting married. Be that as it may, I'd not let gray clouds descend over our wedding. As a very young child I'd learned it's foolish to cry over spilled milk.

I took a shower and began to dress. The wedding dress felt like the stiff body of a swan in my arms as I placed it down on the bed while I did up my hair and my face. I wanted to look gorgeous. I combed my hair back into a Grace Kelly chignon hairdo, applied crimson to my cheeks, combed my eyelashes with blue mascara, and colored my lips cherry-red. I put on the gown and placed the fingertip length crowned veil over my head, then looked in the full-length mirror turning this way and that. I put on my blue silk garter past my knee and picked up my bouquet of red carnations. The waif from O'Brien's Place and one time 'stinky girl' from the Sandymount dump felt like a princess.

It seemed as if Father Harris married us in a minute or else my mind had slipped away. Ed looked manly and beautiful in his new navy-

blue suit, white dress shirt and blue and silver necktie. He had a blue
flower in his lapel and his eyes shone into mine like the morning star,
while raindrops dripped from his mother's eyes. We packed into
Eddie's car and headed back to pick up his father, then we all headed
for the half-sister's farm for our wedding dinner. The ride to the farmhouse in the October sunshine could have been a postcard bearing
the caption 'Autumn in New England, Wish You Were Here.'

When we sat down to dinner in the dining room, I noticed that
none of the guests were young. The elders bowed their heads in prayer
before the meal began then upon rearranging their noggins stared
straight into my face. The big stone heads of Wake Island that I'd
recently seen in the *National Geographic* magazine looked like mer-
rymakers in comparison with the Elders of Zion now facing me at
the wedding feast. Without a word the lot in unison raised drinking
glasses filled with ice-cold sparkling Maine cider and toasted Eddie
and me. Who would have believed there was no thirsty-drunken
drinker amid the lot?

We were all hungry and dug into the roast turkey, baked ham,
and oyster pie, fresh fruit pies, caramel custard and home made
cheeses, all washed down with gallons of sparkling cider. Some ate
as if they had a fear of famine. After dinner the elders asked me all
about Ireland and potatoes. Gladys played some old-fashioned songs
on the piano in the parlour. They begged me to sing an Irish song and
Eddie urged me on. Before I knew it I could hear myself singing as
sweetly as possible:

> '*Lavender blue, dilly dilly, lavender green*
> *When I am king dilly, dilly, you'll be my queen.*
> *Who told you so, dilly dilly, who told you so?*
> *I told myself, dilly dilly, I told myself . . .*'

I liked the catchy non-Irish romantic love song but from the reaction of those present around the table, it seemed a silly song.

After introductions had taken place, I began to feel more at ease.
I had figured by now that the Protestants present were not going to
roast me in hell. After the dinner party, we went back to my in-laws'
house and Mom suggested everyone take a nap in order to be refreshed
for the evening wedding reception at the church. She pointed me up
the stairs to the bedroom and shooed her son onto a sofa in the den. I
felt relieved to be alone and draw breath as I removed my veil and

wedding dress. The stiff tiers of tulle that made up the gown and the headgear irritated my flesh and caused me to itch all over. Picturing myself as a married woman, the wife of an American, and about to settle down in a new country, apparently forever, intensified the itch. I slipped into bed and covered up, feeling a bit numb. While I dozed, off guard, my stupid mind began its unravelling of the past. Christ, if only I could stop some recollections. If only my skull would turn into an ice-ball and snap off the stem, roll all the way from Presque Isle to upstate New York and topple down into the gushing waters over Niagara Falls and sink like a stone into the muddy bottom of the abyss. Instead, in spite of all resistance, bastard memories flooded my brain like a searchlight, beaming back images of my mother and me looking at each other in our room in O'Brien's Place. She is racked with pain. 'Ma you look so sick, why?'

I saw bunches of sores, bright as red berries under her armpits and stacked under the flaps of her white breasts. Da had delivered her dose of pain while home on one of his family leaves from the Army—after having shagged other women while out on military manoeuvres. It took ages before my mother got well. She forgave Da his sin, but the knowledge of what he did to her was a vicious blow to my mind. Of course my new husband had no inkling of what my mind struggled with now, only hours away from our wedding night. I could never tell him such shameful things. He had no ear for such stark reality.

Eddie's mother called up the stairs to me, 'Time to get ready for the reception, dear.' Once more I arranged myself in the mass of stiff white tulle, thinking how quickly a plucked chicken became an elegant swan. I remembered my mother's saying 'fine feathers make fine birds'.

The crowded church hall surprised me—and to think that all the people assembled were related to Eddie one way or another. Eddie's two half-sisters hosted the event. They took each one of us by the elbow and began to walk us down the line of relatives. The robust farmers and their ample wives and children might have been transplanted from County Kerry when you got a closer look at their red apple faces, blue eyes, and round heads. Not one in the lot looked like the scrawny members of my tribe. The pair of us ended up in front of a hefty three-tiered wedding cake with two small doll-like figures of a bride and groom stranded on the top layer of icing, hanging on to each other for dear life. Someone handed Ed a large knife to cut the cake with. He took the implement and sliced it down and through the cake like a brain surgeon parting the hemispheres. He offered me the first bite of the cake, spilling crumbs down the front of my frock. I bit his finger for spite, drawing a little blood amid the sweetened goo.

As I passed out the cake to all, I noticed two large tables filled with an assortment of odds and ends. I thought some church ladies were arranging a jumble sale. After the cake and most of the apple cider had been consumed, we were led to the merchandise on display. I looked at Eddie for a sign indicating that a sale was going to start. Then Ed's mom opened wide her arms to encompass all of the things on the tables and said, 'This is your surprise shower. It's your wedding shower from all the relatives.' It took time to open all the boxes that contained toasters, coffee-pots, pots and pans, knife sharpeners, can openers, a vacuum cleaner. We also had to handle each and every towel, each and every pillowcase, bed sheet, blanket and all the other household items displayed on the table. After we'd acknowledged and thanked all for their gifts, Mom presented us with a double sized patchwork quilt she'd quilted by hand for our bed. Her lovely colourful quilt outdid everything else. I had little interest in all the other things; they seemed like a mass of clutter that could cover a battlefield. I asked myself who needed more than one cooking pot? I'd used one pot for heating wash water, for boiling spuds, for cooking coddle, and as a water dish for the dog.

As the wedding activities came to an end, I felt astonished. There had been no alcohol, no impropriety of any kind or rowdiness, or attempts at bare-knuckle boxing, or a singsong or bouts of upchucking. It was nice just the same.

Eddie had arranged for us to take a car trip to Nova Scotia, Cape Breton and the Cabot Trail in Canada for the honeymoon, knowing how much I loved the sea. We said our goodbyes to the relatives and headed for the first leg of the trip, Houlton, Maine where Ed had arranged for us to stay in a rustic cottage for the night. Each small cottage had its own veranda, flower garden and spiked fir tree pointed to the heavens. We were both exhausted and excited by the time we fell into the bed, but love being what it is we regained our vigour. The following morning telltale signs of lost virginity were obvious on the white sheet. The sight of the bloodstains on the sheet bothered me.

Eddie and I ate like lumberjacks, polishing off stacks of pancakes impregnated with huckleberries, smothered with butter and Vermont maple syrup, along with crisp Canadian bacon. Ed had his glass of milk; I opted for strong coffee. We meowed and licked each other's paws on the way back to the cabin, jumped into bed and began the game again. Later my new husband called out from the shower, 'Angel, imagine — we will be like this for the next fifty years and more!'

'I'll have to hide in the tall grass,' I replied, not making sense.

I walked outside the cabin door into the scented October day. Overhead, crows were 'caw-cawing' like cattle among the treetops. I always loved the argumentative birds, common as buttons in alleyways and fields. Eddie arranged and rearranged our luggage in the trunk of the car. I could have lowered a tank of Guinness stout down my gut as I watched how he packed the trunk.

We stopped at the Canadian border. The border inspector asked Ed to show his social security card. Then he asked me for identification. I showed him my alien Green Card issued by the United States Government. The guard asked Ed why we were going to Canada and if he had any guns with him? 'God, no,' I answered. 'Only people in the army have guns.' The guard smiled, and then waved us across the border and into Canada. We found a small cabin-type motel and stayed for the night.

When I recall our trip, it's the image of the small fishing villages flung out over the landscape that comes to mind. Each village consisted of an assortment of small wooden planked houses that shimmered like bushels of herrings under the bright October sunlight. We stopped at 'trading post' stores owned by various Indian tribes. They sold native carvings, woven blankets, willow baskets, and piles of hand-knitted knee-high slippers known as 'muk-luks.' I bought Ma and Da a pair of muk-luks each which I intended to send back to Ireland as souvenirs from Canada. I tried to image my old fella putting on the muck-lucks, and him three sheets to the wind. Ma would love their colour and pattern and would probably hang them on the wall beside the picture of the Sacred Heart for the neighbours to see.

Sometimes we bought bread and cheese for a picnic in one of the small parks near a town. All of our views were of the Atlantic Ocean. When we got to the Bay of Fundy late in the evening, I swam in the pelt while Ed kept an eye out in case God knows who might see me in my altogether. The lapping ocean waves soothed my senses and everything in between.

The Bay of Fundy became the last leg of our trip. We returned to Maine and from there to our married life in Connecticut. No need any more to fret about being hungry again or to fear being sent off into a Magdalene laundry if I sold my soul on the streets of Dublin.

Ed loaded the collection of wedding gifts into the car to take back to Glastonbury. Mrs Anderson appeared sad for a moment that I was going from under her roof. On the way out, she once again reminded me to appreciate the opportunity of living in the greatest country in the world.

Married life

It felt different being a married woman. As I fussed about the wicker furniture my feet seemed to tap to a street rhyme sung to me by an elderly Protestant woman I ran errands for as a child until her son, Pip, exposed himself to me. The rhyme went:

Good morning, John, your cock is gone.
Your crow will crow no more.
You went to bed with a sleepy head,
And forgot to close the door.

Sometimes I didn't know if the twiggy furniture needed to be watered or dusted. The woodsy feel and smell of the furniture made me think of Goldilocks and the Three Bears, whereas I pictured myself a lover of splendour. My husband inquired if I had given in my notice at work and told them I was quitting the job. I reminded him that I needed to earn some money to help out my family back home. 'My mother does not want me to send her any more money. She wants me to spend it on us. You don't know the story back home.'

'What story are you referring to, honey?'

'The story of Johnny McGory,' I smiled, not wanting to bring up the sharp nails of want and woe.

'I thought you would like being a stay-at-home, lunch with your friends, go shopping and have fun.' I listened to the set-up proposed for me. I didn't want to get into a row about working. Eddie and I did not get into fighting matches. I felt he did not deserve any guff that I might spout. 'It's fine, Angie, if you want to continue working. Of course you would stay home on becoming a mother?' I hadn't given this matter much thought, and hoped cute babies might be found on mounds instead of having to give in to nature's way.

I took down one of the wedding presents Ed's cousin; the professor at Millbury College, had given me — *The New Fannie Farmer Boston Cooking-School Cook Book.* I opened the heavy book, letting a small card fall out. Eddie picked it up and read it out loud for me. 'From an old bachelor who wished he had a beautiful colleen to take care of him, too — with all good wishes, Richard.' I re-shelved the hefty green covered cookbook that would demand a whole life of attention. Bit by bit the tug of domestic life pulled me away from the Land of Youth.

I hoped motherhood would wait a while. Ed wanted to plan for a family. He believed in family planning, something foreign to me. He told me about the various methods of birth control. I told him the Catholic Church forbade birth control and that I was still a Catholic and I could lose my soul if I used it. Ed respected my belief, but I knew he did not like any church dictating his personal life. I was not American enough yet to grasp what this meant to him.

'A letter arrived in the mail from Ireland for you, honey.' I looked at the writing on the envelope and knew it was from Bob, or Robbler as he was called in Irishtown and Ringsend.

> *Dear Angeline, I got your letter with the postcard and dollar o.k. I got a free trip on one of the coal boats to Liverpool. I met Charlie Darby over there. You remember? He picked on the Irishtown Tip with us. It was lovely going over on the boat, but coming back it was terrible. There was a big gale of wind and the boat was bouncing up and down like a cork. The weather over here is terrible at the moment and for the last 4 days there has been terrible gales coming off the Irish Sea. A big tree in Stella Gardens got knocked over by the winds. All the fishing trawlers are wind bound along the Dublin docks. Two English trawlers came up to the docks to take cover. I tied one of them up and the mates on the trawler gave me a big cod and a stack of scallops and plenty of flats and crabs. The only thing that was wrong was it was 2 o'clock in the morning. At the moment I am listening to the Glencullen calling, calling the Glengarry. It is now 12 o'clock in the daytime . . . When will you be back home? Bob.*

Lo called me on the phone to talk. She knew I worked all week and that Saturday seemed a good day for us to chat or visit. I knew her baby would be born soon. I learned more about living in America from her than the copies of *Ideals* Mom sent me from Maine. I expected Lo to give birth to her baby at home, and that the women around her would birth the baby the same as back home. I found out that being up the pole in the new country meant being sick. Lo told me she went to see a gynaecologist and he would be delivering her baby and that she would have to go into the hospital like a sick person in order for it to be born.

First Christmas in America: Connecticut 1957

I had never heard of gynaecologists before and feared even the sound of the word. Then Lo said the gynecologist intended to give her a 'spinal tap' and perform an 'episiotomy' on her. The strange and fearful sounding words caused me to cringe but I asked no further questions, out of fear and not wanting to appear ignorant of something she assumed everyone had heard about. The rest of Lo's conversation was lost to my ears. I'd taken it for granted that being knocked up didn't mean being ill or had anything to do with seeing gynaecologists who performed strange acts on a body. Her discussion about having a baby in America made me want to sew myself back up and hide the darning needle in the Pacific Ocean. I put down the phone and went outside to watch for the postman—or mailman as they say in Yankee Land.

He had a letter for me from Mrs Jenny Cummins, 15 George Reynolds House, Irishtown, Dublin, Eire. The envelope was barely readable after being soaked somewhere during its long journey. Jenny lived on the same balcony as my family in the flats. Her last baby, Bruce, my godchild, had been her eighth child with probably more to come.

> *Dear Angeline just a few lines. Glad to hear you are so happy
> and glad to hear you are contented over there. Well, Angeline
> young Brendan misses you a lot. He is always asking for you
> and when he sees the postman he says it is your postman. He is*

*a funny young fellow; he never forgets you. I was very thankful
for the little things you sent me. They are lovely. Brendan shows
everybody his outfit and tells them he got them from America.
Your mammy still comes to me for a chat. You know she is very
fond of me. Jennie told me to ask you for a pair of plaid jeans
you know what she is for style. Young Brendan says you are to
come home and bring him for a walk I love to hear from you. I
though at first that you had forgotten all about me as you know
I was very fond of you. Bruce is not walking yet, but he can
stand. Your brother Frank's baby has got big; he is like Bridie,
his mother. This is all for now. God Bless you, Jenny, Billy and
the children. PS: Here's X from Bruce in the pram.*

Jenny's eight children were born at home and my mother assisted
in their birth.

My first autumn in Connecticut flipped by in a downpour of falling
leaves, smells of burning brush, and heaped mounds of mulch left to
be covered over by winter snows.

Christmas was on the horizon, and I reminded myself that parcels from America took six weeks to get to Dublin, Ireland. And a
Christmas parcel from America would be viewed as the next best
thing to the birth of Baby Jesus.

Bill phoned Ed to tell him that Lo had had a baby girl. He'd expected a son but got a baby girl instead. Lo gave birth to the baby in
Saint Francis Hospital in Hartford; mother and child were both doing well. Lo told me earlier on that she hoped the baby would look
like Bill instead of her. She wanted to give him a German-looking
baby instead of an Italian one like herself. All the talk about differences between people and how they looked was new to me, having
assumed that the greatest difference in the world had to be how poor
and rich people were treated.

It being early November, Ed and I bought the new baby a warm,
fuzzy-wool pram suit. I'd planned to knit a miniature Irish fisherman's jumper for the infant but never got around to it, working full
time and everything else. The baby appreciated the soft woolly
jumpsuit over any rustic-getup I'd knit.

Baby Gloria arrived in the world the spitting image of her German
father. Her smooth white skin, apple blush cheeks, clear blue eyes,

slender body, were just what the parents ordered. Lo seemed as contented as a mother cat stretched out on the sofa, her feet encased in
pink fluffy slippers. She'd combed her thick curly brown hair into a
ponytail, and her brown eyes, magnified by her glasses, were as shiny
as a pool. I held the baby in my arms under the gaze of both parents.
She felt like a collection of fragile bones that required light handling,
although the infant's head felt heavy as a cannonball sunk in the fold
of an arm. As I looked at the child's angel face, I briefly thought of a
picture of a Nike missile I'd seen earlier on television. I wondered if Lo
and Bill ever thought about such things? The constant radio reports
on the evil things the Russians were up to began to frighten me.

Bill jokingly asked when Ed and I were going to become parents.
He reached for a paperback book and held it out for me to see. 'This
is the Bible of child raising,' he said. *Baby and Child Care*, by Dr
Benjamin Spock. 'Lo and I intend to raise Gloria on the advice given
in the book. We've both read every page. We highly recommend this
book to every new parent.' Lo butted in, 'the chapter called "Parents
are Human" really impressed me.' For some reason, I got a touch of
vertigo and had to sit down. Bill suggested that we all have some
Italian red wine. Earlier in the day Lo's parents had brought over a
case of wine for the new parents. Much to my surprise, Ed slurped
down an oversized goblet of the liquor as if overcome by some fear.
He'd repeated to me dozens of times that he liked us being 'just two'
and hoped that the Catholic method of birth control which we practised, the 'rhythm method', would not screw up.

Da wrote in a letter that Christmas would never be the same for
him and Ma now that I'd gone away. They were not looking forward
to the holiday without me.

> *Dear Love, What a difference a year can bring. Noel and you
> singing a carol or fighting over who got the first bit of Christ-
> mas cake? But, if you are happy, that's all that matters to your
> mammy and me.*

I used my lunch hour to buy Christmas presents. Rufus, Calvin
and Jordan in the shipping department asked me if I were going to
send presents to the folks back home. They wanted to see the presents.
I showed the green shirt for Da, a red jumper for Ma, the red baseball
jacket for Noely, gloves for Bob, a blue shirt for Frank, a green blouse
for Bridie, and a stuffed toy monkey holding a banana for Barney,

the baby. 'Leave all that with us and we'll package it up for you to mail,' the three said, 'and you go back to work.'

At the end of the day, I took the last load of mail to be shipped out and Jordan pointed to the beautiful mailing carton filled with presents from America, and said, 'Ready, baby girl.' The perfectly packaged carton ready for the mail stunned me. The three made me promise to let them know if Noely liked his baseball jacket and the baby its toy monkey. 'Have a good holiday,' they said. I should have kissed each of them instead of settling for a mangy handclasp.

Ed talked about how wonderful our first Christmas would be out in rural Glastonbury. He set up a large Christmas tree in the living room and decorated it with as many coloured lights as the branches could bear. He lifted me up in the air to put a silver star on the tip of the tree then hugged me like some precious gift. The contrast between this holiday and those I remembered back home amid want gave me pangs of guilt. In spite of my misgivings about having so much, I would not go into mourning and gloom. I'd not be 'Deirdre of the Sorrows' and deny Eddie his delight on Christmas Day. I also knew my family and neighbors back in Dublin wanted me to experience a taste of the good life.

I cooked a frozen turkey for the holiday dinner and stuffed it. Ed set the table with the new china and silverware. I felt like a stylish housewife, dressed up in high heels and all, fussing with the bird, that was cooked to a golden brown, displayed on a large china plate flecked with green Italian parsley and hard red radishes. Ed said Grace then carved the turkey as I anxiously awaited his verdict. He inserted a spoon to scoop out some stuffing from inside the bird, giving me a benign look as he rooted inside the turkey. 'What's this, honey?' he asked holding up a smelly pile of something.

'It looks like a bag of guts. I don't know how it got into the turkey.'

'Didn't you check inside the bird before you stuffed it? The manufacturer always packs the giblets of chickens or turkeys in the body cavity.'

'Shit, shite and cauliflowers, who could have guessed that?'

'You need to pay a little more attention to instructions, honey. Still, we can enjoy the turkey meat. Next time you will know better.'

Out of nowhere I had the image of myself crossing over the Ha'penny Bridge in Dublin with my mother on a cold and frosty November morning while Dublin gulls flew overhead flinty as wayward arrows.

Da wrote to thank me for the parcel and to let me know everyone loved the presents from America. Noel put on the red baseball jacket and paraded around the flats like a Yank on holiday and wee Barney screamed at the sight of the stuffed toy monkey, but reached nevertheless for the banana the toy held in its hand. My mother's part of the letter read:

> It's now 9.30 on New Year's Eve and all the kids are piling up all the old stuff off the dumps for their bonfire. The caretaker of the flats got the corporation to cart it off to the dumps. The kids went back to the dumps and brought it all back. Noel is right in the middle of it all. Last year you and I were looking over the balcony at the bonfire but you are a long way from the balcony now . . .

Miss Foley heard me heaving my guts up in the lavatory at work and asked what ever was up with me? I told her that since early March I got sick every morning. I told her it must be all the American food I'd eaten for over a year. She looked at me and said, 'Have you discussed this with Ed?'

'No! It's just a queasy belly. I had something like it before years ago after eating a rotten egg.'

'Come back and sit down by my desk.' I followed her, still feeling as sick as a dead fish. 'Angeline, dear, I think that you are going to become a mother. Call your husband to come and take you home' I sat down to ponder what my supervisor had surmised about my ongoing belly heaves and their likely outcome. I knew a baby wouldn't be out of the blue. Trying to figure the Catholic Church's method of birth control based on times to have sex and times to cut it out had been a muddle. As a convert to the joy of bodily wrestling and its aftermath, I wondered who would follow the 'rhythm system' instead of having on the spot whoopee? I went back into the women's rest room to wash my face before Eddie arrived to pick me up. My face appeared pea-green in the mirror and my eyes a slate gray.

'Honey, I got here as fast as I could,' Ed said.

'I'm all right. I just upchucked again and Miss Foley heard me vomiting even with half of my head in the toilet.'

'Gee honey, maybe you have the flu. It's going around'

'No, I don't think it's that. Miss Foley thinks I'm pregnant. For Christ sake, don't drive so fast!' I looked at his startled face and I couldn't tell if my profanity had caused the expression of amazement or the idea of me being up the pole. He reached out for my hand and held it lovingly. 'I love you, Angie,' he said still not saying anything about a possible baby on the way. 'By Christ, you better,' I mumbled under my breath. As soon as we got inside the house, he held me to him like nothing in the world could put a crease between us. Over a mug of tea, we talked about the possible pie in the oven. We both concluded a baby would be grand. He said that I would need to make an appointment to see a doctor. 'I don't need to see a doctor. I don't have pneumonia, or even a mild case of rickets, so why do I need to see a doctor? Where's the need for a doctor's hand in the matter?' I tried to explain 'lying in' to him, and the ins and outs of having a baby which my mother had taught me at age ten when we lived in the laneway in O'Brien's Place. I explained that the mothers who lived there took turns in caring for a new mother and her infant. Although they had bushels of children of their own, they had an agreement among them to take care of a new mother. They watched over her until her time came to have the infant, then they delivered the newborn mite and cared for mother and child until both were out of the woods and into the sunshine. Ed listened attentively to me then asked if I expected having a baby in the United States would be similar. 'I hope so,' but my heart recognized that this new land favoured the modern and medical over the mystical and magical.

'I'm going to send a telegram home to let Ma and Da know I have a pie in the oven and it's not a jelly tart.'

'While we're at it, honey, let's make an appointment for you to see an obstetrician.'

'What's me eyes to do with it?' He explained the meaning of obstetrician, and by the sound of it all having a baby with the assistance of an obstetrician instead of a mother's helper would be more of a mechanical event than a natural one. I told Eddie that I wanted to discuss the matter with Lo and Shirley before seeing a whatyamaycallit.

Shirley, Lo, and I met at Augie and Ray's diner to have some of their famous broiled hamburgers with onion rings for lunch. Over the delicious burgers we discussed my having a baby. I asked Lo and Shirley if they'd ever assisted a new mother in having a baby at home. The two acted shocked at me asking them such a question. 'I'd faint at the very idea!' said Shirley. 'Me too!' Lo exclaimed. I pointed out that I was going to ask them if they would help me deliver my baby at home, and told them that babies back in Irishtown were born at home without ever a doctor entering the picture. The look of shock on both their faces took me by surprise. My God, I hadn't asked them to blow up Fort Knox or to fight a wild boar with a clothes-pin. While they were getting their wind back, I explained, 'lying in' to them. Shirley and Lo explained they would be terrified even at the sight of someone giving birth. They asked me if I were joking. 'I'm serious.' I said. They explained that in the United States modern women had their babies delivered in a hospital by an 'OB/GYN' in case any emergency came up. None of their college girlfriends had their babies born at home. They consider it a backward thing to do. 'Angie, Ed will insist you deliver in a hospital.'

'I'm not sick.'

'That's not the point, Angie, you need to go into the hospital to have it.' I decided to keep quiet. Sometimes tight lips are called for. Lo and Shirley were highly educated young women, and both of them had given birth to beautiful children, but nevertheless the idea of needing a doctor and going into a hospital solely for having a baby, seemed odd. After lunch, my friends turned to cautioning me about finding an 'OB/GYN,' this being an expert in delivering infants. By now the thought of having my baby outside Irishtown, seemed over-whelming. 'Don't be afraid to ask questions of your OB/GYN,' warned Shirley as a goodbye shot. Ed asked how the lunch went with the girls. 'They advised me to find an OBY something or other to deliver the baby, but not to be surprised if a stand-in delivers it instead. I want you to deliver our baby when the time comes, on our lodge pole-bed. I'll turn it into a soft and fluffy nest, with down pil-lows and feather quilts. I'll push and shove, shove and push until it pops out of the pocket and into your warm waiting hands.'

My appointment to see Dr D, OB/GYN was on a Thursday afternoon. Miss Foley let me off work early. Ed and I went to see the doctor to-gether, and from that day to this, the mysteries of bearing and giving birth to a baby will never be the same, sweet Mother of God. The nurse told us to take a seat in the waiting room, which had the feel of a cozy parlour instead of the medical infirmary I had expected awash with odours from the living and the dead. Pretty young women sat on tufted, rose chintz armchairs placed around the room, each woman in a different stage of baby making.

When the nurse beckoned me to follow her through the inner door where the doctor did the examination, my heart went pitter-patter. I had a terrible dread of doctors, and the sight of the one now standing before me dressed in his white lab coat nearly made me topple. He looked at the chart that Eddie had filled out listing my history, and said, 'Hi Angela', instead of Angeline which was written down on the chart. With that he whisked out of the room and told the nurse to get me ready for my medical exam. She told me to take my clothes off and put on the gown she handed me. I asked her why I needed to take off all my clothes 'It's an internal exam to check on the fetus. Open your legs and put your heels into the stirrups. There, that's it. The doctor will be right in.' He came back into the room and did a chest exam first, and then he put on a pair of rubber gloves and pulled up a stool. He sat down at the base of the examining table, and to my shock, inserted two long fingers into my vagina without as much as a please, and began to fiddle around inside as if looking for a needle in a haystack. I could feel my blood boil with shame. No one had prepared me for such an examination as part of being an expectant mother.

The idea of a man other than a husband taking such liberties seemed a criminal act: an act of extreme violation one might expect from a devil like Jack the Ripper, but from a doctor? 'The fetus feels in the right position,' he said. 'What's that?' I whispered. 'Is that a baby thing, the fetus?' 'Don't you know about human biology?' 'You mean about having a baby growing inside and coming out when ready?' 'I'll have the nurse give you a booklet that explains pregnancy, obstetrics and gynecology. You may get dressed now. Then come into my office.'

'The dirty dabbler,' I said to myself, still shocked at what had happened to me under the end of the sheet. I dressed and the nurse directed me into the doctor's private office. 'Sit down,' he said. I looked at the short, fat man sitting behind a massive wooden desk. 'You're from the Old Country,' he noted. 'Born in Ireland, I see written down here. This is your first pregnancy? How long have you been married? I see your husband is professionally employed as an engineer and you work as a runner for the Travelers' Insurance Company.'

'That's right,' I replied. He took up a small brush and began to buff his fingernails one by one. 'Modern childbirth has left behind the old ways. I only deliver newborns in a hospital setting,' he said.

He now looked at each fingernail intently. He stood up and said, 'See you next month, the receptionist will give you an appointment.' When Ed and I got outside the building, I headed for the evergreen shrubs and nearly threw my guts up. I imagined feeling a cooling sea breeze from Sandymount Strand over my face. I prayed a letter from my mother would be in the mailbox when I got back to Glastonbury. Any news from her would steady my legs about having a baby. I said nothing to Eddie about the shame caused by the posh, slick-haired, nail-polishing doctor who had fingers befitting a street-organ player. I still hoped Eddie's hands could deliver our child in the nest where it took wing but it would be a difficult job.

I found a letter from my sister-in-law Bridie in the mailbox, with her return home address as 6 Camden Court, Camden Street in Dublin. Bridie, Frank, and their young son now lived in a rented room in one of the slum tenement houses that remained out of view in Camden Street.

> *My dear Angeline, Just a few lines. I'm very sorry not answering your letter before now. I don't know what you must think of me. But I never seem to be able to sit down and write a letter. Little Barney seems to take up a lot of my time. Do you know Angeline; I don't know how long it is since I was out on my own. All my time seems to go on the house and Barney. Frank is after havin' the flu; as for little Barney he is well and getting as big as a house. When he sees me getting my coat he knows I'm going out and cries to come with me. He loves your mother and she loves him. He got to know that when he sees her coming that she has something for him, Frank is very proud of him; he brings him down to your mother every Sunday while I get a chance to rest. Angeline I nearly forgot to thank you for sending the lovely thing to Barney. I don't know how to thank you. You asked me in your last letter if I ever wanted to join the 'Puddin Club' again? Your mother tells me that I already have my hands full with Barney. Frank is afraid for me to have another baby, as it was so bad this first time it might be the same again. But what about yourself, would you like a baby yet? I have to stop writing now; little Barney is trying to climb out the window. Love Bridie.*

I guessed Bridie knew by now I'd joined the 'Puddin Club' too. God bless the light that shines on us. I wondered if she knew about the

Catholic rhythm method of birth control. If she did she never uttered a word. Maybe the rhythm method applied to Catholics in the United States who were bolder in challenging the Church than the Irish.

Lo called me to find out how my visit to the doctor went. She said that it was too bad that I went to see a different gynecologist than the one she had. I told her that some guy who worked with Eddie and had five children had recommended his wife's obstetrician, Dr D, who had a house full of kids of his own. She asked me if I liked him. I told her about the medical examination and the fingers up me Swannee River. She replied that she thought I knew about internal examinations as they were considered a normal part of a medical examination for pregnant women. 'By the time a baby arrives, the mother is left without any sense of shame,' she hooted into the phone.

Miss Foley beamed when I told her about having a baby and that she'd been correct about the reason I threw up in the bathroom every morning. She asked me how Ed felt about becoming a dad.

'He's happy about it.'

'Does he want a girl or a boy?'

'Either. But he'd prefer a boy.'

'What about you?'

'Either one would be OK, but a boy would be better.' The thought of having a girl, someone like myself, held little appeal. I knew from the start boys were better.

The girls in the office were delighted to hear that I was pregnant. I felt odd using the word 'pregnant' instead of telling them; 'I'm going to have a baby.' The foreign word 'pregnant' tasted as odd in the mouth as did crunching salty peanuts by the handful.

Thinking about salt made me hungry for pickled pig's feet dug deep into a mound of leafy green cabbage smothered with succulent fat. A vision of my mother's cooking made me dizzy, especially how she halved a pig's cheek on the table, dotted with peppercorns and bedecked with hot mustard. The girls promised to give me a baby shower. I listened to the list of baby items they said they'd give me, thinking all the time of where I could get my teeth into a boiled pig's cheek or a slab of its arse. My fondness for pineapple milkshakes gave way to a liking for chunks of ham, hamburger, and undercooked steak juicy as sex.

Thinking about sex reminded me that Eddie's allergies were getting worse. The doctor advised him to move out west where there were fewer plants and pollens to bother him. You might have thought that I'd be the one with the affliction instead of someone who'd lived in the United States from birth.

Bill and Lois called that evening to tell us that Lo's great aunt had 'passed away'. Eddie told me 'passed away' meant the same as, 'died.' Bill invited us to attend the service at a funeral home in two days' time. Ed asked me if I wanted to go. He said I did not have to, but being curious, I decided to go along, as Lo had made me feel so welcome in America. The aunt had died in the hospital. She'd never married. We arrived at the funeral home in the afternoon to be greeted by a pool of people related to the dead woman.

A sombre man in a black suit, white shirt and black tie came foreword to meet us. 'Have you come to see the deceased?' he asked. Ed did all the talking. 'This way, please,' the man said, indicating that we should follow him into the large room. 'The relatives are in the pews,' he said, 'the departed is resting there in her casket.' Lo came over to us, and led us to look at her aunt in the casket. I held onto Eddie's hand as we arranged ourselves in front of the casket perched on a platform and surrounded with bundles of fresh flowers, seemingly just plucked from fragrant meadows in May. A tiny figure lay deep inside the coffin on a nest of white satin with a pleated pillow under its head. The little woman, wizened as an aged apple, had on a blue dress that matched her carefully arranged pin-curled hair, tense as tinsel. Her aged face looked calm as a lily held beneath a saint's chin in some ancient religious image. Someone had dabbed rose rouge on the old lady's cheekbones, making her corpse look girlish. Her parched hands overlapped on the stilled breast like donkey's ears. She could have been a prize doll being packed away for storage. Tears filled our eyes upon leaving the dainty corpse to the fate of all. Lo thanked me for coming to the funeral parlour to be with her.

Outside, Eddie asked how I felt seeing my first dead person in America? 'Dead is dead,' I replied. 'The baby wants apple pie and vanilla ice cream. See, pat my belly and find out.' 'I wish our baby were here already,' he grinned. 'Takes nine months to make one,' I replied.

'Angie, I think we need a house closer to town.'

'Being closer to a bus route and shops would be better than way out in the country,' I answered. A week or so later, he told me that a guy who worked in the machine shop had a cousin with a ranch-style home for sale in East Hartford much closer to Eddie's workplace and closer to a bus route. Ed pointed out that the house would not be as fancy as Bill and Lo's place in Manchester. We would have to count our pennies to pay for the house and the expenses for a new baby.

Living in the old house in rural Glastonbury for over a year had not been my cup of tea. Cows and horses were odd creatures for someone weaned on cement. The only cows I'd ever seen before now were those that were trotted down some street in Dublin on the way to the slaughterhouse in Ringsend. The mooing of the cows grew louder as they got closer to the slaughterhouse. The sight of the cows going to be killed bothered my mother as we stood on the sidewalk watching the parade. Ma said, 'Them poor four-legged animals know where they're headed. They have brains enough to know.' Ed let me know that the cows grazing in the meadow near our place in Glastonbury were milk cows, and not bred for slaughter.

Our new ranch home on Lorraine Court in East Hartford looked like the rest of the houses that had sprung up on the former tobacco field. The housing estate went on as far as the eye could see. Unlike the more posh housing estates, the families who lived on Lorraine Court earned their living from various jobs not requiring a college degree. The house had three bedrooms, a living room, kitchen, dining room and bathroom. 'Hardwood floors throughout,' Ed said. I thought the naked floors needed to be covered with cheerful linoleum.

The family who originally owned the place had got transferred to some military base in California. Miss Foley and the girls in the office were happy about us getting a 'place of our own'. They were dead set against people renting houses instead of owning them. 'Will you be getting new furnishing to go with the new house?' they asked? Ed told me that he would be taking only one piece of Adirondack to our new modern home. 'Does that mean we're not taking all the twiggy whatnots?' I inquired.

'Only the Adirondack Mountain rocking chair that once belonged to a Scottish relative.' Of course he included the butcher-block bookcases he had hand-made in the Boy Scouts. I preferred modern everything. Sometimes, Eddie acted more like he'd arrived from the Old Country than I did.

After moving in to the new home, I rambled through the five rooms meant for a couple and an infant. All the empty space felt unnatural. I had pangs of guilt knowing that back in Dublin whole families were still crammed into one or two rented rooms, as my brother Frank, his wife, Bridie, and their baby were. I realized that whatever came into my life would be compared with the past, and I might always feel guilty for my good fortune.

When I wrote and told my mother that we were moving from our place in Glastonbury to East Hartford, she immediately thought either the house had been condemned or we'd been evicted. Da added to the letter, 'Did Eddie get drunk and burn down the farmhouse?'

My belly began to get bigger by the week. I had a harder time running back and forth on my feet as the mail girl in the supply department. Miss Foley wanted to know when I intended to give up my job, stay at home, and create a nursery for the baby. Ed wanted me to stay home, particularly on mornings when I had the heaves and could not get out of the car soon enough. My mother wrote that having such bad heaves meant the baby would be a boy and for me to drink barley water before going to bed at night. Eddie searched every store in Hartford for bottled barley water but no one had ever heard of the drink. His mother wrote that when she was in my condition fiddlehead juice fixed her morning pangs. Joni, in the office, kept me going by keeping a supply of Mars bars in her desk that she doled out to me twice a day, commenting that she had no interest in getting pregnant.

My time to quit came and I lost the best job in the world. The office girls and Miss Foley gave me a 'baby shower' as a going away present. I said adieu to my friends in the shipping room. Everyone said they would come to see me in Saint Francis Hospital when I had the baby. I cried like a baby on leaving the place.

Three months later I yelped like a hurt hound when the baby's head began to bore down like a drill within my body, demanding to be let out of the bag and into the world. I'd had my blue suitcase packed for weeks, ready for the trip to the hospital. Ed held onto me with one hand and carried the suitcase in the other on the way to the car. He looked white as a sheet but had the confidence of an Irish cop directing traffic at a busy intersection as he drove to the hospital as if on wings. I worried how the demanding baby could find its way out of my body. The doctor had explained dilation and the expansion of the birth canal but it still remained a mystery to me how a bundle of baby could manage to make its way through a small crack. I hid such worries from others. If only the Great God had put a zipper where a zipper would have been the most use!

Upon arrival at Saint Francis General Hospital a nurse took me by the arm and led me into the 'Prep Room.' She told me to undress, put on a white shift, and get into bed while she fetched a basin of water and a man's shaving razor. She pulled back the lower part of the shift and began to shave my little ball of yarn naked. Feeling stunned as a knocked-out drunk, I asked no questions. The bearing down pressure of the unborn baby bobbing in the belly left me with little breath to utter any protest. After this shaving shock, she led me to the bathroom and told me to get into the bathtub and soak for a while. I felt like the heavens had collapsed on my head. What had either being shaved or being forced into a hot bathtub got to do with birthing a child? I bit into my lip to keep from crying out for my mother to come and rescue me from such treatment. My mother had helped many mothers give birth in O'Brien's Place as well as in the flats back in Irishtown. She and other seasoned mothers were always at the side of new mothers providing them with kindness, guidance and assistance when bringing forth their infants. I'd expected a similar experience. After the long soak in the bathtub, and the pain of struggling to get out, the nurse and an orderly helped me onto a stretcher, which they wheeled into a room, and left me alone to dilate. I called out if I could see my husband, and received the answer that Dr D had told Eddie to go home, as it might be hours before the baby arrived. I could not believe Eddie had followed the doctor's orders and gone home, leaving me alone!

Ceiling lights flooded the large delivery room where other women were in the birth process. Male doctors dressed from head to toe in surgical gowns, some blotted with fresh blood, were working on the women, some of whom cried out like impaled animals. My gynecologist, Dr D, appeared alongside my stretcher, took my pulse and looked under my shift. 'Time to put on the straps,' he commanded the nurse. She buckled my ankles to the stretcher and took each of my wrists and bound them to the stretcher also. Left helpless and terrified, I began to cry. The nurse told me to 'Shush and act like a big girl.'

'Give her the mask,' were the last words I heard as the nurse placed the ether over my shaking face. I remember vomiting and vomiting until my chest hurt. I felt something hard being inserted into me and the baby's head being jerked from my body like a lock-jawed molar. I could sense warm liquid flowing between my legs. 'Get her a blood transfusion,' ordered a man's voice. Someone said in my ear, 'You have a baby boy, weighs eight pounds, two ounces and is twenty-one inches long.'

'Thank you, God,' I mused to myself, wondering how a grand thing like having a baby had become so brutal and grotesque for mothers in America.

The following morning I heard Eddie's voice whisper in my ear, 'Angie, the baby is beautiful. It's a boy, honey.'

'I had the baby? It got out OK? I want to see my baby. Where is it?'

'They keep all the new babies in bassinets in the nursery,' he said.

'Well, for Chrissake, get my baby right now. I want him.'

I looked up and saw a bottle of blood on a stilt above me, dripping down through a tube into one of my arms. 'What's that thing for?' I asked Ed. 'It's a blood transfusion. The doctor ordered it for you.' A young nurse entered the ward and came over to my bedside. 'Congratulations, little mom,' the nurse smiled. 'Ready to see your baby? I'll be right back.'

'I hope the baby likes me,' I whispered to myself. My mouth trembled in eagerness waiting to kiss my baby into the world. My husband held my hand as the nurse went to get the baby. He told me that he'd picked up a box of cigars with the label 'It's a Boy' on the box. He planned to pass out the cigars to the guys at work. I told him to save one for my da in Dublin. The nurse returned with a swish and a bundle in her arms. She came to the bedside and placed the bundle in my arms, slid the corners of the blanket away from the baby's face, smiled and left.

I looked down at my baby asleep. His black hair matched his daddy's crop. His lovely face was peaceful as a dove, blushed with pink. He had a perfect little nose, rosebud mouth, firm chin, and lovely swept brow. His small fists were rolled up. I unfolded one of his hands to tangle my finger in its grip. My heart went hither and thither. Ed took his other little fist and held it. We felt dumbfounded at our good fortune. We both said, 'Hi, little Robert.' We named our son Robert after my brother and my mother's favourite Irish hero, the bold Robert Emmet, and Edward for his daddy. Ed remarked that I had done a great job. 'I laid a golden egg,' I replied, feeling silly and giddy and out of the world.

The next day two orderlies wheeled a stretcher into the room bearing a new mother. A nurse followed and assisted the recently delivered black woman into the hospital bed on the other side of the room. By noontime the Negro mother woke up and lifted herself up in the bed to look around. 'Wow, glad that's done and over with,' she said in my direction. 'They told me I'd a daughter,' she exclaimed. 'This is the second girl for me.'

'I had a boy,' I told her. It's my first.' The nurse appeared with her baby and the mother cried out with joy on seeing her child for the first time. 'She's so cute,' the mother giggled out loud. 'Like Grandma.' Later in the afternoon a nurse came in and told the mother that she was not supposed to be in this ward and would be moved to another room in the hospital. The departing mother waved at me as they pushed her bed out of the maternity ward. An official in the hospital came in and asked me if I were upset about the mistake someone had made by putting Negroes in the same hospital room as a white woman. I could not believe my ears at what he said. I did not know black people and white people were not allowed to share the same maternity ward. How could anything so ugly happen under the wing of Lady Liberty who guaranteed all a nest? What had gone askew?

After work, friends from the supply department came to visit me. The girls brought me flowers, talcum powder, a blue bed jacket, and love magazines. One of them got excited when she saw the bottle of blood dripping into my arm. She asked me if anyone had made sure that it wasn't Negro blood I was getting in the transfusion. I never heard Negro blood was different from mine. The ominous tone of her voice, and what happened early on in the day regarding the Negro mother brought a pain to my side. I observed the red fluid going into my arm and felt grateful for the gift of blood. The donated blood seeping into my vein had meant more than liquid gold.

The doctor kept me in the hospital for five days. He would not let me breastfeed my baby, insisting that I needed rest. When it came time to go home, Ed packed the baby and me into the car, delighted to have the opportunity to daddy us both. He had saved a week of vacation from work to take care of Robert Óg and me. I prayed that didn't mean tuna sandwiches morning noon and night.

Before I left the hospital with my new son, the nurse told me a pediatrician had circumcised the baby that morning. I turned to Ed for an explanation. 'Infant boys have to have the foreskin removed from their penis.' 'Why?' I asked in horror. 'Men are bothered by lint. It's just more sanitary to have it done now,' he assured me. When the nurse returned with the baby, she showed me what the pediatrician had done. The monster had cut and rubbed raw the baby's little teapot. Had I known such a brutal thing would take place, I would have fled the hospital with wee Rob under my arm and not stopped until reaching home. I'd the urge to buckle the father but held my peace.

The infant would be bottle fed instead of latching to my now dripping breasts because the doctor said so. The amazing flow of milk wetting the front of me would have fed half a dozen babies in Africa as well as my beloved little son. I got dressed, packed up my things, Eddie carried the child and we headed for the automobile and Lorraine Court. I still felt woozy from having lost some blood, but I knew the baby and I were in the best of hands with Ed. I longed for my mother like a lost child. 'You are going to be a wonderful mother,' Ed beamed at me. 'With the grace of God,' I answered back, fingers crossed. Since I was a child I'd wanted my own baby—a beautiful black baby. Now I had a beautiful white one.

Ed sent a telegram to my parents informing them I had a baby boy and that Da needed to keep an eye out for a cigar coming for him in the mail. My mother scrambled together the means to buy an Irish lace christening gown and sent it over to me. She insisted her grandchild in America be baptized in Irish lace.

She must have pawned Da's overcoat to get the money, or borrowed it from the only person willing to shell out to the poor, the Jew man. How many times did she and others thank God for someone lending money when it could not be found anywhere else: loans to buy christening gowns, First Communion outfits, Confirmation outfits, wedding outfits, and burial shrouds for the dead. The Jew man performed a service to the Dublin poor like no other walking about in shoe leather.

The nurse gave me a list of instructions to take home with the new baby. The bottles of formula were to be prepared and sterilized every day. The baby needed to be nursed on the bottle every two hours, burped and diapered. The contrast between taking care of a new baby in America and Ireland startled me, all the expected do's and don'ts and underlying grave responsibilities if I did not meet the mark of motherhood. When my mother took me with her to help take care of a new mother long ago, she noted that a *leanbh* loved to be held, cooed to, and above all to be latched either to a breast or a bottle. She warned me to look out for the scourge of the poor—'green diarrhoea'—that carried too many lovely Irish babies to the graveyard.' Ed gave me a strange look when I rummaged over the first small load produced by his son. 'It's Crayola yellow,' I noted. 'Thanks be to God.' Ed pointed out that he had never heard of infants coming down with the dreaded disease in the United States. 'Look around the nursery, honey. All is sanitized and new for the baby.' I nodded in agreement wishing that he did not insist on keeping the baby in the nursery instead of beside me in a crib by our bed, but being an educated person, he knew better.

Little Rob thrived day by day. I loved taking care of him but never expected it would be so much work just taking care of one child. I kept everything spotless, sterilized every baby bottle, measured each and every batch of formula, fed and burped the infant, bathed and dried him, cuddled and held him as much as possible, according to the regulations in Dr Spock's book. By the time seven months rolled around, I wished Dr Spock had kept all he knew about bringing up a baby to himself. I chucked his book in the bucket one bright morning. I lifted Robert out of his protected playpen and sat him on the floor where he and I polished off a bowl of chocolate ice cream for breakfast and jelly, rolled together on the not yet scrubbed and disinfected kitchen floor. We were like a cow and calf mucking in a meadow. After giving the baby his bath—he got one in the morning and one in the evening—I went about doing the daily house cleaning. I'd never lived in such a spotless house: not a flea, fly or spider pestered me like in old times. Sometimes I missed the buggers. When Ed did heavy cleaning with the vacuum every single speck of dust and every household pest were sucked into the snout never to be seen again.

Living in a state of spotlessness could be a lonely thing. I set the table for dinner at five in the afternoon, an hour before Eddie got home from work. I always kept Robert looking lovely for his daddy when he came in the door to pick him up. And I changed my work odds and ends for a nicer outfit for dinner. We ate in the dining room, Robert close by in his high chair pounding on the tray with a spoon. More and more I noticed the cuts and scrapes on my hands from trying to open cans of food. On special occasions I served canned ham decorated with cherries and pineapple. The large tin containers with the sharp edges were a bugger to open with the can opener. Eddie never complained about any food I put in front of him, with the exception of canned peas, which he put to the side of the plate. I figured a person who ate fiddleheads as a delicacy could eat anything. My mother-in-law continued to include recipes in her letters to her son. I figured if he wanted me to fix the recipe, he'd ask. Over the evening meal I filled Ed in on what I did that day, mostly taking care of Robert and cleaning the house even when it didn't need it. He enjoyed me reading out loud from letters I got from home. He had a hard time reading and making sense of the letters on his own. I read him an excerpt from Ma's recent letter while he ate his dinner:

Rob is sitting on the floor with a can of bait and his long line and the smell of ould maggots would give you the headstaggers. It smells like scutter. I am getting to be a better writer every day. The old fella said I went to Trinity College. God help him he is very dry. He is drinking plenty of goat's milk; it is even growing hair on his head IDT [I don't think]. Mrs Fanning was asking for you she is a nice woman and Mrs Coady . . .'

Home again

Eddie exclaimed one day that two years had passed by since I had left Ireland. He would make all the travel arrangement so Robert and I could take a trip back to Ireland and see my family. He could not take time off from work to go with us. The thought of returning home to see everyone at George Reynolds flats, with my new son, felt stupendous. My husband's generosity and love for us constantly amazed me. I'd miss him greatly while I was gone, but he insisted that it was time to reconnect with family members.

Eddie booked our berth on the RMS *Mauritania* setting sail on 8 September 1959. Although only two years had gone by since leaving Ireland, I'd learned some lessons. I realized poor people living in Ireland had a lot in common with poor black people in America. Had I been a poor black-skinned Irish immigrant girl in America I doubt much comfort would have come my way. My life would be still tethered to an iron post unless some advertising agency were to promote me as a black Irish colleen in ads to sell Guinness to Americans.

Eddie drove us to the New York Port and Docks to board the RMS *Mauritania* for our trip back to Ireland. We said a tearful goodbye on the docks. Eddie told me to enjoy myself with my family and not to worry about him, as he would hold the fort until we got back. He told me that Robert and I were his life, and he loved us both. A steward directed me to the tourist cabins on the ship. First class cabins were on the main deck. The cabin contained a bunk bed, a baby cot for Robert, and a tiny sink. The toilets and showers were located down the hallway. The ship began to move and I picked up my son and went upstairs onto the deck, located Eddie on the pier waving both arms in the air to wish us a good journey back home to Ireland. I shouted over all the noise that I loved him. He grinned and kept waving away. Robert got fussy and wanted to be fed. When we went out on the deck again, the city of New York seemed a mirage in the distance. I felt like I was in a dream. The open ocean came into view, massive and restless, and the screeching gulls tagging along with the ship set my teeth on edge. The baby needed changing, so we went back down into the hull of the ship and I unpacked jars of baby food.

I had packed jars of baby food in one suitcase, as well as vitamins, baby shampoo, diaper cream, Band-Aids, disposable diaper liners, a baby toothbrush, and a training potty. These were all the things experts recommended for a 'happy baby and a happy mom' in America.

The passengers I met on board the *Mauritania* included two Irish women who were going home to see their families, especially their mothers. One of the women, Maureen, had migrated to Toronto in Canada, with her husband at the same time as I came to Connecticut. She hailed from Camden Street, Dublin, where her mother had a fruit and vegetable stall. 'I hate Canada,' she said, 'they eat rabbit food for every meal.' It was her mother she missed more than anything while living in Canada. Her husband, 'that fella', loved living in Canada where he earned his living as a bricklayer and went golfing every weekend with his mates. 'He knows he can't do that back in Dublin. Only toffs get to golf not bricklayers. He'd be run off the course. He stayed in Canada. Me mother never really cared for him anyway.' She planned to live with her mother in Camden Street. The husband could 'feck off' and golf till his knees buckled.

The other woman, in her early thirties, met and married an American GI in England where she'd worked as a waitress after leaving Ireland. 'All that I owned fitted in one suitcase when I took off with Anthony for America. He didn't tell me that his parents were immigrants from Italy who'd moved to Boston. They kept calling me the "Irish war bride" that married their son.' Her husband had a job as a foreman in some factory in Boston. She added, 'Anthony has no interest in seeing Europe again; that's why I'm travelling on my own.' She left her three young children with her Italian in-laws who 'stuffed them'. She came originally from Kilkenny. It was her mother she wanted to see so badly. 'Eight years without seeing her has been awful.'

The RMS *Mauretania* dropped anchor in the open ocean miles from Cobh, County Cork, after five days at sea. Departing passengers for Ireland were directed to line up for a smaller waiting tugboat that would take us to Cobh.

I dressed up little Robert in his blue corduroy coat with matching hat. My friend Lo gave him the outfit when her daughter outgrew it. Blue looked lovely on him. I could hardly contain my excitement at being in Ireland again. Puffy pink-hued clouds drifted by overhead and the soft, sweet smell of Ireland took over my body as I held little Robert in my arms to get aboard the tender to take us to land. Da would be waiting for us, having taken the train from Dublin to Cobh. His new little grandson, Robert Francis, would be the treasure I brought home to him and my mother.

When we got to the harbour a young Irish customs officer with a head of rust-brown curls and a Cork accent welcomed me back to Ireland. He held baby Robert in his arms as I went through customs. Liam, the young custom officer, still holding my son, asked if I had returned to stay? And why had I left my native land so young? 'Why don't you consider staying now that you and this little lad are back home?'

I looked to find Da in the crowd. He saw me first and waved his newspaper in the air like crazy to get my attention. 'There's my father waving the newspaper,' I told the smiling customs officer, still holding Robert, as if the baby belonged to him. Da looked surprised at seeing a strange man, not Eddie, holding his grandson as if he'd known the child and myself for donkey's years. 'Congratulations, sir, on your daughter returning home and bringing this little lad with her. Wouldn't it be nice now for them both to stay in Ireland? If not, I'll keep an eye out for them on the return journey to America.'

Da put his arms around the baby and me and tears filled his eyes. 'It's great to see you again, Titch, and to have you home. Is that the wee love, my American grandson you're holding there in your arms? Wait until your mammy sees how well you look and your lovely wee boy. She'll go mad.' Da looked like a swell, wearing a new tweed sports coat and gabardine trousers, and his brown brogues gleamed with a military shine. Ma must have got his new outfit on the hire-purchase plan for me coming home. I joked that he could be mistaken for a Trinity College don, in his new outfit, newspaper under his arm, except he was wearing a matching pair of socks.

After we got on the train for Dublin, and settled into our seats, Da relaxed. He held Robert's little hand and talked to him in fairy talk. The baby listened attentively to the chatter, content to be sitting on granda's lap. While granda played with the baby, I ran my eyes over the newspaper noting a familiar image on the front page, larger than life, as usual. Éamon de Valera and some Spanish nuncio of the Holy Catholic Church stared out at the reader like a couple of plain Janes relishing the spotlight. Similar photographs had appeared in the papers for as long as I could remember: only the faces of the religious bigwigs changed, the other disagreeable puss remained the same.

Reading through the paper, I could tell little had changed since I had left: same stale piss and vinegar and dead-end politics. The baby fell asleep on Da's lap. 'You're a woman of the world now, Titch,' Da said. 'Have you any regrets about leaving us and going to America?'

'I've missed you all a terrible lot. I don't know about regrets, having the best husband any woman could want.'

'I'm glad to hear that, pet, as your mammy and me wonder and still wonder if we should have let you go.' Could Da be completely oblivious to his part in my wanting to get away, never mind getting away from other stagnation? Did he know how many times I wished him dead? Or how many times I wished him to give up the drink? Or how much I loved the fool?

As if trying to read my mind, Da inquired, 'Titch, penny for your thoughts.'

'Ah, just childhood things.'

'You and your wee tin-pot ways,' he smiled.'

'Yep, Da, me and my tin-pot ways.' I took his hand in mine to rid myself of painful thoughts that might come between us, thoughts that made me feel ill. 'I brought you two cartons of American cigarettes.'

'Thanks! Titch. These are good smokes.'

'Coffin nails,' I corrected him.

'American codology,' he replied.

Little Robert slept most of the way on the train to Dublin. I watched the cool green countryside streak by like ribbons worn on Saint Patrick's Day. Soon images of the blue-green seacoast came into view, Ireland's crowning glory. As we came towards Dublin we saw familiar red-brick buildings, church steeples, and clotheslines of family washing strung out in backyards to dance and tumble dry in the breeze.

'We're here, Titch, back in Dublin city.' I held Robert in my arms on the train platform and told the baby, 'We're in Dublin, in Dublin's Fair City.' Da set about finding a taxi as I had luggage by the cartful. The taxi driver greeted my son and me with 'Welcome back home.' Da reminded me my mother, brothers, and sister-in-law, Bridie, along with her two children, Barney and Angeline (my namesake) were at the flat in George Reynolds in Irishtown waiting for me. My heart began racing as the taxi sped and dodged through the streets of Dublin. The pubs and shop-fronts were drying out from a recent shower and now glistened in breaking sunshine. The taxi driver darted in and out between lorries, bicycles, motorcars and slow moving horse-drawn carts that filled the streets. By the time we made it to Butt Bridge, I could hardly contain myself with the delight of being home. The taxi-driver coursed down Ringsend Road like a tossed penny flung by a gambler. The four gray, cement blocks of George Reynolds flats came into view.

The taxi stopped at the kerb outside Mrs Wafer's flat. Ma, Bob, Frank and Bridie called and waved down from our flat on the third floor. Bob and Frank ran down to help us up with the bags. My mother must have taken the stone stairs to the bottom floor by threes, getting to the bottom ahead of the others. She ran to me with arms wide open and enfolded the baby and me like a tea-cosy. We struggled up the three flights of stone steps as if in one mass until we got to the front door of the flat, which my sister-in-law, Bridie, had flung open to welcome me. Bridie held her new baby daughter, named after me, in her arms. Her two-year-old son, Frank the third, nicknamed 'Barney', leaned shyly into his mother's body. The smell of coal-smoke and frying fish greeted me in the hallway. It felt familiar and strange to be home again.

The front room seemed the same as when I left it two years ago. The framed picture of the Sacred Heart was still hanging on the wall, the Bleeding Heart. Ma, Bridie and I sat down on the sofa, the rest anywhere they could fit. Ma held my baby and I held my niece. She had a thatch of black glossy hair with a forelock that fell down over a pair of Irish blue eyes. When tickled under the chin, she showed her dimples amid rosy apple cheeks. 'She's lovely, Bridie and Frank. Can I keep her?' Barney sat on his granda's knee and fiddled with Da's specs that had only one lens and were held together with twine.

Bridie and Frank's rented room in Camden Street, where they lived with their two children, had neither running water nor a toilet. They had to carry their water and empty the slop-bucket outdoors. Their landlord went by the name of 'Mr John'. Mr John, according to my brother, lived in an adjoining dump along with his eighty-year-old widowed mother who ruled the roost like a general, although afflicted with crippling arthritis. The son spoon-fed the mother, gave her a wash-down, fixed her long gray hair into a bun, and made sure she had easy access to the chamber pot. Bridie noted Mr John never uttered a complaint about caring for his mother in case a little birdie might overhear remarks and carry them home to her. She constantly threatened him that she might give the property to the Catholic Church on Aungier Street Street, if he didn't do her bidding. John's dilapidated tenements were firetraps according to my brother, Frank, who had fumigated the rented room he and Bridie moved into, in order to rid the room of funk.

I listened for the sound of the front door opening, hoping that my youngest brother Noely was on the way in. Ma told me that Noely had gone job hunting at the bottle works in Ringsend, and then on to the Dublin Port and Docks to see if they needed an extra worker. In my mind's eye he still remained my bare-arsed younger brother who'd followed me everywhere. Da said I'd be surprised at the stretch he had made since I left. 'He's browned off with being idle, going from Billy to Jack looking for a bit of work,' my mother said. 'He's like thousands of others in the country,' Frank said. Bob was trying to get him a job as a young hand on the coal-boat he worked on.

Ma set a plate of fresh flounders in front of me that Bob had caught at the crack of dawn out on the Shelly Bank on the long line. Bob complained that the bloody seagulls made a beeline for the stranded fish as soon as the tide retreated. They made a beeline for the head of the fish and pecked their eyeballs out. Crabs, he said, did the same thing, headed for the eyes and the face first. 'See the head of that flounder on y'r plate? Caught this morning, empty eye sockets. Blinking gulls beat me to the punch. Not a feckin' blinker.' Frank, if given a choice, would rather have a plate of sausages than any fish in the sea. Bob picked the bones from one of the delicious flounders and fed it to Barney by his side.

After the feed, I sat on the sofa with Robert on my lap. He took in all the new sounds and sights with great interest and let my mother hold onto his hand with contentment. 'Thank God, for bringing you both safe and sound back to Ireland. I wish Ed was here too, 'she noted. 'Sure, such a grand chap be lonesome for you and wee Robert,' added Da.

'Pull the cork on this bottle for me, Bobbler.' Bob gave him a look. 'My hand is tender from a cut I got knocking off the neck of a bottle with the knife a while back,' Da informed me holding up his scarred

In the flat in George Reynolds House, 1960: from left, Da, Ma holding Frank Jnr, Bridie, Noel and Frank.

hand. 'Remember y're on a ration while Angeline and the baby are here,' Bob reminded the auld fella. I'll pull you this one and two more and that's it. That's the pledge — OK?' Da put on his hurt look. 'I know the rules,' he said. Before another word got said, Ma blunted out, 'He nearly set the place aflame. If Mrs Thing-a-ma-jig hadn't seen the smoke coming out the winda, we'd be living on the street. It was an accident.' The auld fella stiffened like an umbrella spoke. 'Sure, don't pay attention to what the pair of them say, love. The box of matches exploded into flames on their own.'

While Da pulled on the gargle, Bob asked me questions about my trip across the Atlantic. I explained that we'd had several days of calm and also times when the sea created huge chalk-white waves that surged over the rail of the ship. 'I'm glad to be on firm ground again.' Bob asked me if I'd seen any sight of 'Mother Carey's chickens' heading towards the Irish coast or, spotted any 'sea pigs' cutting through the ocean?' 'I don't know what Mother Carey's chickens are nor do I know about sea-pigs.'

'Mother Carey's chickens is another name for some Irish sea birds,' he said. He and his mates, while out on the boat in the ocean had spotted flocks of the seabirds flying towards the Irish coast. Sea pigs are just another name for porpoises.' I never knew anyone who loved the ocean as he did even think he worked so hard on the boat, in all kinds of weather to earn a living. I asked him if he'd get the chance to go to the United States for a cargo? He'd heard by the grapevine that a cargo of some kind might be going to Galveston, Texas, and bringing back a cargo of coal for Dublin. 'Remember my chums Charlie and Pat Mullen who worked on the boats?' he asked me. 'It's two years not twenty-two years since I left,' I reminded Bob, 'but I recall Pat and Charlie who never got up the nerve to ask me out.' Bob grinned. 'You acted and dressed like some American young wan instead of an Irish girl.'

I heard Noel coming in the front door. My baby brother now stood before me as a young man dressed in blue jeans and a black zipper jacket and shod in black hobnailed boots. He wore his hair in a ducktail. 'How's me skin and blister?' He laughed giving me a squeeze. 'Is that little Robert? He looks like a baby Yank.' My mother asked Noel if he had any luck finding a job? 'Nah! Mother fuck-all out there, 'he replied in a hard tone. 'Might as well give up lookin and stay in bed.' 'Noely y're bound to find something sooner or later,' my mother assured him. 'Maybe me skin and blister take me back to the States with her?' I smiled feeling a bit edgy with my baby brother who acted like he might have something up his sleeve.

Next day, Ma and I arranged the jars of baby food along the mantelpiece for easier selection. A neighbour in George Reynolds, Mrs D, came over to the flat to welcome me back home. My mother invited her in for a cup of tea. While Ma attended to making a pot of tea, Mrs D let her eyes run along the mantle to where the jars of baby food were. She called out to my mother,

'Mary, what's all them jam jars of paint doing on the mantle. Are ye planning on painting the flat?'

'Them jars are jars of American baby food that Angeline brought all the way home to feed her baby. Show Mrs D what's in some of the jars,' my mother directed. I took jars of processed green peas, carrots, applesauce, beetroot, chicken, liver, and beef to show our neighbour.

'What's in that wan?' she asked. 'Looks like the colour of dead pigeons.'

'Chicken.'

'The child eats that? Poor little pet,' she said.

I pointed out to the two older women that pediatricians in the United States endorsed the baby food I fed Robert, 'packed with vitamins,' I added for good measure. Mrs D exchanged glances with

Ma as if to say, 'Let her be, she means well.'

Mrs D shifted the conversation by asking me, 'What's the biggest differences between the Irish and Americans?' 'I don't rightly know, but there's a difference.' I'd given too short of an answer. The two older women looked at each other. I could tell our neighbour wanted to hold my baby, so did Ma. 'She brushes the infant's two front teeth with a baby toothbrush and baby toothpaste,' my mother informed Mrs D as if such a thing went beyond belief. Mrs D took a closer look at the baby's teeth. The baby gave her a crabby look. Before departing, Mrs D looked at my mother and asked quite blankly, 'Does living in America agree with yr daughter?'

During a chat with Da by the fireplace, I mentioned that some married men in American had a room for themselves they called a 'den.' The auld fella's ears picked up like antennae. 'Give me every scrap of information you have on dens,' he said. Ed's friends, married men, talked a lot about decorating their dens. Some built indoor bars into their dens and stocked them with liquor. The wife and kids were barred from entering the den. Some men had a billiard-table put in the den. Most liked to add some kind of a head of a wild animal over the bar. 'Did you hear that, Mary?' my father called out to my mother, playing with the baby on her lap. 'Holy Moley,' Ma shot back, asking, 'Does that mean the husbands never leave the house? The poor women.' I could tell by the look on Da's face that he had been taken by the idea of having a den, a built-in-bar, and the head of a dead animal hoisted on the wall. 'That's what every man should have in this country, a den,' said Da, quivering with excitement.

'Mary,' he said, 'the next time you go into the Dublin Corporation, tell the fella behind the desk, that your husband, a former Free State soldier wants one of the builders who works for the public housing to come out to number 12 George Reynolds, Irishtown and build on an American den.'

Then he turned to me: 'Titch, will you send me a moose head from America to hang on the wall. Stuff it full of US dollars. That's a good girl.'

After a go round of hugs for me and kisses for Robert, Jenny, our next door near neighbour, sat down for a cup of tea and a long chat.

'What are Americans like, are they like us or not?' she wanted to know.

'Yes and no,' I replied. 'A lot of them eat meat on Fridays. They are not all Catholic like we thought. There's tons of food in America and Americans are always eating. They eat the usual three meals a day and still constantly need more food. I think they are afraid of food — they love it and say they don't need so much. I think they might have heard too many scary stories about the Irish Famine.'

'Do you think American husbands are different than Irish ones?' Jenny asked.

'I never had an Irish husband — couldn't get a fella to marry me.'

'Ah, git out a that Angeline. Tell us about the American fella ye married?' My mother picked up her ears.

'He's great to me and the baby and helps around the house. He gives Rob his bath. Works hard at his job, and he has a hobby of collecting stamps. He gets hay fever.'

'Hay what?'

'Hay fever. It's caused by anything that grows in a garden, field or forest.'

'Does it spread like TB (God forbid) or chicken pox?'

'No, it's caused by something called allergies.'

'Is the child on your mother's lap afflicted with it? Please God, no,' I looked over at baby Robert, comfortable on his granny's lap. 'Angeline's babby's mostly Irish,' said Ma.

After Jenny filled me in on everything that had happened in George Reynolds since the day I emigrated to America, a hazy Irishtown afternoon slipped away like magic.

Jenny continued questioning me about the ins and outs of America. She wanted to know if the women were as glamorous in real life as they were in the films, and if I had seen the mansions they lived in. I knew that Jenny, like the majority of the neighbours, only wanted to hear happy and fanciful accounts of life in the United States. Going to America for poor Irish people meant the same thing as going to Shangri-la or Fairyland, or arriving at the end of the rainbow to find the crock of gold. 'There's a lot of them well off by George Reynolds standards and others who struggle every day.' Jenny was crestfallen at this. Such harsh reality did not fit in with Irish insistence that the big yonder shimmered in a golden glow for all.

I described the young women at the Travelers' Insurance company, and the fashionable wives I'd met through Eddie's friends at work. 'Men in America call their wives "sweetie, honey, and baby" in front of others.'

'Better than "bitch" or "hairy goblin". What does your husband call you?'

'For a terrible time, he called me "angel" this and "angel" that.'

'Did he think he married a nun or a saint? ' asked Ma, with an astonished look on her face. 'He calls me Angie now,' I replied.

Jenny asked me what kind of makeup I had on my face. 'Revlon. Here try some on, and the berry-cherry lipstick.' If the truth be told, Jenny, the mother of seven children, looked less washed out than myself. In spite of a hard life and the familiar gaps in her teeth, Jenny's beauty could enrich an Irish banknote.

Ma ended the conversation by letting out a sharp yelp. Little Rob had bitten her fingertip instead of the pork rib that she held for him to chew on. 'Sharp little American teeth,' his granny said, with a voice mingled with pain and pride.

'Gimme the baby, Ma, and hold y'r finger under the water tap,' I exclaimed, my Dublin tone coming back. 'Y'r mammy loves that baby,' said Jenny. 'She couldn't wait for ye to get home and ye should have seen y'r da sobering up like a bishop days before you were expected to get here.' I looked around our front room as Jenny continued to talk and picked out the bunches of new paper flowers Ma had bought at Woolworth's to decorate the place for me coming over.

'I have to run over to Coady's for a few messages,' Jenny said, getting up from the chair to head out the door. While Ma ran cold water over her bruised finger, Robert and I rocked on the skeleton armchair by the fireplace. I wondered how Eddie was getting along back in Connecticut on his own. Did he miss us? All the time I was away, his letters arrived twice a week, sometimes containing a ten or twenty dollar bill. When my mother sat down again, her finger rolled in a wet towel, I explained to her that Charlie hadn't arrived for over two months and asked her if it were possible to get caught out so quickly after having a baby. She glanced at little Robert scooting under the table beneath us and asked, 'Have you the dates right? Are ye a bit peckish for odd food?' I nodded, 'yes' on both questions. 'I've a mad craving for Bisto gravy and onions.'

'Does Eddie know y're late?'

'I didn't mention it yet. I didn't know I could get pregnant — that's what they say in America, Ma — so soon. '

'Ango,' she said, using her nickname for me, 'bear in mind there's enough juice in the stem of a man's pipe to father tribes around the

*First trip back to Dublin with baby Robert. Noel is
holding the baby. This photo was taken in 1960 on
O'Connell Street by a street photographer.*

world. Some women get in the family way just by asking a man the
time of day.' I decided to ask her a delicate question: 'What can anyone do if they don't want to keep having babies year after year?'

'Other than strapping the mallet to his leg, not much in Ireland as
ye see for y'rself.' Not even the word 'abortion' could be mentioned
in Ireland. 'Ask your husband, he's American with a modern view of
things.' I thought to myself: there's other means for depositing family jewels that doesn't lead to hatching. Ma asked how many children I'd like to have? 'Four,' I replied.

'Don't tear the heart out of yerself, with more than ye can handle.'
I reminded her of the fairy stories told in Ireland that babies were

found underneath cabbages. 'You know better now,' she said. 'It's the camogie-stick ye need to be concerned with.' We both laughed. 'Ma, you're funny.'

'Well, if we don't laugh we cry.'

Little Rob crawled out from underneath the table with a strange expression on his face. 'He's got something in his mouth,' I said with concern. Ma jumped out of her chair and picked up the baby. She forced his mouth open, and out fell a slew of chewed up cigarette butts. 'I warned that child's granda not to toss cigarette butts on the floor, and now look what's happened! He only understands double Dutch.'

Noel and I were alone in the flat one afternoon. He seemed more fed up than usual. I knew he hated being broke all the time and no job prospects on the horizon.

'How about me going to live with you in America?' he asked.

'I'd like it. I'm sure Ed would go for it too.'

'What's me going over got to do with him? It's you I'm asking the question to.'

'I'd have to let him know you would like to go over. Noely, he owns the house.'

'You don't think I'd make the mark over there?'

'Are you going to discuss going away with Ma and Da?'

'No bother there.'

'It would be a sorry bother if you didn't tell them beforehand.'

'Mrs Yank, me own skin and blister, is telling me what to do.'

'I'm not trying to tell you one way from another.'

'Since ye went to the big yonder ye developed a swelled-head; just remember you and me came out of the same belly.' I could feel my eyes getting itchy from his annoyance with me. I didn't want to get into a fight with someone I'd longed to see.

'I don't think of myself as being special because I went to America. It's not all it's made out to be.'

'Let's face it now, me skin and blister, y're a tame house-cat at the heels of its master.'

'Well, let me say to you with y'r slicked back duck tail of a hairdo and pants too tight to fart in, them who looks down their nose don't see far beyond it, and it's you who's looking down his nose.'

'Looka, Ango, just let me have a quid and I'll be off to meet me mates for a pint. Or will a little thing like giving me a quid bankrupt the bank?'

I asked my mother if Noel drank more than his share for a not-yet-sixteen-year-old. I invited Noely to go along with Robert and me into the city for coffee. He acted delighted, saying he would hold the baby in his arms all the way, adding, 'I'll let on to everyone that he's my kid.' 'Fair enough.'

While we were walking across O'Connell Bridge, a street photographer took our photo for two shillings. Noel asked me if I wanted to visit the oldest pub in Dublin.

'Another time without the baby,' I replied. 'Suit y'rself.'

It began to feel like I'd never left home and that I'd always had the baby. In spite of some upset, it meant a lot to be with everyone, especially my mother. Robert basked in all the attention showered on him not only by relatives but also by the neighbours. I asked myself if I'd made a big blunder leaving all the love and companionship behind in pursuit of my Irish-American dream. Eddie, the best of the best, could be better off with an American-born wife instead of a slinger.

There would be no going back to Connecticut without first heading for Sandymount Strand. My mother and I took turns carrying Robert down to the strand. Ma recalled how we'd dug up cockles on the strand with the neighbors and their kids in the past, and the cockle cooks we had in George Reynolds. 'Most of the kids you grew up with in the flats are scattered to the corners of the world.'

Ma took off the baby's socks so he'd feel the sand under his feet. 'Keep him from getting bunions,' she said. Then on a more serious note inquired, 'Did ye baptise the child in America? Did it take the way it does in Ireland? '

'Ma, I told ye Miss Foley in the Supply Department in the Travelers Insurance company is his godmother.'

'Still and all it weighs on me mind whether it took or not. Let's go to that little pool of water left behind by the tide.' Ma knelt down with Robert in her arms and dipped her fingers into the pool sending tiny crabs scurrying for their lives. She shook bright drops over the baby's head with a singsong: 'I baptise our little Robert in the Irish way. In the name of the Father, Son, Holy Ghost, the Blessed Mother, Sun, Moon and Stars.' Robert stuck out a petal tongue, capturing a salty droplet on its way down. She handed over my twice-christened child, and said, 'He's a bit in the nappy. Smells like hen fruit.' As we walked along the strand on our way back to the flats, Ma said, 'Let's sing a song to shorten the road. `Member this one?' Robert listened with both ears as his mother and grandmother sang into the wind:

'Show me the way to go home.
I'm tired and I want to go to bed.
I had a little drink about an hour ago,
And it's gone right to me head.
No matter where I roam
Over land or sea or foam,
You will always hear me singing this song.
Show me the way to go home.'

Seagulls screeched like banshees as they flew towards the Irishtown dump to scavenge for food. The screechy scavengers would be in stiff competition with hungry children from around the area and with the feral men from across the city that rag-picked for sustenance in the wasteland. The gulls heading for the Irishtown dump reminded me of when I'd collected cinders. In 1959, lots of working-class people in Ireland were still on the skids. Many still lacked as much as a hankie to cover a corpse.

Da began to show signs of strain from having to cut back on his drink because of me and the baby being there. My mother and Bob eyeballed his consumption of Guinness. It remained a mystery where he got the money for the drink. He'd told me long ago that he only felt OK when the drink had him in its clutch. For now, with me home, the cursed jar only had a light grip on him, which meant the auld fella could still talk plain. He wanted to know if little Robert would be told Irish stories when he got a bit older, or would only know stories about American heroes. Da obviously favoured Irish mystical and magical charms over Hollywood bang-bangs.

I told Da there'd be no instilling in the mind of my child mystical myths about President de Valera or the hobgoblins who were nothing but tacks in the leader's boots. The auld fella looked at me with a blowtorch gleam in his eye as he greedily inhaled vapours released from a newly opened bottle of Guinness. I knew Ma felt relieved Da had agreed to limit his intake while his daughter and grandson stayed.

'*Oileán-na-Naoimh*—remember what that means, Angeline?' Ma asked. 'I remember all the bits and pieces of Irish you taught me, Ma.

'What does it mean then?'

'Island of Saints,' I replied.

'The time is running fast. Then you and little Robert will be gone away from us, from his granny. It might be a long time before ye get a chance to come back to Oilean-na-Naoimh, with another baby on the way and everything else in between.'

'We'll swim back if we have to, Ma. Keep buying a chance in the Sweep.'

'Those who really need a bit of money never win in the Sweep, only auld mad solicitors and wealthy farmers who won't marry,' she reminded me. She and I cried while packing my suitcase, while little Rob, sitting on the floor beside us bit into a well-buttered bread crust.

I parted once more from Ma and the rest of the people I loved. I hated this part of being an emigrant: the leaving behind of my close family ties. Ma's parting words chimed in my ears, '*Slán abhaile*, my little loves. I'll be waiting till y're coming back home.' Da accompanied little Robert and me on the train back to Cobh. We parted in friendship and tears. The baby and I boarded the *Britannia* for our trip back to New York where Eddie would be waiting to take us back to the nutmeg state.

I'd sit and sort myself on the ship going back to New York for the good of little Robert. I'd turn myself inside out to play being a corporate wife, hygienic homemaker and disciple of Dr Spock, who, some Dublin grannies declared, must have fallen on his head as a baby.

As the transatlantic liner slowly entered New York harbour on an October morning, I held Robert tight in my arms up against the ship's rail to get a good look at the Statue of Liberty hailing us back to America. A great cheer went up from the passengers on board at the sight of the statue. Little Robert held onto me tighter as the noise continued to escalate. I explained to him how fate had ordained that we go from the arms of one mother into the embrace of another. The giantess with the massive crown, holding the flame of freedom, appeared stern and unflinching in her demeanour as if mandating, 'Come hell or high water, I'll not go back on promises made in my name. So help me God.'

Eddie met us at the dockland in New York holding a bunch of golden autumn flowers for me along with a new red snowsuit for his son. We made a tight little circle as we embraced on the dock. 'You both look wonderful. The baby's grown and put on some weight. So have you, honey,' he joked.

'We can discuss that later, ' I replied, squinting from the brightness of the day.

'Does Robert need formula before we head back home to Connecticut?'

'He doesn't like that stuff anymore. He drinks regular milk from a cup or out of a saucer, he loves fried sausages and black puddin` and even the bitter taste of porter. He's a great little traveller, and when in Rome he did what the Romans did.'

Ed's dad died that December at the age of eighty-four. He could not be buried until the following spring because the graveyard in Presque Isle froze solid in winter. He remained like a frozen popsicle inside his wrapper until spring thawed the earth once more. In May that year our second son, Stephen Francis, joined the family; everyone said he looked like the 'Gerber baby'. Lo and Bill were his godparents.

Being the mother of two young children, keeping the house spick and span, and being an attentive wife kept me hopping, but I finally got acquainted with the neighbours who lived on either side of us.

One family had grown children who worked but continued to live at home with their parents. Every Monday morning, Mrs Schook hung out a long line of beautifully washed clothes and linens. She arranged each piece on the clothesline as if stringing charms. We said 'Hi' back and forth over the fence. Her husband, Omer, worked as a mechanic at the New London shipyard. He drove the long distance every day. I got to know the couple better after I heard a scream coming from their house on a Monday morning. I put the baby in the crib and Robert in the playpen, and rushed over to investigate the commotion next door. Mrs Schook had got the front of her apron tangled in the roller of her washing machine and could not get loose. I pulled the electric plug from the socket in the wall but not before the tip of her breast had been pinched. Heaven only knows what would have happened had I not been at home with the window open. The woman could have been rolled flat as a pancake.

The next day, her husband showed up at our door to thank me for saving, in his words, his wife's 'titty'. He handed me a covered dish that smelled like cooked cabbage. When Eddie walked in the door he called out, 'What's that wonderful smell, Angie? Smell's like real food.' I got his hidden meaning: that the smell from Mrs Schook's Bolonka casserole heating in the oven beat the hell out of any dish I ever put on the table.

Mrs Schook recovered from the washing machine ordeal and continued to send her husband over every Saturday evening with a homemade dish. Eddie counted the days until the great grub appeared although pretending he preferred my dinners.

I wrote home and told my mother about rescuing the neighbour from getting mangled in the washing machine. She wrote back saying she thanked God for not having such a thing in the flat and for having little to wash, otherwise the same thing could have happened to her and thousands like her in Ireland. Da asked in the letter if the woman had been pickled doing the washing. I had a postcard also from my brother Bob; he wrote that the cargo boat he worked on as an able-bodied seaman was named *Wimbourne*. He wrote a PS on the bottom of the card: 'Hard to believe y're married with two boys.' Boys were a major part of my existence. I had three brothers, two sons, and our close neighbours also had boys instead of girls.

The two boys next door, Larry and Dave, both played Little League baseball and both were in the Boy Scouts. They managed to sell me chocolate bars, cookies, Christmas cards, flashlight batteries, magazine subscriptions, and other unnecessary items in their efforts to raise money for some project or another. They both told me, 'You don't talk like an American.' The boy's parents, Bab and Dutch, invited us to a cook-out at their home. Dutch explained that his grandparents originally came from Holland and settled in Windsor Locks, Connecticut. Bab worked, unlike most of the housewives on our street; she was a secretary in a doctor's office. Dutch worked in Hartford. When he got home in the evening he played baseball with his sons in their backyard. You could hear him call out as if wanting all the neighbours to hear: 'Heads up. Play ball. Slide! Slide! Grab that bat. Hit that sucker no matter what! SLIDE!'

At one of the cook-outs I got the chance to meet Dutch's dad. The older man asked me what I knew about the Dutch. 'I've seen pictures of dykes, tulips, and windmills.' He smiled. 'Let me tell you our folks had it tough when they first came over. I guess it's to be expected that everyone starts at the bottom, that's just the way it is.' I nodded, not completely getting his drift. Then he repeated a ditty that he'd heard as a child in Windsor Locks.

The dirty, dirty Dutch
They don't amount to much
But they are a damned sight
Better than the Irish.

'It's funny,' I laughed.

'Funny? What's funny about it?'

'The way it's made up and put together. It's silly and funny.' The older man's face took on a look of disapproval at my remarks. Ed stepped in to help me out. 'She doesn't mean it's funny like we mean funny. She sees the serious side.'

'I remember rhymes we heard on the street back in Dublin. They were never taken seriously. Like this one:

Hitler's granny has a shop down in Hell,
She sells ammunition and is doing very well.
A halfpenny for a bullet and a penny for a shell
Hitler's granny has a shop down in hell.

'Who taught rhymes like that to children?' Bab wanted to know.'

'I don't know. They just went in one ear and out the other.'

The conversation turned to how Larry and Dave were going to lead their Little League team to victory in the championship game of the season. They were the stars of the 'Oak Leaves' thanks to their dad, Dutch.

We went to the game. Larry was hit in the head with a fast flung ball and fell to the ground. He died a month later, and the neighbourhood went into mourning. The death of the child stunned me. I thought only poor children died. Larry never wanted for anything; his parents loved him. He didn't die of disease, or lack of food or lack of medical care or neglect of any kind. A stupid, pitched baseball killed the blond, blue-eyed American boy. 'Death's dagger is never blunted,' my mother often said.

Dutch and Bab were in great grief over Larry's death. Their remaining child, Dave, only had eyes for the ground as he went back and forth to school. Not long after, the family put their house up for sale and moved to Florida.

Ed's sister in Los Angeles sent him a letter in which she explained that the aircraft companies in the area were looking to hire engineers.

He'd have no trouble finding a job, she said, and the dry, hot climate in Los Angeles would be better for his hay fever than working in Connecticut. 'Maybe we should move to California, Angie?'

'It would be like emigrating again,' I responded, upset at the suggestion. I asked why they needed so many engineers in America. 'Sputnik,' replied Eddie.

'You mean the little red fart far in the sky, not hot enough to light the tip of a cigarette?'

'It's much more than a spark to the government, honey. They can't let the Soviets get ahead of them in space.'

The IRA's obsession with the English didn't hold a candle to the obsession that America had with the Soviet Union. Every news item on the radio had to do with something terrible the Soviets had done. I wondered if anyone ever met or talked to a Russian in Connecticut. My brother Bob, as far as I knew, remained the only person I knew who'd met 'Ruskies', as the Yanks referred to them.

In a letter to me, my brother wrote about some Russian trawlers having to shelter from a bad gale in the Irish Sea. He helped tie up the trawlers at the Dublin docks. Bob and other Dublin dockers exchanged fags, tea and newspapers with the Russian seamen, who in return gave them bottles of vodka, which, according to my brother, could knock a carthorse off its hind legs. I wondered why de Valera didn't feel the same way about the Russians as the Americans did.

Eddie and my friends kept asking when I intended to apply for my American citizenship. I thought about it, but continued to put it off until Eddie got very earnest about it.

'Angie, I would like you to consider applying for US citizenship. The children and I are citizens. You have been here almost three years, but you don't have citizenship and the rights you'd need to have if something were to happen to me.'

'Are ye hinting that President Eisenhower would take the boys away?'

'That's not likely, but it's important for you to have the same citizenship as the children, and it would make me happy if you were to become an American.'

'Be the hokey. I never realized how much it would mean to you. I'll do it right away.'

'Just think it over, Angie, is what I'm suggesting.'

'I'm glad y're not forcing me into anything. The kids and me'd be better off on the same passport.'

He nodded.

'I'd never try to change you. Like asking you to become a Catholic or go to Mass once in a while with me and the boys.'

'I appreciate that,' he replied, not getting it.

'Would you ever change religion? Become a mackerel-snapper like me and the kids?'

'I can't foresee it,' he said.

'Just kidding,' I replied. Kidding me backside, I mused. When such differences were brought to light between Eddie and me, the sun felt awry. In order to dispel such feelings of isolation, I'd inquire if he still remembered the bits of Irish language that I fed him on occasion.

'*Súile an chait?*'

'Afraid I don't recall, he replied.

'*Súile an chait,*' I'd repeat. 'It means "The cat's eyes".'

'I'll try to recall it next time. By the way, what's for supper this evening? I'm famished.'

'Parsnips and spuds, that's what's for dinner. Rob and Stephen eat the roots like little pigs going to the market. What does *an mhuc,* mean?'

'Holy cow, I forgot that one too.'

'It means the pig. What's a camogie-stick?'

'It's a curved stick you hit a ball with. I remember words associated with sports. Angel, what's for supper one more time?'

'Parsnips. Pot of parsnips or baloney sandwiches.'

I became preoccupied with the thought of becoming an American citizen. It made sense, especially for the children not to have an alien mother. Being an alien felt like having one foot in Ireland and the other on a banana skin. I wanted Ma and Da's advice about taking such a drastic step. Becoming an American citizen meant not being in their category any more, and not belonging to Ireland. Wasn't I part of that place like no other? Part of the empty cobblestone building sites, the stubble weeded fields speckled with bright flowers, the dirt and decay, the hate and love, the hills and the sea — the whole mixed bag of dreamers, schemers, devils, saints and whore-mongers?

Ma and Da wrote back in their letter that it would be a good thing for me to become an American citizen, like Eddie, for the children's sake. Da wrote that he understood my dilemma of having to give up one country in order to be accepted by another. As usual he used a four-legged animal to make his point: 'Titch, you're like the donkey who stands between two bales of hay, debating which to eat first.' The advice made my belly cramp, as if from hunger. Both my mother and father reminded me that I'd always be their daughter, Irish or American—or Hungarian for that matter.

In my eighteen years of growing up in the Irish Republic little or no mention of citizenship ever made it on the plate. Had we understood that citizens had rights, maybe we could have demanded the right to be lifted from the gutter. The notion of being a citizen began to take root in my brain, growing stronger than a lion. With a sense of trepidation, I enrolled in the civics classes required for naturalisation and citizenship at the local library in East Hartford.

I became a citizen of the United States on December 8, 1961, four years after leaving Ireland. After the swearing-in ceremony in the state courthouse in Hartford, Connecticut, I suggested to Eddie that the importance of the occasion demanded a shot of Irish whiskey. He grimaced at the suggestion, looking at our two boys as if to say, what kind of an example is that for a mother to set? The double shot of whiskey caused me to see stars and stripes and other optical illusions. Lo and Bill had a cocktail party at their house to celebrate me becoming One of Them.

After all the fuss had settled, I thought more about what it meant to be a new citizen. I read the brochures they'd passed out with my official papers about 'the duties of a citizen' the 'rights and privileges of a citizen,' and the most impressive part of all was that I had the right now to life, liberty, and the pursuit of happiness. The latter represented, to my mind, the best part of citizenship in America: no priests or nuns or their counterparts had the right to impose their beliefs on me. No clique, political or religious, owned liberty as they did back in Ireland. I stuck the small, coloured picture of the Statue of Liberty in my prayer book, and sent another one home to my mother to put in with hers. I tried to explain some of the meaning of the Statue of Liberty in my letter home.

She is called the 'Mother of Exiles' and the 'Queen of Heaven.' Her head from ear to ear measures 10 feet and the length of her nose is 4 feet, 6 inches according to my information book. The French government gave the Statue to America as a present. They sent the statue in 200 packing crates and the people in New York

had to take all the bits and pieces to reassemble the lot into the
'Mother of Exiles.' There is a verse inside the plinth of the statue.
Give me your tired, your poor,
Your huddled masses yearning to breathe free,
The wretched refuse of your teeming shore.
Send these, the homeless, tempest-tost, to me:
I lift my lamp beside the golden door!'

Da wrote back that the ideas of the Statue of Liberty were grand, but my spelling and writing needed improvement.

Eddie reminded me that I would be able to vote in the next presidential election. When the time rolled around, I took notice. I heard on the news that the vice-president, Richard Nixon, and John F. Kennedy an Irish American Catholic, were both running to become the president of the United States. The two planned to hold a set of debates on television. Eddie had already decided to vote for Nixon. 'Which party does he belong to?' I asked. 'Republican Party,' he replied. 'He's our best, most experienced candidate.'

'I don't know that for myself yet,' I exclaimed, a bit put off by his insistence. Kennedy would be the first Catholic and the youngest man ever to be elected president of the United States if he won. There were groups shouting out in protest that if Kennedy got to the Oval Office he would be told what to do by the pope in Rome. I wondered about this myself, knowing that every move back in Ireland got rubber-stamped by the bigwigs in the Roman Catholic Church, and I hated the Irish government for allowing that. If you ask me, the separation of church and state might be the best reason for moving to the United States.

Interviews and photographs of John F. Kennedy began to appear on television. I thought he must live by the ocean because the photographs always showed him either walking along the seashore or out sailing in a small boat. He had a wife and a little girl. On the night of the debates, he looked like a person in an advertisement. He had the perfect set of American teeth that showed when he smiled, and he smiled a lot. Those big white strong straight teeth spoke to American pride. Some say Nixon lost the debates because he looked like he needed a shave. He didn't have a chance when it came to the Kennedy teeth. Of course, Kennedy had a head full of brains but those jaw-breaker smiles clinched the election. I never thought that President

Kennedy had much in common with the common people in the USA, even though some made a big deal about his poor immigrant forebears. He seemed more like an English gentleman to me than an Irish squire type. The Irish at home and abroad loved him like family. My mother bought a coloured photograph of him in a shop in Ringsend. She wrote that she hung the picture next to the Sacred Heart of Jesus on the wall over the fireplace. She said they looked a matched pair.

Bob wrote that he would send me some Oxos in a parcel he'd put together. The *Wimbourne* was to pick up a cargo of coal in England, to take back to the North Wall in Dublin. I never realized while living back in Ireland that we got our coal supply from England. Bob told me that he hoped to get a transfer to work aboard a deep ocean cargo ship operating out of Birkenhead or Liverpool with cargo for Boston, or Galveston, Texas. He hoped by doing so that he could come and visit us. He finished off his letter by exclaiming in a PS. 'I have a head of black snot now instead of Irish green.' I read some of the letter to Eddie, excluding the part about the effects of inhaling coal dust.

Eddie's sinuses continued to drain as a consequence of ragweed. Being red eyed and miserable each summer began to take a toll on him. He made a decision for us to move from ragweed-filled New England to the arid desert of Los Angeles, as his sister had earlier suggested. His bouts of hay fever were getting harder to put up with. He didn't have a dry eye in his head from the beginning of Spring to the end of Fall. I hadn't any intention of refusing the request in spite of the fact that I had already followed him across the Atlantic Ocean, sunk new roots in Connecticut, and now needed to traverse one end of the United States to another. At that time I didn't feel in the whole of my own health either, and my two rambunctious little boys took my every breath. We put the house up for sale. The real estate man told me that in the advertisement for the house he stated 'You could eat off the floor.' Lo and Bill were surprised when Eddie told them we were moving out West. They gave us a going-away party which drew together the people I'd first got to know in America: Lo and Bill, Al, Shirley, and little Chloe, now three years old, lovely as daylight. Nancy and Les showed up, too.

My former supervisor at the Travelers' Insurance company, Rose Foley, cried when I told her we were moving to California. She told me to call her day or night if I needed anything and that she felt a great loss at us

Connecticut shore, 1963, with Robert and Steven.

going away. I had a good mind to tell Eddie to forget about us moving away because it had taken a lot of effort to create the home and friends we had, and uprooting ourselves for a new place far away made me feel homesick all over again.

We sold the house in a month. Eddie had a job waiting for him in Los Angeles and had already rented an apartment in the small community of Lomita, California. The sight of tall palm trees growing out of the cement sidewalks stunned me, as did the yellow-coloured sky above, and the heat of the day, though it was still winter. I felt once again like a foreigner standing in Los Angeles, only now I had two small boys in tow. A wave of sadness washed over me; already I missed my friends and neighbours in Connecticut and I missed my family back in Ireland even more. Eddie said that we could all go swimming in the Pacific Ocean even though we were in the middle of November. 'I've no bathing suit,' I muttered, hot under the collar. It would be a different matter if we were going to Hollywood to be in the movies, but in fact it would be the usual bread and butter with oranges thrown in.

We moved into the apartment and arranged the furniture. I let Eddie do all the arranging. The boys took to their new surroundings and loved it — so many young children were playing outside in the com-

mon area we shared with our new neighbours. That evening, I told
Eddie that I suspected another child was on the way. He'd put me in
charge of the fertility test kit the doctor in Hartford had recommended
as a means of birth control. The kit supposedly determined when sex
was safe and when it wasn't. It never took into account the spur of the
moment kind of thing that excited me. The monthly planner, based on
safe days and non-safe days, was confusing; and the calculations
took the spin out of merrymaking. Who wanted their marriage bed to
be a place of ifs or buts or do's or don'ts? I didn't have a head for sums.
Eddie was surprised and alarmed on hearing he'd be the father of
three in the near future. 'When do you see the doctor?'

'Soon. I'm not feeling up to steam.'

Eddie's sister Ruth and her husband had invited us over to their
home in Torrance for a barbecue the following evening. 'Ruth can
give you the name of a doctor,' said Eddie.

Ruth and her husband Bud, greeted us at the front door of their
ranch house with their two young children, a darling little red-haired
girl, and a blond little boy. They were all tanned by the California
sunshine, and looked like a movie family. Ruth had on bright blue
pedal-pusher pants, a white cotton shirt, and toe sandals. Bud wore
tan shorts, a red and white plaid shirt, and toe sandals too. Rob and
Steve and their two cousins ran out into the back yard, and the four
of them jumped fully clothed into a round plastic children's swimming pool.

Ruth and Ed talked about their mom back in Maine. Neither one
seemed to have a lot of guilt about leaving the elderly woman living
on, what seemed to me, the edge of the wilderness. They discussed
with each other how self-sufficient their mother was, how she kept
busy doing charity work, sewing in her church circle, and getting out
for walks on her own, even during the winter months. Neither seemed
concerned with the possibility that a bear or a moose could emerge from
the wilderness and charge headfirst towards their helpless old mother.

While Eddie and Ruth talked about old times, Bud asked me lots of
questions about Ireland, saying he had always wanted to go there for
a visit. He asked me if his name, 'McCoy' happened to be Irish. 'Scots,'
I replied not knowing one way or another. He asked if I'd heard of the
Hatfields and McCoys who were famous for their feuding. I lied and
said I did in order to keep the comfortable conversation going.

Over hamburgers and beans, Eddie announced that I was pregnant and needed the name of a gynaecologist in the area. Ruth sprang up from her chair and ran to get her phone list of names. She assured me that I'd have no trouble meeting new people and that California had the friendliest people in all forty-eight states. Her husband nodded in agreement, having been born in the Golden State. He and I went through a pack of cigarettes like a knife through butter. Eddie kept quiet about me puffing my head off, but nodded in the direction of my pregnant belly.

'I belong to a sorority-sister group and we have a lot of fun,' my sister-in-law exclaimed. 'I'll bring your name up at our next meeting to see if you can become a member. It's by invitation only. We do fund raising for charity, go out to lunch, go shopping and do fun things like that.'

Ruth's gynaecologist told me I'd give birth to my third child within the next six months. He performed a blood test that confirmed I was anaemic. He acted like I'd done something wrong upon reading the test results. 'I'll eat more liver,' I volunteered, hoping to change his mood. 'I don't want any haemorrhage to happen on my shift.' He insisted that I take iron pills and a series of iron-rich injections until the baby arrived.

'Christ,' I said out loud. 'I hate injections—especially since you say they will be painful.'

'Are you from Poland by any chance?' he quipped. 'Missy,' he said, talking to me like I only had half a brain, 'find a relative or friend to lend you a hand until your delivery. What area of Poland did you say you were from?'

'The best part,' I replied. Why were some doctors so cold-hearted, so detached from human feelings, whether in Ireland or America?

Eddie worked hard at his new job; they expected him to work overtime and bring home piles of paperwork. I wondered why he'd ever left his old job and the good friends he had. But, like magic, his hay fever attacks ended.

Ruth phoned to let me know her sorority-sisters, over lunch at Trader Vicks, had decided not to let me join their club. 'Sorry about that,' she whined over the phone, adding, 'some of the gals were concerned about you being foreign born, and you might be linked to the IRA. The gals felt it might be better for you to join another group, join a bowling team.'

'None of your friends have ever met me,' I pointed out.

'I told them that you had met my brother overseas, got engaged to him, and came to this country and married him.' I hung up the phone, agitated as a caged weasel.

Eddie called from the living room, 'Interesting phone call, honey?'

'Your sister called to let me know she and her sorority-sisters turned me down for membership in their social club. Fucking cheek,' I fumed.

'Please, honey, don't let the boys hear you swear. Say "fish" instead of the gutter word; remember we substitute other words for cuss words — fish, dang-nab-it, phooey, fiddlesticks, gosh-all-mighty.'

'That's cursing up your sleeve, if you ask me,' I hurled back. Plainly my curse words bothered him more than his snooty sister and her snooty friends bruising my pride. The exclusion stirred painful, old feelings of being unwanted back in Ireland, by either the state or the church.

'I'll make reservations for us at some nice place, Angie. Cheer you up.'

'I don't cheer up that fishing easy after being insulted. Them dang-nab-it bitches can kiss me fiddlesticks fishing Irish arse.'

'OK, honey, why don't I take the boys out for a doughnut and you get some rest. We love you and that's what matters. We'll bring you back a jelly-filled doughnut.'

'Make it two.'

After my family left for the doughnuts, I lay down on the bed and thought about my reaction to the mean-spirited decision made by the uncharitable whores. It summoned up the desperate, gut-twisting feeling of rejection I'd suffered when the head nun at the national school in Sandymount turned me down for admittance when she discovered that I collected cinders on the dump to earn a living. She did not want a poor cast-off child in her school.

The nun's turning me away from the school door made hot shame blister over my body and soul. From that day to this I'd felt that I was never quite good enough. But that was then, not now, I assured myself, hugging the pillow. Furthermore, a new baby nestled inside me. I had two lovely little boys and a husband who had never uttered an unkind word to me in four years of marriage, and there was a possibility my mother might come to Los Angeles and stay with us a while.

I fell asleep on the bed while Eddie and the children went out for doughnuts and milk. A stream of orange sunlight coming through the bedroom window woke me. The intense heat and light of the ray reminded me I was in Los Angeles instead of Connecticut or back in Dublin.

Our apartment looked out onto a lush landscape of orange and yellow foliage. I opened the window and the fragrance from the rows of orange and lemon trees outside entered. The perfectly shaped citrus fruit on the branches resembled Christmas decorations gleaming in the sun. I inhaled the fragrance from the citrus trees, whiff after whiff of the aroma of paradise. The babe in my belly fluttered like a butterfly upon each breath I took into my lungs. I got up and went outside.

The family across the way from us had a little girl. The mother and daughter were outside in the flower-fragrant air hanging out their laundry. The little girl appeared to be around two years old, the same age as my son Stephen. The child looked like a miniature copy of her mother. The pair had on matching sleeveless sundresses in bright canary yellow with sandals to match. The mother wore her black hair in a bouffant style. When she turned in my direction to say 'Hi', I noticed how she had enhanced the shape of her dark brown almond eyes with liner. Her lips were tinted a coral pink, and when she smiled she showed perfect pearl white teeth. She gestured for me to come over for a chat. This was the first time that I ever got to meet a person of Asian ancestry.

'I'm Sue and this is my daughter Valerie. Our name is Wong.' Valerie covered her face in the hem of her mother's dress. 'She's shy,' her mother said.

'I have two small boys,' I told her. The little girl picked and pecked over the clothing in the wicker laundry basket before deciding what to take out and hand to her mom. She gave her a tiny red sock then found the mate. Then the child picked out a small silk shift, delicate as an orchid, and gave it to me to peg on the clothesline. 'I do all the wash in Ivory Snow detergent,' Sue told me, adding that her husband, a physician at Harbor City hospital, recommended it above the harsher detergents on the market. I took note of her advice. Sue stopped a minute and asked me where I came from originally, as she'd detected that I had a foreign sounding accent. 'Originally I came from Dublin City, Ireland to marry my American husband. He came from the state of Maine.'

'Aaah! So you married a GI.'

'Yep.'

Her family lived in the Chinese part of Los Angeles. 'Big Chinese family,' she laughed. 'Lots of relatives.' She noticed that I was pregnant, and asked my due date. She patted her tummy saying she too expected a new baby, and hopefully, it would be a boy. 'My husband's family want desperately for me to have a son, a grandson for them. They'd rather have grandsons.' The Chinese and the Irish have something in common, I thought. She and I became friends over the clothesline and little Valerie, beautiful as a summer butterfly, appeared to like me too. Having a little girl like her would be wonderful, but I had fear in my heart about having a girl. Before going our separate ways, I told Sue that my mother might come to Los Angeles to visit and help out with the new baby.

I heard Eddie honk in the carport signaling he and the boys were back with my two jelly doughnuts. The baby moved inside my belly as if licking its lips at the thought of getting a taste of fresh jelly doughnuts. I wondered if it tasted my weekly liver injections — hopefully not. Robert and Stephen ran from the parked car and into my outstretched arms nearly causing me to fall on the grass. Eddie offered me the doughnuts with love in his eyes.

Having summer weather every day, the lovely flowering plants everywhere, and the bright clothes that everyone wore, even grown ups, made it seem we were all on holidays; we made trips to Redondo Beach, and took rides to Riverside. Nothing bad could happen in such a perfect world. Then, on a Thursday afternoon, a terrifying scene took place in our serene apartment complex.

I had just met Peggy from across the way and her two children. Peggy explained she and her husband Lars and the children had recently come to live in Los Angeles from Kentucky. Lars had found a job as a police officer. 'It's his dream come true,' Peggy said. Her eight-year-old daughter Darlene loved LA, but five-year-old Billy wanted to go back to Kentucky because he missed his grandpa and grandma. Lars came home occasionally for lunch and parked the police car, attracting young children in the apartment complex to view its bells and whistles. Mothers and their children were outside in the common area one Thursday when Peggy ran out of her apartment and shouted out to us, 'Git them kids inside right this minute! Billy got hold of his dad's service revolver and he's out in our patio aiming the gun at Darlene. He got the safety off! Git! Go inside! Lars is trying to get Billy to give him the gun.' I grabbed Robert and Stephen by the arms and dragged them indoors, my heart pounding with dread. The three of us sat under the table. I tried to explain to my frightened children what was happening. 'My God, my God,' I prayed, 'please don't let Billy shoot his sister, father, mother or anyone else.' The children around, including mine, played cops and robbers often, pretending to have imaginary guns, which they aimed at each other calling out, 'Bang! You're dead.' It had been a make-believe game — until now.

The roar of police cars entering the apartment complex further frightened us. Police officers, fingering their holsters, criss-crossed the complex. 'Everyone stay inside,' warned a bullhorn-enhanced voice. Because of my belly, the boys and I moved from under the table to sit on the sofa. To reassure my little boys everything would be all right, I turned on the radio and heard the happy voices of the Beach Boys singing 'Little Surfer Girl'. I held my children's suntanned hands in mine and we pretended we were somewhere out on the ocean on a surfboard bobbing up and down to the happy rhythm of 'Little Surfer Girl'.

After Billy was disarmed by his daddy, the facts came out about how he had got hold of his father's gun. Peggy told us what had happened.

'I knew Lars would be home for lunch so I went up to Taco Bell for their special of five tacos for one dollar. I bought five dollars' worth. Lars ate half a dozen of the tacos, and then felt bloated. He unbuckled his gun holster and laid it on the back of the chair while he ran into the bathroom. Billy took the gun from the holster, he knew how to shift back the safety catch, and then he ran out to the patio after Darlene. Maybe if Taco Bell had only had three tacos for a buck, Lars wouldn't have eaten enough to cause him to run for the bathroom, and this whole mess would not have happened. We're going to pack Billy home to his grandpa and grandma. Darlene will stay here with us.'

I wondered why police officers in America walked around with loaded guns. Back home in Ireland, police officers were only allowed to carry a wooden baton. Whacking someone on the noggin with a baton didn't usually kill. Shooting a bullet into it would blow their brains apart. The whole disturbing episode with Billy and the gun had been upsetting for everyone. I didn't want to dwell on it.

I turned to thoughts of my mother, hoping she'd be able to come over. It would be wonderful to have her around, she being normal and down to earth like no other person in the world. I'd take her to Taco Bell when she came over. She'd never seen or heard of such food. The restaurant continued their special of five tacos for a buck. I now savoured each bite into a crunchy taco since I'd had massive dental work done. I wondered if my mother would be able to bite into one of the spicy wonders. Like other Irish people with scant funds, Ma had four usable teeth in her head. Hibernia didn't concern itself with any health problems faced by its poor working-class people, let alone their dental health. Americans' teeth, real or false, could chomp the head off Godzilla in one bite.

The mailman brought me a letter from home. Ma had enclosed a lace-edged souvenir handkerchief ink-stamped with a green and red outline of the map of Ireland surrounded by shamrocks. I knew she could ill afford the small treasure, but she went ahead anyway. I shared my love token with Eddie. Next morning he suggested that I write a letter to my mother and ask her if she would be willing to come and help with the new baby, Robert and Stephen until I got back on my feet. I asked him how he could afford to bring her over, 'We'll manage. I'll be able to foot the bill for the baby, too,' he joked. 'We'll cut down on doughnuts,' he called out heading out the door for work. The idea of having my mother come to Los Angeles lit me up like a firecracker. My two little boys were so lively and lovely. 'Life's grand,' I assured the heavens with heartfelt thanks.

My mother was to arrive from Dublin on the 26th of July 1962, at Los Angeles International Airport after a journey of some 6,000 miles. When we arrived at the airport to meet her, no sign of her could be found, even though the plane had landed. We made inquiries at the airport desk. Eddie asked if it were possible that she never got on the plane in Europe. We were told that she'd been through the customs. But she was nowhere in sight. We searched the airport high and low looking for my mother but to no avail. The children asked, 'Where's Granny? Did she bring me some sweets?' I began to panic. I should never have asked her to make such a long journey when she had never set foot out of Dublin City, never mind travelling to the Big Yonder. Eddie took us back home and made a telephone call to Coady's shop in Irishtown to see if he could get Da on the phone. I felt contractions and thought I'd give birth right on the spot. I scooped my arms under my bulge, protecting it like a balloon. If my mother were lost, stolen, or strayed, it would be because of me. Before calling Irishtown I asked Eddie and the children to join me in a prayer to Saint Anthony, the saint of lost things. Eddie nodded bowing his head while I jabbered to Heaven. The children were exhausted from the whole ordeal, but continued to inquire if Granny would have goodies in her shopping bag.

Eddie made contact with Coady's in Irishtown and Mr Coady sent one of his kids to fetch Da over from George Reynolds. At last Da came on the phone, breathless from running the whole way. 'Hello Da,' I said.

'Oh hello love! Did you call to let me know your mammy is with you? That my little Mary arrived safely in America to be with her three little loves?'

'That's why I'm calling. Da, don't get upset. We went to the airport to meet Ma's plane coming in and we can't find her. Did she get on the plane for sure?'

'What's that you said, Angeline? The phone's crackling. You didn't say your mammy's lost? God bless us and save us tell me that's not what I heard! Don't say such a terrible thing!' Eddie took the phone from my hand and said, 'Hello, Mr Kearns this is Ed. Let me describe for you what has happened. Please don't faint. Please sit down and I will continue.'

Fourteen hours and a sleepless night later, we received a phone call from someone at the Los Angeles airport inquiring if we knew a Mrs Mary O'Connor Kearns. Apparently my poor mother, after she got off the plane and through customs, sat down behind a screen and dozed off. Hours later, an airport official woke her up, and asked her if she was waiting to be picked up by a relative. Ma had lost the paper with our address and could not recall where we lived. The agent took her home to his family to spend the night. He brought her back to the airport the next morning and that's when we got the phone call. 'Oh thank you Saint Anthony for finding my mother!' I prayed. We phoned Coady's shop again to let Da know that his beloved wife, his Mary, my mother, had been found alive and well. We piled into the car and headed to Los Angeles international airport to get my mother.

We found her in the terminal, sitting in public view, waiting for us. As soon as I spotted her, I grabbed the children's hands and ran down the concourse crying like a banshee with relief and joy, my belly on the verge of exploding. I enfolded my mother in my arms. She asked, 'What took you so long?' We hugged and hugged. After greeting her, Eddie explained how he'd phoned Da back in Irishtown. He directed her to a public phone booth and called Coady's shop one more time. When Da picked up the telephone Eddie put my mother on the line. I could hear my father cry out, 'Is that you, Mary, is that you, Mary? Oh, Thank God. I thought I might never see or hear from you again.'

'Why?' asked Ma.

While driving back to Lomita from the airport, Eddie began to twitch his nose. I noticed a bit of a sour smell. 'What's in that stuffed shopping bag, Ma?' I joked. 'Sweets for the little lads, and things that you loved to eat back home.' Then she began to sniff and made a face. 'I think the parcel of pork link sausages I put at the bottom of me shopping bag has gone a bit off, love. You mentioned in a letter how you longed for a few Dublin sausages, so I dug room for them in the shopping bag. Wonder if they're still good to fry up?'

Over a cup of tea in the living room, Eddie advised my mother not to ever go anywhere with a stranger again. His voice shook with emotion, comprehending what might have happened to his mother-in-law on her first few hours in Los Angeles. I nodded to my mother that Eddie had her best interest at heart and told her that talking to a stranger in America isn't like it is back in Ireland. 'He might have been Bluebeard or a cold-blooded killer, like James Cagney in *White Heat*.' My mother assured us that it was all right now, and not to worry. The airline worker and his family had been kind, and turning to me, she said, 'Bluebeard is English.'

My mother looked worn out and in need of care. Her dark hair had sprouted tufts of gray. Her eyes were still a vivid bluebell color. She had only a few teeth still in her head. Her dull, secondhand Dublin clothing made her an oddity amid the colourful, stylish women in Los Angeles. But their granny's smile and lovely eyes drew Robert and Stephen to her like waves to the shore. After seeing me kiss and hug her a thousand times, the boys did likewise. Stephen tried to figure out why he had so many teeth in his mouth while Granny had so few. Robert touched her curly hair, then his own. Eddie wanted to know if my mother would like him to call her Mary, Mrs K or Mom? Ma savoured the inquiry as she would a strong peppermint. 'What comes from the tip of the tongue is closest to the heart,' she answered. 'Call me Mary.' 'Mary, it is,' said Eddie unaware of any coolness in her reply. 'Sure a person has only one mother,' said mine to my husband.

I handed the oilcloth shopping bag filled to the gills to my mother.

She dug out Irish chocolate bars, candy, and colouring books and gave each grandson an equal share. She brought me tea, gravy powder, chocolate bars, and Irish toffees. She asked me what I wanted to do with the smelly sausages. Eddie jumped up and said he'd take care of that. He took the leaky package and went out the back door. I heard him remove the lid of the garbage can. When he returned, she handed him a box of Irish handkerchiefs. The half dozen starched handkerchiefs, when unfolded, made three sets of pillowcases. In my letters home I had mentioned Eddie's allergies; obviously Ma took it keenly.

Over breakfast the following morning, my mother filled me in on the neighbours back in Ringsend, but not before we each leaned over the table to bump foreheads over our teacups like in the days of yore. Maisie had got married, Anna had had a baby, the Currys across from our flat in George Reynolds had moved to England. Old Mr and Mrs this or that had dropped dead in the middle of the road, on the way for a pint at the pub, or on the way to Mass. Ma closed her eyes as the sun beamed in the windows. The warm sun coming in from outside made her stretch out her limbs in the chair like a contented feline. She liked the roomy apartment, especially the picture windows that let in so much daylight. She raved about the modern kitchen and the bathroom. She would not use the shower, but loved me fixing her a bubble bath. I'd hear her singing to herself as she soaked in lavender bubbles. In spite of saying 'It's lovely' to everything, she finally asked: 'Angeline, where's the holy pictures? Have ye given up being Irish?'

'Ah, let's not get into that. Let's go outside on the patio and tan our skins to look like film stars.' She gave me a smile and patted my bulging belly. Robert and Steve followed us out into the sunshine. I asked my mother what she thought of President John Kennedy and his wife Jackie. 'He's loved like a son by everyone back in Ireland. His photograph hangs beside a picture of the Sacred Heart on every wall in Ireland, and it's not 'cos he's a Catholic.'

'He's the youngest President ever, and the only Catholic.'

'His wife's got terrible tonsils. I need a hearing aid when she talks,' said my mother, adding, 'she needs to have her throat blessed by a priest on Saint Blaise's Day. Cure her tonsils.'

'I think she likes to sound like that, Ma, soft as a kitten.'

'Still, Mrs Kennedy needs to gargle with salt and water. Someone should fix her up a silk stocking filled with coarse salt and wrap it around her neck for a week. Great cure in that. Remember how Granny

Martin fixed one for you when ye had terrible sore throats in the winter?'

The rest of July, August and September passed by with my mother by my side offering advice on many things and making me laugh about a whole lot of stuff. 'Old wives' tales,' I thought dismissing what I once took as wisdom. Old wives' tales held little footing in America.

On October 18th, the date of my birthday, and two weeks before my delivery date, shocking news hit the airwaves. A US reconnaissance plane photographed an installation of Soviet missiles in Cuba, missiles aimed at the United States. The Cuban missile crisis grabbed world attention and lasted twelve days. On October 22, President Kennedy gave a televised address to the nation. He laid it out in a nutshell: if the Soviet President, Mr Khrushchev, did not remove the missiles from Cuba, holy hell would be unleashed. If a nuclear war broke out between the US and the Soviets it would likely result in the destruction of life on earth.

After the speech, Eddie reached for my hand. I'd never seen him so concerned. My mother said she could not believe anyone would start a nuclear war over anything. 'To even have such a dreadful thought flies in the face of God,' she exclaimed, rounding up Rob and Steve for their evening bath. We were upset and did not want the children to know anything was amiss. My baby may not be born, I realized, if a war breaks out. We would all die along with millions of other people. I could hear the children singing one of their favourite tunes for their granny as she rubbed and scrubbed them:

> *Oh I wish I were an Oscar Meyer Wiener*
> *That is what I'd really like to be*
> *Because if I were an Oscar Meyer Wiener*
> *Everyone would be in love with me.*

I tossed and turned in bed, unable to sleep. The President's talk instilled a fear I'd never known. I'd never thought about how a few powerful men had it within their grasp to destroy everything. My taut belly felt as tight as a new drum. How many other women were pregnant at this moment, wondering too if their unborn babies and children were safe from harm? God made me a mother, quiet and kind up until now. But now I felt like an outraged madwoman, locked up and shackled in a tower with no exit, helpless to defend my children from harm. Either Kennedy or Khrushchev would have to back down to save the world.

The deadly word game going on between leaders in the Soviet Union and the United States made me sick. Who could fathom anyone debating such life and death issues as if they had a right to even joke about such hideous fantasy? I vowed if peace got restored by some miracle, I'd never be indifferent to politics again. I'd keep more of a close eye on things and get involved. Didn't people realise that a nuclear war would be the same thing as burning the body of Christ?

Khrushchev took the courageous step to back off from nuclear war allowing the earth to spin on. 'The coast is clear — no war,' sighed my mother with relief listening to the news report on the radio. One of the announcers said, in effect, 'The President of the United States, and our great military, made Khrushchev cry uncle.' 'Little apples will grow again,' I cried out loud. Eddie kissed me, noting, 'This baby is about to pop its pouch!'

Eddie Jr arrived on November 1. My water burst in bed like a tidal wave, nearly sending my husband and me swimming to Redondo Beach instead of Torrance Memorial Hospital. 'Eleven pounds and two ounces,' said the grumpy doctor as he held up my new son. 'Let's stitch her up, nurse, then it's down to the cafeteria for coffee and bacon.'

I looked at my new son and he smiled at me. 'Glad y're here at last,' I purred into his ear.

'Another boy, Angie, that's fine! How are you doing, honey?'

'I'm going on the pill if I can ever sit down again.'

The morning fog lifted from Lomita and the sun spilled its rays. My mother, up since six, had the baby bathed and dressed in a long cotton gown that came down to his rosy, bare toes. Rob and Steve had on their short pants, short sleeve shirts, sneakers and socks. As usual Granny got her folding chair and set it up beside the glorious clusters of the bird of paradise plants. She bundled the baby up in a blanket and took him outside along with his two brothers. Other young children around came out to play in the California sun. I puttered around in the apartment for a while, thinking my own thoughts: Will my figure ever return? How can I keep from getting knocked up again? Should I go on the birth control pill and risk going to hell? Why do I have such a feeling of being unreal? Am I Irish, am I crazy, or happy as a lark?

I looked out of the picture window in the living room. My mother smiled while she held little Eddie on her knee. Robert stood on one side of the chair and Steve on the other guarding their granny and baby brother like sentinels. Ma seemed to be getting younger since she'd shed the dull Irish garments, styled to hide any hint of glamour among Irish women her age, or any other age for that matter.

Sue announced she had something to ask my mother. She wanted to know if she would be willing to take care of Valerie when she went into the hospital to have her baby. She would pay her for the babysitting. Her husband, Stu, the doctor, thought Ma would be the ideal person to babysit their little girl. Later my mother talked the arrangement over with me and decided she would help the family out by watching Valerie, and the opportunity to make a little money to take back home to Dublin would be grand too.

Ma decided to stay with us until after Christmas. She felt torn between me and her grandchildren and her own family back in Ireland. She fretted about the auld fella back in the George Reynolds flats, if given the chance he would drink himself to unconsciousness with a lit cigarette implanted between his fingers.

The auld fella wrote to Ma weekly, keeping her up on the news about the neighbours. He missed her 'terrible' and hoped to see her return soon, but knew that I wanted her to stay as long as possible. Da mentioned that he cooked for himself, sausages for breakfast, dinner and tea. He missed his bit of grub Ma made for him, especially a bit of boiled cabbage and a few spuds and the occasional parsnip she mashed with creamy country butter and black pepper. I knew my mother missed him and missed her old life back in Irishtown, so different from life in Los Angeles. She brought up the issue of getting the baby baptised before she left. 'I'll return home to y'r daddy soon as the babby gets baptised. Thanks be to God, y're back on y'r feet, Angeline. Stay that way. We'll have a small celebration with Eddie, Robert, Stephen and y'rself, before I go home to y'r daddy.'

'Ma, I wish you could stay forever. I'll get the baby baptised. Eddie and I want you to be his godmother as well as being his granny. How's that for double Dutch?'

Dr Wong rang our doorbell in the middle of the night to let my mother know that Sue's time had come to deliver. Ma followed him back to the apartment to take care of Valerie while he drove Sue to the hospital. Later that day, Stu telephoned to say that he now had a son. Ma took care of Valerie for a week, mostly at our place, and received fifty dollars for her service. My mother thought she'd fallen into a fortune, and envisioned great plans for the dollars when she got back home to Dublin. Somehow word got around the apartment complex that my mother was available to babysit. She got requests from nearly all the young married couples to babysit for pay. By the time she left for Ireland, she'd earned nearly a hundred dollars. At first she didn't want to take any pay for babysitting as she felt neighbours did it for each other without any heed for making money. I told her 'Ma, y're in America. If you want to make hay while the sun shines, do it.' She babysat in the evenings when young married couples wanted to go out. They treated her like a queen.

'What would y'r daddy say about me earning money on me own?'

'If you let him know, he'll expect half to piss up against the lamp-post.'

'I'll get some things out of the pawnshop that's been in for months. And help Bridie and Frank with their children. It will be nice to do up the flat with new wallpaper, something with a print of roses or sailing boats.'

'Buy something nice for yourself, Ma.'

'I want to get Eddie something nice as he is so good to you, and has been like a son to me.' Ma was delighted at her good fortune in being able to earn money of her own. It brought to mind how I had enjoyed working as a mail-girl at the Travelers Insurance company and getting a paycheck, my own stash of cabbage to use for extras or to share. Eddie gave me money to spend, but there's nothing like the freedom of earning your own.

My mother became very popular around the apartment complex and got invited in for coffee and cake more than I did.

Eddie reminded me that he preferred to own his own home, and said that after my mother returned to Ireland we should consider finding a new home of our own. Rob and Steve enjoyed playing with the other children and the baby slept through all the sounds of noisy play. I knew that if we moved into a new house in suburbia, life would be a lot duller. Besides, I knew that I wanted to grow in my mind, instead of spending my time on endless household chores. When things settled down, my plan was to find the local public library and obtain a library card. Hopefully, the library would be in walking distance for my two boys. I'd put the baby in the buggy and off we'd go. In the meanwhile, the children, Ma and I enjoyed the company of our neighbours and took in the splendour of beautiful days and the dreamy perfumed afternoons.

Ma asked me if I remembered Ann Kelly, the old maid who lived in O'Brien's Place when we did. Ann found out that Granny Doyle (known to O'Brien's Place inhabitants as the Gasbag), dearest companion to Granny Martin, had died in the old folk's home unbeknownst to the old neighbours. 'She choked while sucking on a round bull's eye sweet. Got sucked into her windpipe. Could've been worse. Doyle might have come down with galloping pneumonia or broken bowels. It's a known fact that if elderly people accidentally soiled the bed sheets in one of them Godforsaken holes, they get clattered left and right by some on the staff.'

I was sure Ma was right about that. 'Had she any family at all?' I asked. Ma shook her head and mused, 'Who stood by the lonely grave after that bull's eye? On her soul Sweet Jesus have mercy.'

My mother's complete faith in the love of God continued to surprise me. With all the hard knocks she'd taken in life how could she still believe in God so uncritically? She'd told me since childhood that poor people had only God to turn to.

'He turned more than a deaf ear to our family and others,' I reminded her.

'Anyway, in spite of everything you can always turn to Him and he won't turn away,' she said in earnest.

The thought of her going back to Ireland felt unbearable. I wailed, 'Ma, why don't you, Da, and the rest of our family move to America? You can move in bag and baggage with Eddie and me. We'll make room.'

'I've eaten the loaf and drank the water of Ireland for too long now, love, to switch habits. If Da and I ever left Ireland for anyplace else, we'd die in a week.'

I asked her what she liked best about her visit to the United States; she said the people she met in the apartment complex, all the smiling waitresses, the friendly people who worked in supermarkets, the mailman, and the children she got to know for a little while. She enjoyed the odd pancakes (pizzas), blueberry pie with whipped cream, hamburgers, smoked pork chops from the Narbonne Market, hash browns, and Phillip Morris cigarettes. She'd never eat spaghetti (reminded her of other things) or hotdogs (weren't sausages), and tea bags were a fright. Her favourite tourist memory: the blooming banks of scarlet red poinsettias at San Juan Capistrano Mission.

Even Eddie noticed that Ma no longer looked tired and weary. Her stay with us had done wonders for her as well as us. Her parting words of love and wisdom were: 'Nothing breaks the cord of love that holds a family together. God has you, Eddie and my three little loves in His keeping. I have you in my prayers.'

My mother made friends with more people in America than any Irish Ambassador coming to the White House on Saint Patrick's Day bearing a bowl of shamrock to present to the President.

In a short note scribbled on a postcard, Bob wrote: 'Da met Ma at the Dublin Airport with flying open arms. He wanted to know who made her so glamorous.'

My mother's visit caused me to think again about religion. I hated the overbearing knuckle rapping of the national schools in Ireland. Of course there were the odd nun and priest who practised what they preached, but they were as rare as a white blackbird. Not being part of a church in America left me feeling at odds. I believed in God, but getting back in, bag and baggage, with any Catholic parish would be a big step.

Robert and Stephen showered great attention on their baby brother. Most of my time was spent taking care of the children, cleaning, polishing and cooking, doing a bit of gardening, while trying to remain attractive, sexy, in the eyes of my husband. When I felt my energy ebb, my doctor gave me a prescription for pep pills. I'd enough pep left to enjoy reading books from the public library.

I checked out my first book, Harriet Beecher Stowe's *Uncle Tom's Cabin*, the story of African people used as slaves by Southern plantation owners. I read about how slaves were bought and sold for money by their white owners as if they were cattle at a country fair. The second book I borrowed was John Steinbeck's *The Grapes of Wrath*. It told of the hardscrabble lives of fruit-pickers trying to survive and make a living working in the orchards of California. Both books provided me with a different view of the United States than the Hollywood one I'd cherished from the movies I'd seen back in Dublin. They shook me to the roots. I began to realise rich and powerful people, when given the power, would trample over the poor.

I refused to move into one of the new homes in suburbia where outside life depended on owning and driving an automobile. I had no interest in getting a driver's licence because I had a tendency to daydream when not running around like a chicken with its head cut off. Besides, the thought of driving on the Harbor freeway jammed with thousands of automobiles, giant trucks, and loaded buses hurtling along switchbacks of cement at seventy miles per hour, caused massive confusion in my brain. Eddie gave up trying to get me behind the wheel of a car.

We finally did move into an older house in Lomita, California a short distance from a public school, a Catholic church, the wonderful Narbonne Market that sold everything from imported beer to fresh bales of hay; and the public library. Eddie continued to work long hours and took care of things outside of the house. He loved planting and pruning the yard. The boys enjoyed the loaded-down avocado tree in the backyard. I'd no idea what to do with such strange and lovely shaped fruit. Robert and Stephen used to pick up the windfall avocados and played hand grenades and pitch ball with them.

I'd finished folding the wash when I heard the news on the radio that President Kennedy had been shot in Dallas as he and Jackie rode in a motorcade. I turned on the television and listened, with heart in mouth, as Walter Cronkite described the events. I sat down on the sofa as if I'd been hit by a log, and like millions of other Americans waited to hear if the President would live or die. 'Spellbound' is how I'd describe the country during the week that followed the assassination, spellbound with grief and dismay. How could such a horrible thing happen? In despair, perhaps because my brain refused to grasp the bigger tragedy, I pondered how to remove the blood stains from the First Lady's pink outfit in order to make it new again: coarse salt? Tide detergent? Ivory Snow? Or some of the Twenty Mule Team Borax, hawked on TV?

Eddie tried to comfort me and expressed his deep regret over the President. Although I'd teased him to vote for Kennedy, I knew Nixon, with his deep-shadowed jaw, had got Eddie's vote. Everyone in the country seemed to be in tears except the late President's wife. The news announcers commented endlessly on her 'stoic control' as she went through her husband's death and burial. How could she have refrained from screaming her lungs out and pulling her rich brown hair out by the bunch at the loss of her love, her husband, the father of her children, the Commander in Chief, the handsome, stylish mischievous man any woman would give her eye teeth for? An Art O'Leary reincarnated in the Land of Immigrants.

I wrote the First Lady a letter of condolence. Nearly a year passed, then I got an unexpected reply of acknowledgement printed on an official note-card I continue to revere.

When President Lyndon Baines Johnson replaced President Kennedy it seemed as if Christmas had forever come to an end. The handsome prince was vanquished, and his beautiful princess was in exile; the magic, the romance, and the glamour were gone forever.

Soon the carnage of the Vietnam war would stagger my mind, and make me aware, for the first time, that America's government and its leaders were not as benevolent, upright, and moral as I had believed them to be. Opponents of the Vietnam war, mostly young university students like those at Berkeley, openly denounced the war, the deaths of American soldiers, and the slaughter of Vietnamese civilians.

I had lived for eighteen years in Ireland where the attitude had been 'hold your tongue' to those who voiced disagreement with de Valera's government or the powerful arm of the Roman Catholic Church. The young Americans opposing their government amazed me. And it wasn't just the Vietnam war that these Americans were opposing. The civil rights movement also caught my attention: the bravery shown by the civil rights marchers in the face of bricks and bullets, and the courage of the Reverend Dr Martin Luther King Jr. And what Irish immigrant didn't want to hide their head in shame at seeing brutish Bull Connor, with leashed attack dogs, threatening harm to the peaceful civil rights marchers?

When I discussed the political events I saw on television with Eddie, he told me not to worry. He worked hard; as did all the people I met at his workplace. American workers were worked to the bone. Hard work seemed natural to Americans. No leaning on the shovel for a breather. No wonder engineers like my husband fell asleep in the evening. Their brains were worn to the bone working to get a man on the moon.

Robert was now five years old, Stephen four, and little Eddie almost two. My boys were my whole life, it seemed. Because of their father's involvement in the space programme they played endless games of astronauts gearing up to go into space, and they always wanted me to go along. We were delighted when we found a discarded cylinder tank at a dumpsite. I badgered their dad to bring home the tank so the boys could use it as a space ship in the backyard. A few neighbours were miffed at seeing the large aluminum sausage in their neighbour-hood. Our children and others from the neighbourhood painted the 'Space Banana' with bright stars and stripes and imaginary wiggle creatures from outer space. The constant sunny weather in California meant that the children played outside most of the time. They looked like golden Californians devoid of any Irishness, in contrast to the photographs of my young nephews and nieces posing outside in cloudy, drizzling Dublin.

Eddie came home from work one afternoon and told me we were expected to attend a fundraising event for Ronald Reagan, the former Hollywood screen star who might run for governor of California. Eddie's boss at the aerospace company urged the scientists and engi-neers working there to get behind Reagan in his run for governor. I'd never met a real live film star and could hardly hold my water with excitement. I'd seen *Bedtime for Bonzo* starring Ronald Reagan from one Saturday to another while working as an ice-cream girl in Dub-lin picture houses. The Saturday matinee featuring *Bedtime for Bonzo* attracted hundreds of kids from the surrounding tenements. Ronald Reagan acted a bumbling professor who tried to rear a chimpanzee. The bare-arsed, snot-nosed kids in the audience jeered and flung spit wads at the screen, at the ushers, and at the ice-cream girls if Ronald Reagan lingered on the screen more than the chimp. My brother Noel raved about Reagan in *Hellcats of the Navy*. I wrote to tell him that Eddie and I planned on going to see the Hollywood star.

Crowds of men and women filled the civic hall where the fund-ing event for Reagan took place. At least a half dozen Old Glory flags decorated the stage. Dozens of police officers patrolled the civic cen-tre. I'd noticed a crowd of young people protesting the fundraising even as we went into the hall. Obviously the throng of young people outside did not see the campaigning candidate in the same light as the crowds inside the hall. A man on the stage began to chant 'Reagan for governor' and everyone joined in except me, causing a crescendo of noise fit to wake the dead. Then a high school band came on the stage and began to play American patriotic songs, bringing smiles and tears to the faces of the audience. After that, the crowd began to chant 'One for the Gipper. One for the Gipper.' I thought it might mean Reagan in Irish. After a while Nancy and Ronald Reagan came on stage looking as sweet and dainty as a pair of waltzing figures in a Swiss music box. I recall some remarks he made, like charging tuition to students going to the universities in California, and he kept repeating: 'Reduce the tax burden on homeowners and small businesses'.

Roars of approval went up from the audience when the actor finished his speech. Reagan's wife Nancy, outfitted from head to toe in bonfire red, kept her gaze on her husband like a laser holding on to his every word.

On the way home Eddie asked if I were going to vote for Reagan for governor of California over the Democrat Pat Brown. 'No.' I said. 'Reagan reminds me of de Valera in the way he gets misty eyed going on about the mystical and magical destiny of America, while turning a blind eye to citizens in need.'

'Honey, you would never rampage through the streets protesting some cause would you?'

I hummed 'Ah, let's stop at Long John Silver's for their Friday fish fry.'

'Politics can be a dirty game.'

'Y're telling me.'

Eddie grew concerned about me skipping church in favor of skipping outdoors to frolic with the children. Going to Mass made me exceedingly sad. When I did go, I cried into my prayer book and didn't understand why. Ed suggested that he take the boys with him to Sunday service at the Methodist church. The children said their prayers with me every night before they went to sleep. They were greatly aware of the love of God, His Blessed Mother and other heavenly beings. Robert and Stephen knew the prayer to their Guardian Angel backwards, and little Eddie babbled in with his rendition of 'O Angel of Dod.' Eddie wanted his sons to attend church: it would be wrong not to let him take our sons with him to his Protestant church just because I no longer wanted to attend the Catholic church. But I remained too Irish to allow my children to become Protestants. Echoes of Oliver Cromwell's atrocities against Catholics in Ireland still held sway and my relatives both living and dead would never get over me straying so far from the fold.

I made an appointment to meet with the parish priest of Saint Margaret Mary's Catholic Church in Lomita, to see if I could get Robert enrolled in their Catholic school. A big rotund man in late middle age, dressed in a long black cassock, opened the door of the

Christmas 1964: with Eddie Jr., Robert and Steven

parish house, and beckoned me to step inside. 'I'm Father Harley,' he said with a rural Irish brogue thick as custard. After the expected interrogation, a commitment to go to Confession and Holy Communion, attend Mass on Sundays and holy days of obligation, keep the fast, say the family Rosary, and pay the school fee on time, Robert was admitted into the school.

Robert looked lovely in his new school uniform. He had some qualms about leaving his friends in public school, but after his first week at Saint Mary Margaret's he had made new ones. The school had two lay teachers; Miss Buffalo (true as God) and Miss Camel (true as God). The young women were as immaculate looking as a pair of long-stemmed church lilies in a vase. I bumped into the parish priest occasionally while taking my son to school. He'd stop to chat with me, say something to Eddie Jr in the stroller and Stephen holding my hand. 'How is the little family this fine morning?' went the usual remark.

'Fine and well, thank you, Father,' went the expected response.

'Have you met the mother superior of the parish school, Sister Rita?' he asked.

'I've seen her rushing around.'

'The sisters teaching here are missionary sisters from Italy,' he said. I could hardly believe he or the sisters from Italy considered themselves missioners, living in such lovely and swanky surrounding without a starving mite or hordes of sightless unfortunates rattling begging bowls. If given the chance to go on a mission to Saint Mary Margaret's compound with its groves of lemon and orange trees, banks of brilliant coloured cacti, and dreamy religious garden shrines, half of Ireland would take up the call.

Demands were heaped on the parents with children enrolled in the school, especially the mothers. Mothers put on bake sales, white elephant sales, used uniform sales, holiday sales, dessert tasting sales, book sales, religious statue sales or anything else that could bring in a buck. Being part of the church gave me instant contact with women from everywhere: Margaret, originally from Scotland, Colette from Paris and Winnie from Bristol, England, who all married Americans and Irene from Germany who married a man from Holland and emigrated with him to the United States. Irene told me that her husband planned to get rich quick in the States and the family would return to Holland. He had a fulltime job, another job, rented out apartments, and in the middle of the night, at age forty-one, died of a massive heart attack.

The Mexican mothers did most of the work in the parish. The women worked their hearts out in order for their children to attend school in the parish. They made Wednesday the day to look forward to. They made and served sloppy joes with hush puppy potatoes for lunch and coconut flan for dessert. The proceeds went to the Catholic school and allowed the Mexican children to attend the school for a lower fee. At noontime on Wednesday, Father Hegarty stood first in line for lunch. The delicious homemade grub, all you could eat for two dollars, also attracted elderly people to come out of their homes and join in.

I got to know the mother superior, Sister Rita, by volunteering at the school. She appeared to be strict with the school children but never hit or slapped any of them or allowed corporal punishment in the school, as did mother superiors back in Ireland. Sister Claire, also from Italy, enjoyed having a chat. She took a great liking to my three children and offered me words of advice on motherhood. 'A good mother is God's gift; mothers are sails on the ocean; young mothers are like roses.' Sister Claire told me that she missed her mother back in Italy and did not expect to see her ever again. Sister Claire's not being able to see her mother again brought tears to my eyes and my crying made her rush inside the convent and return with four hot-cross buns.

'I recognise that voice,' said Father Harley to me in confession one day.

'I am originally from Dublin City.'

'What sins have you committed against God?

I reeled off the usual list until the end. 'I'm taking birth control pills.' Deadly silence except for my beating heart.

'Then you are committing a mortal sin. Your immortal soul is in danger.'

'The doctor told me not to have any more children because I could haemorrhage and die. That's why he put me on birth control pills. He didn't want to see me back in his office.'

'Did you tell this doctor you're a Catholic?'

'Yes, Father.'

'You are to stop taking birth control pills or you will lose your immortal soul. I can only give you absolution if you promise God in this confessional to destroy the doctor's prescription and stop using the birth control pills. Do I make myself clear, child?'

'Yes, Father.'

The word 'child' rang in my ears all the way back home. A twenty-four-year-old woman, wife, and mother of three children could not be regarded as a child. As much as I wished to remain a practising Catholic and belong to the Church and all it offered, I knew that having another baby would be very dangerous for me. If I died in childbirth, who would take care of my children? I knew Eddie would take excellent care of them, but no doubt his sister would put in her dime's worth on how to raise my kids and with whom they could associate.

The doctor was surprised when I called to tell him my monthly periods were more like monthly floods. 'Taking the birth control pills should have corrected that matter,' he said looking into my eyes like a preying hawk. 'You are taking your medication that I prescribed?' he asked authoritatively. I said nothing. 'Have you been on the pill like I recommended?' he asked more quietly.

'I'm a Catholic and the priest in the confessional told me to stop taking the pill.'

'He what? The priest did what?' he shouted. 'No priest has the right to interfere with what a physician prescribes for a patient. Give me the name of the priest. I am going to call him and tell him how serious this matter is.'

'Father Harley.'

'In the meanwhile young lady, you are to take this new prescription to the pharmacy and fill it. You are to take the birth control pills to control the bleeding during your monthly periods as well as for you not to get pregnant. You're twenty-four years old and already have three children. What does your husband say about this? Do you want to keep your husband or drive him away?'

Jesus, my God, I thought as I waited in the lobby for Eddie to come and get me. What a mouthful the doctor had said. Why would Eddie stray should I happen to get pregnant again? Why would the doctor say that? I felt I was damned if I did, and dead if I didn't. Why bother falling in love, getting married, becoming a mother and trying to put down roots in a new land with so many men pulling me in different directions? I reminded myself that I did not have to kowtow to any one religion in America, no matter how much favoured. I refilled my prescription for the birth control pills, thinking that thousands of other young Catholic mothers had made the same decision.

Next time I encountered our parish priest he wanted to know if I intended to keep the commandments of Holy Mother Church? Or succumb to American paganism? 'I'm not just a rib, Father. I'm back on the pill.' He turned away from me, switching his black robe closer to his body as if a hurricane loomed on the horizon.

A new missionary recruit arrived from Ireland to minister at Saint Mary Margaret's. He came into the school office where I was doing some voluntary work. If the colleen was a picture of the ideal Irish girl, then Father Gorman was the Hollywood version of the rustic Irishman with his head of blackberry curls, fierce blue eyes, healthy set of teeth, standing tall and trim. He looked like Rock Hudson in *Farewell to Arms.* I met him at the school during recess. He came over to talk to me, and we looked into each other's eyes for a long second. He asked if I'd like a cup of tea in the school cafeteria after the kids were back in their classrooms. Imagine, a priest getting a woman a cup of tea! He not only got me a cup of tea but cookies too. I asked him why he became a priest. 'Either that or a postman,' he joked. 'Few choices for a lad back in Wexford.'

I finished the tea saying I needed to get home to get dinner ready.

'Be seeing you,' he said.

He must be lonely, torn as he was from familiar moorings, I thought.

'Just a minute,' he said, 'do you smoke?'

'Yes, if I can get one.'

He handed me a cigarette, struck a match and I inhaled, watching the blue flame flickering between us.

That Sunday after Mass an older Irish-born couple invited our family to their house for cake and tea. Dave, the elderly man, told me that he had had to get out of Ireland on account of the troubles in the 1920s. He met his wife Mary in Los Angeles. They had a son, an only child, John Michael. John Michael was killed fighting for the United States in the Korean war. Mary told Eddie and me that Dave longed to return to Ireland so he could die in peace. He wanted to be buried in the land of his birth, beside his parents in the old country grave-yard. Mary didn't care where they put her bones. I looked at the hand-coloured photograph of their son on the piano, and Dave showed us some old brown-tinted photographs of himself holding a rifle cross-wise in his arms taken in some Irish field.

Mary handed me a glass of sherry. As I sipped the sherry, some-thing very strange happened. I looked down at my fingers twined around the step of the crystal goblet and my fingers were covered with hot, sticky, thick blood. Images of violent death flew before my eyes and I felt faint. I tried to wipe my fingers but the blood remained congealed there. From that day to this, I don't know how to explain the episode.

The tragedy of the war in Vietnam became personal with the death of a young parishioner. I attended the Mass at Saint Mary Margaret's. Father Hegarty and four altar boys from the school moved slowly down the nave of the church in front of a coffin draped with the American flag. A grieving young woman dressed in widow's black followed the coffin down the aisle to the altar. Other members in the funeral proces-sion led her into a pew. The parish priest told the gathering that the young man in the coffin had been killed serving his country on active duty in Vietnam. It seemed unreal that he had died so far from home. Everyone in the church cried at the terrible loss. They reported on the news that the war in Vietnam would soon end, but instead it got worse. I could not grasp why the government of the United States would wage war on people so far away. I did not know of anyone who'd ever met a Vietnamese person or heard of Vietnam until the war. I could not bear to watch all the fighting and killing on television. I redoubled my prayers for peace but it seemed peace would never come. The picture of the young Vietnamese girl running naked down the street in panic after a US plane napalmed her village broke enough hearts, I thought, to put an end to the war. In my mind I could never separate her tormented little girl's face from the image of the war.

Idaho Falls

In 1969, Eddie asked me if I'd like to move to Idaho Falls, Idaho to get away from the crime, racial strife and traffic of Los Angeles. The Watts Riots had frightened a lot of white people, and caused a number of people we knew to move away from Los Angeles. When the riot broke out, it made news in the Irish newspapers so that Da in Dublin called to make sure we were all right. The news accounts of the blazing riots and black people getting killed were terrible. Why had the government let things get so bad for black people that they had to destroy the place? The people who rioted, it seemed to me, had plenty of cause to be upset, as did the deprived back in Ireland, who lived on a par with the impoverished Negro families in Watts. The Dublin poor and those elsewhere around Ireland didn't bother to strike a match to protest their miserable lives. Instead, too many gave up, died or found an exit out of the place. At times I feared that more riots would break out. More and more knife-fights occurred in the junior high and high schools in Harbor City and Compton, areas nearby. Local politicians appeared on the news programmes constantly to assure everyone in Los Angeles that they were going to take care of the violence in the schools, and help people get out of poverty, but little changed. It seemed that most elected officials, whether in Los Angeles or Dublin City, took you up blind alleys or down rabbit holes.

Eddie had been offered a job at the Idaho national atomic site. The offer included a large increase in salary and a safer place to raise a family. But it seemed rash to ask me to move yet again away from my friends, and take the children out of Saint Margaret's school. I'd put down roots in the neighbourhood, and the thought of pulling up stakes again seemed awful. I knew Idaho was part of the United States, but nobody I knew ever mentioned having gone there or come from there. I knew nothing about a nuclear site. I'd thought my hardworking husband was content with his job, working along with thousands of others to put a man on the moon.

The children were still in primary school but it would not be long before they went to the public school in Los Angeles. Eddie saw the job offer in Idaho as a chance to raise the boys in a less crowded place, with plenty of open space, opportunities to fish for salmon, ski and hike. None of the rugged outdoor things appealed to me. I liked shopping centres, restaurants, lying in the sun, inhaling the perfume of flowering citrus trees, and doing whatever volunteer work came my way.

Robert, Stephen and Eddie Jr, on hearing all that Idaho offered, according to publicity sent to us from the Idaho National Laboratory in Idaho Falls, were anxious to move. Knowing my husband always did what he believed best for our family clinched it. Of course I would move.

Our friends gave us a going-away party. I said a sad farewell to the people at Saint Margaret's Catholic School, hugged grizzly Father Hegarty, embraced Father Gorman sorrowfully and bid good by to the children in the neighbourhood. We left California, the home of Hollywood, land of everyday sunshine, of sweet-smelling flowers and the great big blue ocean in order to reside in a sparsely populated wilderness.

We travelled to Idaho Falls by station wagon; loaded down with kids, toys, and odds and ends forgotten by the moving company. Eddie planned on driving to our destination in four days. We drove from Southern California through parched desert until we got to Reno, Nevada, that home of the 'five-minute marriage and the ten-minute divorce' according to a signpost along the way. We stopped to eat breakfast at Hog Haven café where the garish sign read 'All you can eat — breakfast 99 cents'. It felt like Hog Heaven living in the United States where food cost so little. For less than one dollar each, we'd bellied up to slabs of bacon, eggs any way you like them, honey, tyre-sized pancakes and as much coffee as the human bladder could hold. The immense Western desert recommenced at the edge of Reno and loomed ahead vast and wide as an ocean. The bare landscape was dotted here and there along the way with clusters of wooden shacks and aluminium trailers. Such poor housing appeared unreal set in the land of millionaires. These impoverished dwellings, in the middle of the twentieth century, in the middle of the American West, were a disgrace. I'd read that the era of the hardscrabble, grubstaking pioneers had long since given way to better, more liveable homesteads. The pot obviously had not sweetened for many people in the States.

'Penny for your thoughts, Angie? The boys are sleeping like babies in the back under their sleeping bags. They see going to Idaho as a great adventure,' said Eddie.

'Yep, hopefully it will be a good one,' I said, missing our home in California more and more with every mile of dun-coloured desert and smoky mountain ranges we covered. We passed pockets of cattle either bunched under a lone tree on the range or lined up along the barbed wire fences staring into Christmas. When the wind outside gusted, it gathered loose sagebrush and purled the prickly fibre into cannonballs that blasted the car windows and made the wheels rumble as if we were driving on cobblestones.

'Are we there yet? Are we there yet?' groaned the kids in the back of the car, getting more and antsy. 'Let's go home, I wanna go back home. I want to see my friends. I miss my friends,' they pleaded. 'We don't want to go to Idaho, anymore. We were just pretending.'

We stopped the car by the side of the road and let the boys out to run about and look for anthills, rocks, insect eggs, lizards, ladybugs and butterflies. I wondered if the boys would like the desert creatures as they did the creatures found along sections of the beach in LA: sea stars, anemones, crabs, limpets, sponges, and polished agates along with other treasures thrown up on the shore by the Pacific Ocean.

Lightning bolts booming in close made us scurry back to the car and continue on. We drove through the endless desert, canyons, and mountain passes. 'Are we there yet? I have to go pee,' went the refrain from the back seat. 'Quiet down in the back,' their father called out as if suffering from a pinched nerve. In a softer tone he said, 'We should be there tomorrow evening. Look ahead and see which one of you spots a motel sign first.'

'I will,' said Steve.

'I will,' Rob challenged.

'I will first,' chirped Eddie Jr. straining to see over the back of the car seat. Two hours later coloured lights flashed MOTEL VACANCY. 'Son of a gun,' said Eddie Sr. After the children were tucked in their beds, I looked at him and whispered into his ear, 'Are you too pooped for a game of paddywhack?' He bolted from the easy chair into the bed like a Border collie hearing a gun shot. 'Let's play.'

In all the hundreds of miles across the plains, desert, bluffs and mountains we saw not a sign of an Indian or a buffalo. The Indians had long since been moved to reservations, and the buffalo hunted to the brink of extinction. What a stiff price to pay for creating the Western frontier. We passed the Fort Hall Indian Reservation on the outskirts of Blackfoot, Idaho, then went on to the small town of Shelly, Idaho which declared itself the 'Home of the Russet Potato' and finally on to our destination.

'Welcome to Idaho Falls' read a sign on the freeway exit leading into the downtown area. 'Population 36,000' declared another highway sign. I gulped, seeing a city that appeared to be not much larger than the frontier town in the movie *Shane*. Lord Almighty, I thought to myself as our automobile inched through the town, where have we landed? Ed pulled up at the library to get a copy of a booklet that provided information on Idaho Falls.

> Idaho Falls is steeped in the tradition of its pioneer Mormon founders, who tilled the soil, built the schools and homes, and conquered the land in 'barn-raising' community cooperation. .... Mormon influence is reflected in the city's beautiful white marble Latter Day Saints Temple. Idaho Falls is headquarters for the US Atomic Energy Commission's testing program for the peaceful use of the atom at the National Reactor Testing Station, located 40 miles west on the mile-high plateau covering an enormous tract of 894 square miles known locally as the 'sagebrush campus.' America's nuclear navy was born here with the design of a prototype nuclear engine for submarines. The first ships' reactors for surface vessels were developed here. Electricity generated by a nuclear reactor lights Arco, Idaho, the first US city to use atomic energy.

After reading the leaflet, I felt like we had arrived in the strangest place on the planet. Robert, Stephen, and young Eddie complained about being hungry. I spotted a large sign in front of a shoebox-sized eatery. The advertising read: 'Bob's Arctic Circle Drive In. Come in and sample Acey's Appeteasin' menu.' We devoured plates of ranch-fried chicken washed down with cans of coke. I figured for a town out in the middle of half nothing, we'd discovered a decent place to eat. And Bob's Arctic Circle had three locations in Idaho Falls. We headed to the West Bank Motel & Restaurant, located a stone's throw from the man-made falls that gave the city its name. We unloaded the car and took our luggage into the motel, glad to be off the highway. The boys fussed over who got to sleep in which bed. They were tired after the long journey and missed their friends and familiar ground.

Eddie's employers picked-up the tab for our room plus meals at the

Westbank Motel & Restaurant until we moved into a home of our own. They also gave us a list of recommended real estate agencies. The following morning Ed would begin his job at the nuclear site forty miles from town. He needed to get the site bus that left Idaho Falls at seven in the morning. I'd be responsible for the three boys and finding a house while he worked out in the desert until six in the evening. Wives were discouraged from contacting their husbands at the site. There were no direct phone calls allowed. All phone messages had to go through company headquarters in Idaho Falls.

Ed took the three boys with him to explore the falls spanning the Snake River. The churning waters flying over the falls and into the dark abyss of the Snake River gave me qualms knowing our three daredevil boys would risk life and limb to catch a fish. After unpacking and stashing our stuff away in the motel, I joined Ed and the boys along the riverbank. The September evening breeze felt cool on my skin after so much California sunshine. Willows fringing both sides of the riverbank bore the look of hammered gold. Ed said he needed to get some things organised for work the following day. We headed towards the restaurant to feed our brood before bedding down for the night. Over smoked salmon, my husband reminded me that I would be on my own when he left in the morning for the day.

Ed told me only site workers were allowed anywhere near the gated facilities in the desert. Each gated facility had armed guards with cocked guns ready at the hip to use should anyone go beyond the 'no trespassing' signs. 'I'm not planning on taking the kids out there for a picnic,' I replied, annoyed at such secrecy out in the middle of nowhere.

Ed promised he'd take us all out to see the site from the main highway when time allowed. When he left for work the next morning, I waited for the boys to wake up, feeling a bit lonely, with Ed gone for the whole live long day. The guys grumbled about having to go eat breakfast in the coffee shop instead of having their cereal in front of the television as they used to. Worse yet, if they wanted to eat they had to dress and wash before heading out for breakfast.

The waitress in the coffee shop obviously had encountered disgruntled, displaced children before. She tempted the lads with blueberry pancakes, colouring books, and free candy. While serving our meal she wanted to know if I were a new 'site wife' in town and in need of the name of a reliable real estate agent? I nodded yes to both questions while sipping the hottest and strongest mug of coffee this side of the Atlantic. She reached into an apron pocket retrieving a business card, and gave it to me. 'Jim's a wonderful realtor. I'd recommend him to my own relatives.' I thanked her and said I'd give Jim a phone call after breakfast. I added on a generous tip knowing my husband's employer would pick up the tab. On the way out of the coffee shop the waitress, Rose, cautioned me not to move into a Mormon neighborhood if I were not of that religious persuasion. 'They will try to convert you and if they don't you will be left out in the cold.'

As a child growing up in Dublin City where fistfights broke out between Protestants and Catholics, my parents drummed into our noggins, 'Live-and-let-live.' It seemed odd that the friendly waitress would feel obliged to warn me about the Mormons.

Before calling the real estate agent, I thumbed through the booklet published by the Greater Idaho Falls Chamber of Commerce for another look.

> The people of Idaho Falls are stable, conservative, conscientious, God-fearing, hardworking citizens . . . The city's religious leaders provided a strong moral fiber, unique in this permissive era . . .

Be that as it may, as an Irish-American by choice, I firmly believed in the American value of the separation of church and state. If holier-than-thou types operated all the ropes in Idaho Falls, I'd be madder than a monkey with a thorn in its paw.

I phoned Jim and within two shakes he arrived at the motel in a big shiny new Buick. He showed me a list of available houses and invited the boys and me to climb aboard and go look at some neighbourhoods. He jangled a set of door keys in the air asking the question, 'Which key will be the key to your new home? Bet you buckaroos are anxious to have your own bedrooms?' I asked Jim why people were leaving Idaho Falls. He shrugged and said, 'Some site wives just pack the kids in the station wagon and head back east. Husbands come home from the site, call out "Hi, honey," not knowing she's up and left. Most of our engineers and scientists at the nuclear site are from Michigan, Massachusetts or Chicago, Illinois.'

'I see,' I said.

'The husbands love their work at the site. Imagine wives taking off like that,' he said. 'Where is this little family from?'

'All over the place,' I replied feeling like a rolling stone.

We stopped to look at two-storey homes, split-levels, and ranch-style houses. The wives and children in each house had up and gone back east. Getting concerned, Jim suggested he take us over to look at a new home that had just come on the market. The house was located in a lovely residential area next to Tautphaus Park which housed the city zoo. 'Fewer Mormons live in this neighborhood. I guess you're not of LDS religious persuasion. Am I right about that?' I let him know I wasn't concerned about the religious beliefs or non-beliefs of people. He found my face in the car mirror, and smiled. I figured he probably had a double of himself selling real estate in Belfast, Northern Ireland, where arrows of prejudice also were aimed at the hearts and minds of strangers.

The house, a low, rambling, ranch-style home was set on a large lot surrounded by a log pole fence. Jim assured me I'd love this one. He unlocked it and nearly pitched me inside. Once inside he spread out his arms, as if doing an impression of Saint Michael the Archangel, in order to emphasise the church-like spaciousness of the interior, empty of even a housefly.

'If you're like my wife, Angie, you want to see the kitchen first.' Two cookie trays sat on the kitchen countertop containing baked cookies that had never been touched.

'She and the kids left in a hurry,' Jim joked, annoyed at the sight of the cookies, burned at the edges and beginning to buckle like old earlobes. 'The husband, sweetheart of a guy, works as a physicist at Westinghouse reactor testing station at the site. Surprised the heck out of him when he returned home and realized his wife and kids up and went. He is anxious for a quick sell. Now's your chance.'

The boys ran in and out of the rooms and down to the basement, loving the space after being cooped up in the motel.

'How would you cowboys like to move into this house right now? And what about that park and zoo, guys?' asked Jim.

The three impetuous voices hollered back in unison, 'Let's move in right now, Mom.' I explained to the real estate agent that Ed needed to see the house before I could decide. I asked Jim how long it would take to move out the furniture and the trays of cookies. 'Right away. As I said, the scientist is anxious to unload.'

Two weeks later we moved into our new home. After unpacking and moving in furniture the new place began to seem like home. Then my sons screamed for me to come outside to the back garden and look at a giant rat padding its way across the lawn. Mother of Grace, I never clapped eyes on such a bruiser of a rat even when I picked cinders on the dumps in Irishtown. My heart leapt at the sight. I let out a scream that made the neighbour next door run from his yard into ours. I pointed to the giant rodent inching along over the lawn, stopping here and there to sniff, sniff, and take in all the odours of nature.

'Oh, that's a mature male muskrat,' offered the neighbor. 'I'll be right back.' He returned with a spade and before a word could come from any mouth, lifted the spade and chopped the animal in two.

'Welcome to Idaho,' he said holding up the long tail still attached to half a rodent carcass. I nodded at the neighbour and went back into the house, not saying a word. The children followed me. 'Mom needs to lie down on the couch for a minute,' I said.

My sons noticed my trembling and the drops of sweat beading on my forehead. 'We'll get you some water, Mom. Shall we try to phone Dad?'

'He's forty miles away in the Arco Desert. I'll be fine after a cup of tea.'

'Mom, what if that rat had of been a bear? The neighbour said black bears still roamed the hills just miles from here.'

Ed liked our new home although, because of his work, he had little time to enjoy it. I made inquiries about enrolling the boys in a Catholic school. Holy Rosary Catholic School was located in an older part of Idaho Falls. The square brick building, shaded over the years into various hues of red, looked naked when compared to Saint Margaret Mary's school in Lomita. Instead of a school building surrounded by a garden of citrus trees, bird of paradise flowers, and orange poppies, Holy Rosary surrounded itself with long, skinny, spear-tipped dark green fir trees inhabited by clusters of jet black crows cursing their heads off at passersby.

Robert, Stephen and young Eddie looked so crestfallen when they saw the place that their dad and I decided together to enroll Rob and Steve in one of the public elementary schools. They began to attend second and third grade at Longfellow School. Within a week both had made friends, and liked their new teachers. Eddie Jr needed to enroll in private kindergarten because the State of Idaho did not fund public kindergarten. Children of low-income parents had to wait until first grade before they could attend school. I wondered what kind of backward place we had come to, where the state government didn't fund kindergarten.

I sat down to write to Ma and Da back in Dublin to give them our new address and let them know we had settled in. Idaho seemed further away by the minute from Ireland and its ever-changing wild sky. Pangs of despair and loneliness crossed my heart when I thought of my friends and family back in Dublin. I'd toss our new house away for a penny, truth be told, for the sense of community and neighbour-hood that existed in George Reynolds flats back in Irishtown, or even just to return to the deepening roots we'd planted in Los Angeles. Eddie told me in case of an emergency to contact someone at the US Atomic Energy Commission headquarter in Idaho Falls, instead of trying to phone him at his work place. When he left for the far away atomic site and the children were at school, I felt completely isolated and alone. I couldn't get excited about decorating the new house. The radio became my companion.

I knew that being a good mother to my children and taking care of my husband should be my full-time job, but I felt like I wanted something more in my life. Most of the news on the radio centred on war, and the tactics of the Soviet Union. I stopped in my tracks one morning, hearing the reporter say, 'the Soviets attacked Santa Claus as a tool of American capitalist interest.' I had no idea what the state-ment meant. The endless posturing and quarrelling with a far away place seemed childish. I wondered if they did the same posturing and quarreling in Russia. Back in Ireland when politicians or their representatives were on the wireless, we could tell the difference be-tween shamrockery and reality.

Since the Cuban missile crisis, I had felt that the world was no longer a safe place: politicians, on both sides of the world, had the power to blow up the earth. I prayed to God that the flag of the United States would never be the flag of fire to ignite the horror. Eddie acted like he had a pinched nerve if I mentioned politics of any kind. One of my mother's sayings went, 'The cat has leave to question the king.' My in-laws were inclined to follow the slogan, 'Let sleeping dogs lie.' I had no one to talk to about my fears, so I tried to focus on my family.

A health expert on the radio talked about the importance of feeding children homemade brown bread instead of white store-bought bread. I thought about getting out the cookbook and figuring out how to make the more mother-loving loaves of bread, but I was too unhappy to do anything at all. Instead I fantasised about drinking a long draught of Guinness to make the time slide by. I wondered if there were any Irish atheists. I'll take driving lessons and use the station wagon parked in the garage. Feels like the sun's astray. Take me off; take me off.

The mailman broke the silence of the morning. A letter arrived from my mother. She thought it odd that Eddie had packed us up to move to Idaho.

Dear love,
I went to the wedding I had a lovely time. I wore the lovely
cardigan you sent me. I wore it and I bought red skirt and white
shoes. We are grand. Bridie, Frank and the kids are grand. How
is my three loves tell them that I love them and you love. How
is Big Eddie? It is very cold Bag of Cole is going up 2.shillings.
This is al love. God Bless you all Ma.

I noticed Da didn't include his usual note with her letter. Probably drifty from drinking; in a state like that he'd forget his own name.

Robert and Stephen brought a note home from school to invite me to join the PTA (Parents and Teachers Association). I seized on the offer to get involved with other people and help at the school. Eddie thought it a good idea. He never complained about working longer hours at his job than he had in Los Angeles. He never complained about anything. It amazed me the serene outlook he had; day after day, year after year. Didn't he ever want to kick the fucking bucket about?

I went to the PTA meeting at Longfellow School, met my children's teachers, and other mothers. The public schools were, in my estimation, the greatest thing about America. They offered an education to all children, rich or poor, with dignity and respect that I had never experienced in Ireland.

One afternoon I opened my front door to be greeted by two women. 'Hi, we came to welcome your family to God's country,' one giggled. 'We live in the neighbourhood,' explained the other.

'Please come in,' I said, glad to meet some neighbours. They sat down on the sofa in the living room and smiled like matching angels. I asked if they would like some coffee or some tea or maybe something a little stronger? After telling me their names, Harriet and Winifred, they said they were members of the Church of Jesus Christ of Latter-

Day Saints, known as Mormons. The soft-smiling, soft-faced, soft-haired, soft-dressed, soft-shoed women raised their hands in front of their faces and said, 'We don't drink coffee, tea or alcohol; we don't use tobacco, or drink coke.' Instead Harriet and Winifred drank glasses of orange juice and polished off a half gallon of Peppermint Patty ice cream. They invited me to attend one of their Relief Society lunches and get to meet some of the other 'sisters'. They admired my house and asked if I had a basement. They explained the importance of having my husband build shelves in the basement for food storage. Practising Mormons stored a year's supply of non-perishable food in their basements.

'Food for a whole year,' I said aloud. 'That's like buying half a shop out.'

'Food storage is about self sufficiency for your family in case of the unexpected. It's sisters who arrange the food storage for the family and keep it up to date.' The two women had eleven children between them. Next, they gave me a day-by-day account of how their church leader, Brigham Young, and his followers travelled, some in ox-drawn, canvas-bonneted wagons, others pushing handcarts, from Nauvoo, Illinois to Salt Lake City, Utah.

The story the women told me about their ancestors would make a great Hollywood film. The scrapes the travellers encountered on the way included encounters with Indian tribes trying to keep settlers off their lands, running into herds of roaming, nearsighted buffalo, dealing with prowling bears, hungry wolves, and even some white Americans who aimed to shoot Mormons because they didn't like them. Some of the Brethren died of fever along the trail; canvas-bonneted wagons sank in the mud, not to mention skeins of poisonous snakes licking their chops.

By the time the two finished, the children were home from school.

'Hi, Mom, what is there to eat?'

'We're all out of ice-cream. I'll make some fruit punch. How did school go to-day?' 'Stinks.'

I went to a Relief Society meeting with Harriet and Winifred in one of the Mormon stake houses. (A stake is like a diocese.) Over helpings of home-made food cooked right in the church kitchen by the women, Harriet and Winifred began to address me as 'sister' like I'd already joined the Mormon Church. Then they went on about how great their religious beliefs were compared to other non-believers. I thought they might be interested in the 'westward ho' story of how Saint Patrick brought Christianity to Ireland. From the blank look on their faces, Saint Patrick the Apostle might have been a flute player in McNamara's Band. The two asked if my children would like to attend 'Primary' once in a while to meet new children. Primary is like Sunday school. They explained that Mormons liked their children to play with other Mormons. Suddenly the creamed-chicken and carrot casserole they had served me for lunch tasted pasty. I respected people who made religion the pivot of their existence, but pushing the same existence onto others so forcefully ignited my rebellious spark. Having failed to convert me, the two gave me a stiff brush off.

Within a mile of where we lived there were fields and fields of potatoes. The farmers used all kinds of water pipes, sprinklers and other contraptions to irrigate the fields. The bumper crops of potatoes were harvested by Mexican field hands. Rumour had it that Idaho potatoes were 'hot' because of growing so close to the atomic nuclear facilities. I never saw such whoppers of spuds. Idaho spuds were giants compared to the Irish potatoes that grunted forth from black rainy mud. Every eating-place in Idaho Falls offered potato dishes by the bucketful. There were baked spuds, mashed spuds, scalloped spuds, potatoes au gratin, potato cakes, French fries, hash browns, country-style potatoes, and fried patties. If meat were needed to go along with the spuds, the forests, desert, and mountains around Idaho Falls had wild game: elk, deer, bear, moose, mountain lion, and wild birds galore, as well as beaver and muskrats. I thanked goodness the town had a couple of supermarkets where one could buy a bit of meat wrapped in cellophane without the trace of a wild anything.

Life continued to revolve around husband, kids, and a bit of volunteering when needed at the children's school. Now and then Ed talked about his work at the 'sagebrush campus', the world's largest collection of power, propulsion, research, and testing nuclear reactors, forty-eight in fact, with another two under construction. I asked him why all that was needed just to light up the town of Arco, Idaho, a town not much bigger than an ant heap. He just looked at me and smiled his darling smile. Another thing he'd told me that I could not figure out was that the United States nuclear navy was born at the atomic site. I'd see young sailors dressed in either their summer or winter uniforms waiting for the site bus. The sight of seamen in the desert seemed very odd. I wondered where they kept and floated the nuclear submarines when the only running water came from the falls in front of the Westbank Motel or Rain Bird sprinklers.

I had a letter from my brother Bob, home on leave from his work at sea.

> *Dear Angeline, Eddie and Boys,*
>
> *Well I got your letter ok and was glad to hear from you. Well the weather is lovely here at the moment. Rickie O'Brien is home at the moment his father died last weekend. He came from Los Angeles he had plenty of time his father died on Friday and was buried on Thursday. His father was a very quiet man. He said he likes it in the States. I just see on the news five Irish soldiers were killed. They were training with mortar bombs. One bomb got stuck in the launcher and exploded killing five and injuring two.*
>
> *Well the killings are still going on up North. They caught 3 guys 28-24-16 years of age for murder of the ten people 7 Catholics and 3 Protestants. They cut their victims throats. They were so called loyalists who did the killing. It is about time they caught them they were looking for them for ten years.*
>
> *They were going to build a nuclear power station here but had a meeting and reckoned they could get as much power on the West Coast where the wind blows all the time. What will they think of yet?*
>
> *Give Eddie my regards and give the kids a dig for me.*
> *Love Bob.*

Bob's letters kept me up on events back in Ireland. He knew how much I loved the place and the interest it had for me, but my feeling about the past remained shut up. I wondered if the kind of nuclear power station some wanted in Ireland had anything in common with the atomic site in Idaho. The wind blew constantly in Idaho Falls, and could also be used to make power, so why the scary nuclear domes in the desert? When Eddie took the family out to see the sites from the main highway, the domed buildings made it looked like a photograph of the Sahara except no camels wandered amid the perfumed sagebrush.

I got to know two site wives, Pat and Linda, who lived on the same street and had noticed me passing by. They stopped me and invited me in for coffee. Linda and Pat were married to men with doctorates in nuclear engineering who worked at the sagebrush campus in the desert. They both had two young children and originally came from back east before moving to Idaho Falls with their husbands three years earlier. Much to my surprise, instead of offering a cup of coffee, Linda had Pat bring her a bottle of scotch; she poured me a generous glass and then refilled her and Pat's glasses. 'Let's drink to living in Idaho Falls, the spud capital of the world,' said Pat. 'I'll drink to that,' chimed Linda holding aloft her full shot glass, adding, 'Here's to never seeing your husband and being stuck with the kids.' The loose lips of both took me by surprise—they didn't act like regular wives and moms but out-laws. Both had university degrees and met their husbands while in college, following them all the way to Idaho. Pat wondered why Anne hadn't showed up yet. Anne's husband also had a doctorate in nu-clear physicists. 'She's probably getting over last night's hangover,' giggled Linda. 'She and her husband were over for dinner and the four of us tied one on. Charlie barely made it to the site bus this morn-ing. He forgot to take his neck pillow.' I sipped on my scotch and felt its smooth texture causing my rigid brain to feel loose and girlie. They wanted my opinion about living in the wilderness after Los Angeles. 'I'll have another scotch,' I said, assuming such intelligent females understood my thirst. 'We guessed you were one of us, seeing you walk around the block so often, instead of acting like the prescribed site wife,' said Pat. 'Anne will think so too. You're welcome to bitch with us.' Anne did not make an appearance. Linda and Pat jokingly speculated that their friend might have dropped in at the Stardust Lounge for a drink and decided to stay for the afternoon. Linda men-tioned that Anne could not have children and it caused conflict with her husband, the nuclear scientist. And maybe that's why Anne acted as she did. Linda and Anne's husbands worked together on some experimental project. Sometimes they stayed at the site for as long as a week overnight if it was deemed important. Anne felt extremely iso-lated in Idaho Falls.

I thanked God for my three lovely boys and a husband who loved and cared for us. What the hell else can one want? Only an ungrateful person would think of what she might have become in different cir-cumstances. I read books from the library serious as sermons. I won-dered if they had comic books at the library?

Linda called me to come over for a chat. She had just got home from her part time job at Sacred Heart Hospital where she kept count of cancer deaths for the cancer society. I asked her if she got sad about keeping such records. 'I need to work outside of the house. I'd work at anything.' She told me that the hospital did not want her to enter the names of anyone who worked at the atomic site who now had cancer, or had died of cancer, into the state's cancer register. 'That's the set-up,' she said. I wondered why anyone as smart and informed as Linda went along with such a stunt and asked her outright. 'They would let me go and hire someone else.' She played Simon and Garfunkel albums as we sipped scotch and coffee. She did comment on how worried she got about rearing her children in Idaho Falls because of all the nuclear reactors only forty miles away, especially knowing of the radiation releases that came out of the chimney stacks from the chemical plant. I still did not know anything about radiation and re-processed plutonium, thinking still it had to do with keeping the tiny town of Arco, Idaho supplied with electric light. She laughed into her coffee when I said that. 'They make material that's used in atomic bombs out there, don't you realize that yet?'

'You mean — like the bombs dropped on Japan? My God, you don't mean that?'

'Precisely.'

'What about the "peaceful atom" I read about it in a booklet issued by the Chamber of Commerce?'

'It's all mixed up with the United States government and the Communist government in the Soviet Union. '

On another visit to Linda's home she wanted to know if I had heard of Holly Near, the folk singer. 'I've got Simon and Garfunkel's albums, ' I replied. She put a Holly Near album on the stereo and we listened. Near sang a song about the US military dropping two atomic bombs on Japan. She sang how the eyes of the children melted in their head after looking up at the heated blast caused by the bomb. I'd seen black and white photographs of the bombing of Hiroshima and Nagasaki in magazines and soon forgot the horror, but Holly Near's singing of the event and what happened to the children's eyes left a lasting impression. 'You won't hear Holly Near's songs played over the radio in Idaho Falls,' said Linda. 'Know why?' 'Yes.'

The afternoon sun spilled its warmth over my body while walking home from Linda's large split-level home. All the high-paying jobs at the nuclear site made it possible to afford such homes. Thus, few site employees or their families wished to be told disturbing tales about what took place in the shimmering desert where American Indians once roamed. I remember a religious person saying to me 'He lights the light of the sun,' referring to a heavenly creator. Scientists were playing God in the sagebrush campus out on the desert. Ed insisted the work that went on at the site had to do with finding more uses for the peaceful atom. The thought entered my mind: do elected leaders in the United States government really strive for peace or not? Sometimes, I had a mother's urge to take my family back to Ireland.

My sons were the only kids in our neighbourhood whose mom did not know how to drive an automobile. Some of their friends asked if I were 'retarded' or had been arrested for some crime or other. What other reasons could there be for a mother not driving? I began to appreciate more and more the importance attached to having a mother with wheels at her command instead of legs. For now, the boys' dad continued to do all the driving around town. He dropped us off for Mass on Sunday mornings at Holy Rosary church before he headed over to the Methodist church for his hour of prayer. The boys attended Sunday school classes while I went to Mass.

One of the priests who officiated at Mass might have stepped out of a book on Dracula, so serious and emaciated he seemed, almost lost in a cloud of clerical garments. He hurled thunderbolts from the pulpit like a baseball pitcher week after week. He constantly threatened damnation unless there was repentance for grievous sins, sins such as 'onuses' or something sounding like that. Ah, I said to myself when he first started in on the odd-sounding word, he's referring to Ireland. Can he be referring to something about Oisín of Irish legend who ran off to Tír na n-Óg with Niamh? Or was it Fionnuala?

'Wasting a man's seed for the wrong purpose is a mortal sin,' he kept screaming from the pulpit, Sunday after Sunday. 'A man's seed is precious in the eyes of the Lord and a woman who causes her husband to willfully destroy his seed, for convenience sake, is guilty of mortal sin.' He's not talking about Oisín of Tír na n-Óg, I concluded still mystified by the strange word, 'Onuses.' Ed collected the boys and myself after church and we headed home. On the way I asked him if he had ever heard of the word 'onus' or something to that effect.

'Angie, I think the word you are looking for is "onanism". I will let you look it up in the dictionary for yourself, honey.' Later on in the week, I fumbled through the dictionary to find the damning word that translated into *Coitus interruptus* or in my understanding of American parlance, 'Pull the plug.'

Since we had moved from Connecticut, I received occasional letters from Lo, and from my former supervisor, Rose Foley. They promised to make a visit out to Idaho, but events interrupted. Lo's husband, Bill, Eddie's close friend, died at the age of forty-two, from kidney disease, leaving Lo a widow with two growing children. Lo later wrote in a letter that she had gone out to work as a pharmacist, starting a new career outside of the home. Rose Foley wrote to me that she had finally retired from the insurance company and wanted to travel, with a new-found companion, to all the ports of Europe or until her legs gave out.

My sons loved going fishing in the streams, rivers and lakes of Eastern Idaho and up into Yellowstone Park, with their dad. They waited patiently for the opening of the fishing season on Memorial Day, in May. By then the frozen streams, rivers and lakes were becoming free of ice and snowmelt. The boys became adept at fly-fishing and reeled in lively, jewel-toned, silver-skinned fish. Ed, being originally from way up in the Maine woods, enjoyed the great outdoors as his children did. He felt more at home in Idaho than in Los Angeles. Idaho Falls and Presque Isle, Maine suited him fine. Both still felt alien to a person who grew up in Dublin City, amid the hustle and bustle of people coming and going, and ever ready to talk a person's ears off. Sometimes, amid all the open space of Idaho, I felt like a duck out of water: endless waves of sagebrush had to be trimmed back if memory were to keep an image of green shamrocks from the past.

As the years passed by, my ties to Ireland and home were being frayed although letters from my family in Irishtown continued to come. My sons earlier on had asked me questions about growing up in Ireland. I skirted their questioning by telling them about leprechauns and fairies, never wanting to dwell on pain or sorrow. They did not know much about my life in Ireland. I didn't want to pick at scars or make them worry about their mother. I tried with all my being to keep my sons safe, sound, and happy.

Out of the blue, asteroids hit. Two weeks before his ninth birthday Stephen felt sick and complained of a bad pain in his leg. I though he might have pulled a muscle. He acted and looked so sick and he had a high temperature. The doctor took one look at him and put him into the hospital. My darling fun-loving mischievous little Stephen became one of the sickest children I'd ever seen. He cried from the awful pain in his leg and my heart broke. The doctor who put him into Sacred Heart Hospital could not figure out my child's problem only that he had a very sick little boy on his hands. Eddie took time from work, as broken hearted as myself and did everything for his son. Robert and Eddie Jr were shocked that their brother was so sick. A bone specialist was called in, the only one in Idaho Falls, and he did not know what had caused my child so much pain and suffering. I went to the hospital every day and stayed late into the evening. Some of the women I had got to know in the neighbourhood, God bless them, took care of Rob and Eddie Jr, while we went back and forth to the hospital, still not knowing what had caused Stephen to be so ill. I prayed like I never prayed in my life. I called my mother and father in Dublin and asked my mother to have a special Mass said for her grandson. Stephen spent his birthday in the hospital, too ill to come home.

The specialist still had not diagnosed the problem and called in another specialist. While sitting with Stephen in the hospital room, another child was admitted. The nurse tucked the small Hispanic boy into bed, covering him tenderly with a blanket. She told me that his family had brought him to the hospital not knowing what had caused his illness. The boy's parents did not speak any English. The father and mother, along with other family members, worked as migrant field workers planting and harvesting Idaho's famous russet potatoes in outlying areas around Idaho Falls and Shelly. Looking over at the small face on the pillow with the blanket tucked up to the chin, I sensed that the little boy was gravely ill. How could God be such a bugger to let children get so sick, I thought to myself, now looking at my own son flushed as a red rose from some unknown infection. Jesus, Mary and Joseph please don't leave us stranded in this way, I prayed, fear coiling my mind like a snake.

Later that afternoon an older man and woman came softly into the hospital room, looked at me, and then recognised the boy in the other bed as being the one they were looking for. Must be the grandparents, I though. Too old and worn-out looking to be the boy's parents. The woman touched the face of the sleeping child who woke and cried out, 'Mamma.' She bent over him, kissing his forehead. The father lifted his son up in the bed, careful not to undo the drip going into his arm from overhead. I detected the smell of sweet onions drifting across the room. The father turned in my direction as if on cue and uttered in broken English, 'Pick onions. My boy sick.'

'Mine too,' I replied looking at Stephen biting his lip in pain. My eyes swam with tears.

Later in the week when I came to be with Stephen the nurse told me that the doctor had not finished his rounds yet. I didn't know which child the doctor was lingering over. I heard the nurse who had come out from the boys' room say to another nurse coming on duty, 'Give the boy anything he wants. Anything he wants — doctor's orders. He has leukaemia.' My heart nearly stopped beating. Which boy in the room had leukaemia: Stephen or the Mexican boy? Oh, my God, I cried into my sleeve for both children. The regular nurse came into the room after the doctor had left, and said to me with tears in her eyes, 'That little Mexican boy is sick with leukaemia. He worked alongside his parents in the field until he could no longer do so.' I could only nod, the news being too bitter for words.

The new specialist explained that our son had a very serious infection of the leg bone and that it might be life threatening. He put him on some new 'miracle' pills that he hoped would work; we'd know in a week or ten days. Eddie told me to call him if Steve took a turn for the worse while he was working.

He told me later how he dreaded getting a call from me while out at the site because of the distance. Steve remained in the hospital until the medication took hold. The pain in his leg continued but it was not quite as bad because of the medication. He needed crutches to walk. He finally got out of the hospital and had to use crutches for months. He got better slowly, thanks be to God. When I thought that my child might die, I made up my mind to die with him. I knew Eddie would take great care of Robert and Eddie Jr — he loved them every bit as much as I did. I could not let my child be buried alone. Our prayers were answered and Stephen continued to get well.

A couple of years later, Eddie went into the same hospital for hernia surgery. Being around the hospital where my son had been so ill gave me a fright. Ed's surgery went well but he needed to stay in the hospital for four days. I visited him every day. An elderly man was put in the room alongside Ed. As Ed napped, I struck up a conversation with the old westerner who told me off the bat: 'I'm here for cancer surgery. Getting castrated in the morning to stop it spreading.' My jaw dropped. 'Surgeon tells me castration is the only treatment left. I'm over seventy years old. I'm not scairt of getting gelded.' How could a doctor cut an old man's coconuts off for any reason under the sun, I wondered. The old man told me he ranched in Mud Lake, Idaho, not far from Idaho Falls. 'Been on the ranch all my life. Used to be my folks' place. Hearing of more and more folks getting cancer in the Mud Lake area. Blame it on whatever is being released out of them smoke stacks out there on the desert. Atomic site. Blows in downwind towards Mud Lake.'

Ed woke up so I turned my attention to him. I poured him a glass of water and gave some to the rancher. I told him about his new room-mate. 'That old man is here to be castrated in the morning, doctor's cutting off his you-know-what.'

'What?'

'Getting gelded to stop the spread of cancer.'

Ed looked over at the rancher gazing into space. I had to contain myself from advising the tough old westerner to get the hell out of the hospital bed, put on his jeans, jacket and cowboy boots and high tail back to the ranch in Mud Lake while he still had flint in his musket.

The thought that radiation was released out of smoke stacks at the nuclear site alarmed me. Idaho Falls, populated with thousands of families, was only forty miles from the site in the desert. Were we getting irradiated and did not know it? Who would admit such a thing? I knew of very few people who would be willing to go beyond the 'hush-hush rumours' lipped about incidents that took place out at the site. An Irish immigrant like myself, a foreigner who pursued rumours about the site, would get ostracised by other site wives who were not willing to risk losing their cushy lifestyle.

Ed recovered rapidly from his surgery, but still required the OK from one of the physicians at the site before he could return to his job. The boys were glad to have their father fit to take them fishing.

I decided to take driving lessons and passed the driving test. The boys were delighted that I could take them to and from school on cold days which were a dime a dozen in this remote location. They saw me as being more like an American mom. I also decided to go outdoors during the winter instead of staying in the house waiting for the kids to come home from school. I took one of the boys' sleds and headed for the hills at Tautphaus Park. One thing I liked about America was that a grown-up person could do what would be considered silly back in Ireland. I bundled up and headed through the snow, pulling the red sled behind me. Mid mornings were best to go to the park because I had it all to myself. The cold air kept the hills icy and slick — perfect to sled down, sometimes going headfirst, other times full length on the back. After a couple of hours of sledding and tumbling into the snow, the cares of the world disappeared and the beauty of the surroundings flooded into my pores. While sledding, I could hear the bellowing of the animals in the zoo nearby. I had the urge to climb over the high-wired fence and let the deer, elk, and antelope head for the hills. One morning, while sliding down the hill, Connie and her two children showed up with their sled and joined me. Connie had spotted me going to the park alone with the sled and decided she'd rather sled than clean the bathroom bowl. She and her husband Jim were originally from Laramie, Wyoming. He worked in the chemical laboratory at the site. She had encouraged her husband to take the job at the site to get away from an interfering mother she could never please, but she missed her home town.

The weather in Idaho Falls only begins to warm up in May. The lilacs and other flowering trees wait until the middle of June to put out their buds. By June everyone hailed the coming of summer and the chance to go camping in the abundant woodlands where deer, antelope, elk, moose, and brown bears roamed. The wild things of my childhood and youth were rats, mice, cockroaches, alley cats, mangy dogs, and crippled pigeons. Bigger Idaho game were spellbinding.

We went camping in the Idaho forest one summer. While Eddie and the boys took off to explore the fishing areas, I sat beneath a grove of fir trees to read my then favourite author, Erica Jong. I knew Eddie would not like to think of me reading 'obscene' books. He got antsy when he glanced through one of my favourite books *Borstal Boy* by Brendan Behan. It is Brendan's account of being imprisoned in a British jail for his part in trying to plant a bomb in England. Behan, only sixteen years old at the time, viewed himself as a brave IRA man. I asked Ed if he would like to read this book about another Dubliner? He flipped through a few pages and stopped after he spotted the word 'fuck' in the text. 'Obscene. Why do you like it?' He'd faint if he knew how much I enjoyed Erica Jong's account of a 'zipless fuck'. Her vivid descriptions of sex were more interesting than books on traditional families or quaint accounts of the lives of saints, which I continued to get as gifts. Ed and my mother-in-law continued to give me books that related to family life, Maine history, and Christian ideals. In stories about family life in New England and Ireland, moms were always to be self-sacrificing and anointed chief bottle washers.

The guys returned with a string of pink-toned silver-mottled fish. I put the frying pan on top of the red coals, dropped in two large gobs of butter and let it melt until it foamed. I plucked off a sprig of sage and threw it into the pan before dropping in the washed and gutted fingerlings, heads still intact. Two seconds on both sides and the crispy golden carcasses were ready to eat with the fingers. 'Mom, keep frying the fish — we're starving!' Into the pan went three more and three more and so on until only the long string remained. The smell of fish, burnt butter and fresh sage hung over the tent-site for the night. Hopefully, the smell would not tickle the fancy of some bear, raccoon, or skunk on the prowl. Before going into the tent to sleep, I looked up at the night sky gleaming with stars galore; lady moon bore a full luminous face, My husband, a fine cut of a man, waited for me in the sleeping bag.

Connie and her two-year-old came for coffee on a lovely morning in August. She got up early, saw her husband off on the site bus, got her six-year-old to elementary school, and stayed at home to care for the two-year-old. She told me how much fun she had sledding the previous winter and how much better off she felt outdoors in the fresh air. She confided in me that she had a problem. It revolved around her six-year-old. 'He looks and acts too much like me. That's why I can't stand him, my own son,' she said. 'That's why I hurt him,' she said. I knew kids back in Ireland, including myself, who got belted by nuns teaching in the Catholic schools, and small boys having their ears reshaped by some Christian Brothers. Until now, I had never heard any mother or father say they deliberately hurt their child, in the way that Connie described. Connie's six-year-old played with my six-year-old son and I never saw any bruises on her child; as a matter of fact, the boy never had a hair astray on his head or a smudge on his clothing, and he could not have been any sweeter. I wondered what my mother would do if she were here listening to Connie instead of me. She'd hold her tongue, keep the yap shut, I thought, that's what Ma would do. So I let Connie continue. 'I see a doctor weekly about how I feel towards my son. He is trying to help me understand why I did it.' I nodded. 'I deliberately stomped on his feet and squashed them. He'd cry out "Mommy, please don't hurt me!"' I remained silent and shocked by her statements. 'I also pinched him black and blue where no one could see it and told him that I hate him. My two-year-old looks and acts like his dad and I just love him to pieces.' Then she talked about her mother and how she could never please her. She also told me that her white 'Tea Cup' pure-bred white poodle came as a gift from her mom in Laramie. Her mom hated dogs. Connie had it washed and blown dry once a week. 'It's the meanest little fucking yappy thing I ever met,' I told Eddie after visiting Connie.

'Language, Angie, remember,' he said which ended that conversation.

Connie came over for a chat whenever she felt upset and left her younger son with me when she needed to visit the doctor. Sometimes her husband went along with her. The doctor expected Connie would get over her mean feelings towards the look-a-like child. I thought, if Connie can't contain herself from hurting her small child, I hope the boy briskly becomes a wrestler or pole-vaulter and fends off his troubled mom.

Since getting my driver's licence, I drove the station wagon round Idaho Falls every day. Sometimes I felt silly driving around without a destination, but driving suited me better than being housebound. When Ed and the boys left in the mornings, the big empty house felt like a cavern. More and more I felt the loss of home in Ireland since coming to the desert and canyon lands of Idaho. I wished that the fairies would take us back to the land of bread and butter and a sup of tea. The thought of dying in such a remote place as Idaho Falls brought pangs into my heart that would not melt away. I never let my true feeling about anything show through to my family or anyone else. I often compared all the space I now had with the room I lived in with five other people for twelve years as a child. Sometimes I yearned to switch back to that time, in spite of everything.

Ed came home from work one day with exciting news for me. He told me that he had had a phone call from someone in the personnel office who noticed that I came originally from Dublin, Ireland. The person had told Ed that a new scientist had been hired at the site, and that his wife originally came from Dublin and thought that she and I would like to get to know each other. Surprised by his news, I asked him how the personnel office knew I had emigrated from Ireland. 'Remember, you had to be fingerprinted with me when I got the job at the site,' he reminded me. 'Here's her phone number, her name is Eileen, and she used to work for the Irish airline, Air Lingus, as a stewardess.'

I telephoned Eileen, excited to meet a fellow Dubliner. By the sound of her voice on the other end of the line, Eileen seemed a bit posh and not as friendly as I expected. She told me over the phone that she had attended a private school for girls in Dublin, Loreto College, a Catholic institution. She invited me over for tea that afternoon. I put on my best outfit to make a good impression. I hoped she'd like me and we would become friends. Eileen opened the front door in a dressing grown, and with a sweep of her hand invited me in. She explained that she had put her baby, Brandon, in the crib for a nap. She looked me up and down as if trying hard to determine what branch of Irish society had shaped me. She served tea from a silver tray as she gestured to me to pick up an Irish linen napkin. The tea (weak as piss) was poured into two delicate cups. Eileen sat down opposite me in a large floral armchair in the style of some Louis this or that. She wanted to know where I grew up in Dublin: the tenements, public housing in Irishtown. Left school at thirteen to work as a scavenger on the dump, worked as a factory girl and ice-cream girl in picture houses, and married a Yank I met on the streets. She put her cup down on the coffee table.

'I didn't show him the edge of me knickers, until after our wedding,' I joked, wanting to break the tension.

'I worked as a stewardess for Aer Lingus,' she said. 'In order to be hired as an Aer Lingus stewardess, you had to be able to speak fluent Irish.'

'Ah! One of those beautiful Irish Aer Lingus colleens,' I thought wistfully, observing her with stars in my eyes.

'My husband recently got his Ph.D. in Nuclear Science from MIT in Boston. He is currently doing research at the site in the desert. That is what brought our family to Idaho Falls.'

I asked her how she met her American husband.

'The Professor and I met when he took a flight on Aer Lingus from Boston to Shannon Airport. Eventually, we got engaged and later I came to the States where we got married.'

'What a small world. We both chased Yanks.'

'It's not quite the way you just put it,' snapped Eileen, looking as if I'd splashed her with icy water. We resumed sipping our tea.

'I miss my mother still. Don't you?'

'You must be over that by now. Look how well you've done for yourself. I heard you're married to an engineer at the site?'

'Yep, I am and I have three boys.'

'Brandon is our first.'

I asked Eileen if she had been out to see the ataomic site in the desert, noting that hundreds of workers were out there doing all kinds of work shifts. She did not reply but winced as if she needed to pass wind or hoped I would not. 'I've never been a baby person or wanted to be a homemaker so early. I miss all my friends in Aer Lingus and our getting together for lunches in Grafton Street.'

'I bet you do. It must have been wonderful being one of the famous Aer Lingus stewardesses. All the girls I knew wanted to be one.'

'My husband and I are now inquiring about hiring a nanny from Ireland to care for Brandon. We expect we will be entertaining a lot of visiting professors who come from Japan and Englandas visiting fellows at the Idaho National Engineering Laboratory.'

She'd lost me by now. I explained that my sons would be on the way home from school and I needed to get home, but if she needed any help or needed anyone to baby sit in an emergency, I'd be delighted to help her. She showed no interest as she led me out the door. She let me leave without seeing Brandon, the baby, asleep in his crib. Obviously Eileen did not have me in mind as a possible friend — too below her station in life. Weeks later I saw her alongside the Irish nanny pushing Brandon in a buggy in the park. She pretended she didn't see me and began to fiddle with covering the baby in the buggy. I hope he squirted a full measure of wee wee up onto her expertly made-up Aer Lingus face. The friendly attempt to bring Eileen and me together like a pair of exiled daughters from Mother Ireland failed. The more democratic Americans were unaware of the class structure back in the Old Country, rigid as any royalty.

Breakdown

That spring I stopped for a traffic light on the main street in downtown Idaho Falls when the driver behind ran into the back of our station wagon with the force of six horses. I only got a jerk to the back. The other driver got a bloody nose. Although shaky, I drove the station wagon back to the house. The other driver got cited for inattentive driving, the second such citation in a month, according to the helpful police officer. Eddie and the children were very upset about me being in an accident though I reassured them no harm was done. Five days after the event, my neck and lower back felt stiff. I went to see Dr B who prescribed bed rest and traction. While in bed at home with a neck brace on and the rest of the family at school and at the site, my days were long, lonesome and cheerless. My mind kept drifting into sadness and I started to vomit as if there were something in my mind that wanted to be spat out here and now. The doctor said he did not understand why I'd started to vomit but that if it persisted he'd put me into the hospital for needed fluids. I spend the Easter holidays in Sacred Heart Hospital in Idaho Falls. Eddie and the boys came up to see me every day. The children were afraid and anxious about me being away as I had never left them except to deliver the younger two. After a week in the hospital, I went home. The vomiting continued. Something in my mind wanted to purge itself through my throat and out into the slop bucket, but I'd no words to describe how it felt. I went back to see Dr B. He examined me and said my neck and lower back had improved, and the vomiting must be caused by something else. He asked me if everything was OK with my husband and children. I said 'of course', adding that something was bothering me but I didn't know what. And sometimes I felt I was falling apart. He said, 'I'd like you to see a friend of mine, a psychiatrist, and have a chat with him.'

Shocked by his suggestion, I replied indignantly, 'Psychiatrists are only for mad people, for people who have gone off their rocker.' 'That's not so, Angie,' he said, taking my hand. 'Just talk to him.' With that he picked up his office phone and made an appointment for me to see the psychiatrist.

The doctor told Eddie about the appointment. The more I thought about the doctor encouraging me to see a madhouse doctor the more I hesitated about going. How could I explain in my letters home that I needed to see such a person? Who ever heard of an Irish emigrant with everything going her way, needing a loony-bin doctor?

The thing that bothered me the most and convinced me something had gone awry related to the blueness of the sky. It seemed unreal. It made all the colours in the vicinity come alive. I wanted to say to someone, to my husband, to anyone, 'Why has the sky taken on such blueness? Why have my face and mouth become numb? Where did I see such colours before?' I kept quiet about it all.

Dr C invited me to sit down. 'Having some problems?' he asked. 'Dr B informed me that you were in an automobile accident. You OK now?'

I looked him over before replying, trying to figure out the difference between a madhouse doctor and a regular one. 'I'm doing better. My neck and back are not so stiff any more. I'm feeling out of kilter.'

'Out of kilter? Explain that.'

'I feel unreal, as if I don't exist in reality.'

'I see,' he said. 'Not a good way to feel. Dr B explained to me that you originally came from Ireland, and have been in the States for going on eleven years?'

'Yes, the lingering light of girlhood and the past is long gone.'

'You're my first Irish patient,' he smiled. Is that so, Mr Bighead? I thought to myself, not wanting to say another word to him or anyone else.

'I'm going to ask you a series of questions that I want you to answer. Can you tell me the difference between a mouse and an elephant?'

Jumping Jesus, I said to myself, what kind of a doctor is this who can't tell the difference between a mouse and an elephant?

'You don't know the difference between a mouse and an elephant, at your age?' I asked him.

'Just describe the difference between a mouse and an elephant for me.'

'Unless you need eyewear, the first thing you notice is that a mouse is tiny and an elephant is large. One has whiskers on its face, the other has ivory tusks. One squeaks, the other bellows like a bull. One is a rodent and the other is a mammal. Everyone knows the difference between a mouse and an elephant.'

He looked up from his notes.

'Do you ever see visions or images no one else can see?'

'Do you mean ghosts, banshees, fairies, leprechauns and restless spirits?'

He stayed mute.

'Every second person in Ireland sees ghosts and things.'

'Leprechauns, of course, are part of folklore,' he said.

'They eat oatmeal and butter,' I responded, begging to differ.

'Do you ever hear voices telling you to hurt or kill yourself?'

'Yes.'

'Tell me about that.'

'A stern voice tells me to jump out.' I started to feel faint.

'You have thought about hurting yourself?'

'It feels like I'm in a dream, like I could walk in front of a speeding truck and I would not feel it.'

'Do you know why you are sad?'

'I'd like to sleep.'

'You are twenty-seven years old, far too young to end your life. If you killed yourself what would your children think? Maybe they would blame themselves for what happened to you?'

This last remark jolted me like a bolt of electricity. I thought my husband and children might be better off having an American wife and mother instead of a second-class Irish immigrant. The doctor said he understood Irish people would not have the same temperament as did people who grew up in the States.

'Nationalities are different. I'm aware of that.'

'Come into the hospital for a rest,' he said. 'You need some professional care.'

'I'm not cracked. I don't need a psychiatrist. I'm Irish and we don't go mad.'

'Your husband will take care of the children for a while.'

'I don't want to be in a madhouse . . . OK, I'll come in for a few days but that's all.' He called in a nurse and told her I would be staying for a while. As a parting shot he said, 'I know I can help you, Angie. Let me help you. You are my first Irish patient.'

The nurse put an arm around my shoulder and led me to my room.

I began to cry, feeling like a failure. 'It's OK, cry, you don't have to hold feelings back in here, that's what it's about. Let the dam bust.'

'Let the dam bust' became an understatement. I cried out of control for hours. I could not help crying. It frightened me not to be able to stop crying. I went to sleep hearing my mother say, 'Draw up close, love.'

Bonnie, my nurse, noted next morning that I had slept a good fourteen hours. 'Where am I?'

'You are in the hospital for a rest.'

'I have to go now, my children will be looking for me. Where are my clothes?'

'You are here for a rest, and I'm afraid only the doctor can grant you permission to leave.' Bonnie helped me to get out of bed, shower, and put on my own clothes. 'Dr C insists his patients wear their own clothes,' she said as if delighted at such an arrangement. She took my arm and we went out of the room to look at the patients' recreation lounge. Ed would be up to visit me in the afternoon. The fourth floor, the patients' section of the hospital, looked like the foyer of a motel with sofas, armchairs, coffee tables, television, and a piano in one corner. Who would have thought such an inviting place represented an updated version of a madhouse?

Bonnie said 'Hi' to 'residents' who were women around my age. They sat sunk into the large leather sofas and armchairs as if lost at sea. Some had intravenous drips in their arms attached to stands. Bonnie sat me down, and she began to fiddle with some of the drips, making sure the fluids were flowing into the veins of the young women with bandaged wrists. Male orderlies sat nearby at a table like weather watchers alert for any storms. I got out of my chair to look out the window. 'We are four storeys up,' said the orderly who'd stepped to my side like a lightning flash. I spent the rest of the morning staring out the large window at the ground below where small men and women scampered about as if life mattered. I had an urge to open the window and step out.

The nurse informed me that I would be seeing Dr C for 'sessions' every day. I wanted to tell her that I didn't want to talk to someone who could not tell the difference between a mouse and an elephant. 'Dr C makes miracles happen,' she said.

'I want a new head,' I whispered to myself. I wondered how long I'd be a patient in a Mormon Hospital. If only I'd fall down a rabbit hole or vanish.

I asked Bonnie why the young women were walking around the ward linked to contraptions. 'They got depressed and tried to end their lives.' It stunned me that they would think of doing such a thing. Back in the tenements when I lived in O'Brien's Place and later when I lived in George Reynolds public housing, there were some young men who killed themselves either by hanging or by using a razor blade. Hadn't I almost gone with the tide myself on Sandymount Strand at the age of fifteen, due to unbearable conditions? Native wisdom told me not to discuss that painful episode with a psychiatrist who held all the cards, never mind the key to the outside world.

Eddie looked like he hadn't slept a wink all night when he came to see me. He told me that he had had no idea that I would be admitted into the hospital after seeing the doctor. He told me that he had called Dr C and wanted reasons why I went in as a patient. The doctor told him I had done so of my own accord because I needed some professional help. 'He said you are very depressed,' said Eddie holding both my hands in his, tears filling his eyes. 'I'd no idea you were unhappy or depressed.'

'I didn't know either,' I answered. He assured me that our boys were doing fine. He had hired a housekeeper to stay and take care of them. Of course, the boys were worried about me and couldn't imagine what had happened to their mother. He reassured them that I needed a little rest and would be all right and home in a short time. I told Eddie that I did not know when I signed in to the place that the ward would be locked. The nurse told me it had to do with keeping too many visitors from coming and going. Eddie reassured me of his love, the children's love and everyone's concern at his office for my getting back on my feet in a hurry. 'Did you have to tell your boss that I'm in a psychiatric patient and not in for a ruptured appendix or a broken leg?'

'Yes.'

'They'll think you're married to a nutcase,' I replied bursting into tears.

'You're not a nutcase, honey, of course not. You need a rest and you were smart enough to know that.' He reminded me that Eddie, Stephen and Robert would be up to visit me as soon as the doctor gave the word.

'Do I look like wreckage tossed on the shore?'

'No! You look fine, Angie. Try and rest and don't worry abut anything. We love you.'

Nurse Bonnie came to get me for my appointment with the doctor. The doctor led me into the office and invited me to sit on the chair next to his desk. He asked how I felt. Had I been in a joking mood I would have answered, 'With me hands.' He wanted to know if there were things I liked to talk about. I shook my head. 'No.' He swivelled his chair to sit facing me and I looked into his face for the first time. Blurry round outline of a face, I thought. 'Are you sure there is nothing you want to get off your chest or talk about? You can tell me anything. Nothing shocks me. I'm trained as a doctor to listen to everything you have to say.'

I couldn't say a word.

'You don't have to talk to me if you don't feel like it for now. It bothers me to see you so sad. Depression is worse than cancer. I became a doctor in the US Army, returned to Idaho Falls, got married, and set up practice.'

I just looked at him. It took too much effort to bat an eyelash.

'On my medical trips around the state I met a lot of people suffering from depression. So I decided to go back to medical school and become a psychiatrist to see if I could understand the disease and help more people than I could as a family physician.'

I listened to his story and thought, 'That's nice of him. He's a nice man.'

He called the nurse to come get me. 'See you on Wednesday, Angie,' he called out as the nurse and I went down the hallway.

'What does he want me to talk about?' I asked Bonnie.

'Maybe some things in your past need to be brought into the open.'

'I've nothing in my past that needs to be brought to the open.'

'We'll see,' she smiled. 'Like some coffee?'

'No, thanks. I just want to look out the window.'

I can't recall how many visits to Doctor C in his office it took before I felt like talking to him. He told me about how his brother had been killed in the Korean war and how he hated the thought of Memorial Day coming up because his mother got depressed and cried all day. I told him, 'I'm sorry he died in the war,' and held out my hand, which he took in his, and for the rest of the hour we just sat like that.

During the night an orderly and one of the nurses wheeled a stretcher into my room with a new patient whom they put into the vacant bed in my room. The patient was hooked up to a drip — obviously another stray in the land of opportunity.

The new patient, Barbara, woke up the following day in the late afternoon. The nurse and orderlies had been in and out of the room checking on her. Barbara raised her red-haired head on the pillow and looked at the drip in her arm, glanced around the room, and then looked in my direction.

'I'm supposed to be dead,' she sobbed. 'I swallowed a whole bottle of aspirin.' She began to bawl like an infant.

'I'm glad you didn't die,' I said, annoyed that someone as nice looking as her would do such a thing. She went back to sleep. I asked the nurse why she had put Barbara in my room. 'Dr C wanted her in with you. He thought you could learn something from each other. Barbara has three children under the age of twelve, as you have.'

Dr C asked if I felt like talking about my growing up in Ireland. He noted that I'd feel a lot better when things came out. He tried to get me to say something by asking, in a joking way, 'Is it true the Irish have a fiery temper?'

I heard myself replying to his question as if in a fog, 'It's more like "Yes, Father, no, Father" than fiery temper.'

'Are you talking about Church leaders? You were raised in the Catholic Church?'

'Most Irish people are Catholic left, right and centre,' I replied. 'The government let the nuns and priests get away with nearly murder.' I noticed he wrote down on a writing pad whatever I said.

'What are you writing down about me?' I asked.

'It's just part of the job,' he replied, shifting in the chair. 'Why don't you tell me about growing up in Ireland?'

'I don't want to remember and I don't want to talk about it either.'

'What do you want to talk about?'

'Nothing. I'm feeling numb. I think everything is a dream and nothing is real. I want to shake these feelings off.'

'Can I ask you about your childhood?'

'I don't want to talk about my childhood for Christ's sake. Better to forget it, if I could.'

'Many adults have been hurt by what happened to them in the past. They need to talk about what made them upset with a person who will understand.'

'Everybody gets hurt one way or another in life.'

'That's very true, but some people are hurt more painfully than others. Have you been hurt?'

'No! It's just the image of a gray girl lodged somewhere in my mind.'

'Tell me about her.'

'Nothing to tell.'

'Is the gray girl you or someone you know?'

'She's who she is. I don't want to remember.'

'Why?'

'I feel dead when she enters my mind so I have her smothered.'

'What if we can make the gray girl happy again?'

'I don't want to remember. Are you some kind of magician? I suppose you believe in white blackbirds.'

'I don't get your meaning.'

'It's an Irish thing, forget it'

'Why don't you tell me about growing up in Ireland? What comes to your mind right now?'

I looked at him and then began:

'Old Johnny Duggan lived in a room above ours in the tenement. On his way down the stairs to empty the slop bucket in the backyard, he'd stop as he passed me, "There she is, the girl who nails thing down in her head."'

'You grew up in poor circumstances in a tenement. I would not have guessed that.'

'That supposed to be a back-handed compliment?'

'No, it's not meant to be a back-handed compliment.'

I felt the fog clouding my mind shifting a bit.

'Time's up.'

'OK, Angie, see you later.'

'Not if I see you first,' I mused under my breath.

'Say something?' he asked.

'Just a cough.'

'Are you still having thoughts about wanting to jump from the window?'

'That's for me to know and for you to find out. None of your business.'

'It is my business what happens to you. You are under my care.'

'OK,' I said with remorse.

'We will talk later, OK.'

'Let's hope not,' I muttered on the way out the door.

'Excuse me,' he said. 'Did you say something?'

'Coughed again.'

He gave me a dry smile.

On the way back to my room with the nurse, I had to admit that the conversation I had with the doctor had brought a sense of relief. God, did you finally find someone I could talk to about my life and I don't have to worry about inflicting pain on them? This stranger, this total stranger who is willing to listen to me and won't be disturbed by anything I have to tell, or can talk about? Thank You!

Barbara sat on the side of the bed combing a red hairpiece with a brush. She brushed and brushed the matted mess of a wig as if all life depended on it. 'My husband's coming up to see me this evening,' she said. 'He's mad about what I did to myself. I wish it had worked.'

'Do you like your husband?' I asked, not knowing what else to say.

'I love my husband. He is a righteous man, husband and father. He is president of our ward.'

'Is that a big thing like being a parish priest in the Catholic Church?'

'Maybe.' She spoke in the voice of a sweet little girl. 'This is my second try at this,' she said, as she began to brush every knot out of her hairpiece lying across her lap like the pelt shorn from a poodle. 'Would you turn the other way while I get dressed, please. I wear special blessed church underwear that only practising Mormons in church standing can see on one another.' I tuned my face to the wall and heard her struggle to get into her Mormon underwear, panting as she did so — she was still hooked up to a drip. From the corner of my eye I saw her put on loose drawers and a chemise over her regular knickers and vest. The vestments added at least ten pounds of weight to her frame. When she stood up she wobbled for a bit. I held her drip steady as she fitted this piece of clothing and that piece of clothing to fashion a silhouette out of 'Home on the prairie'.

Barbara pinned her hairpiece on, blending it in with her natural hair. She began to put on makeup and ended up looking a ravishing beauty. I could not believe that someone as attractive as her, so particular about her looks, about pleasing her husband, and caring for her children could still wish to be dead. 'She needs to get back on her rocker,' I thought, looking at her.

Her husband, a third generation rancher and a Clint Eastwood lookalike, walked slowly into the hospital room to see her. He looked at his wife with misty eyes as he whirled a wooden toothpick between his front teeth like a drill. I turned to the wall waiting for Eddie's visit. I could hear Barbara and her husband trying to reach out to each other.

I wondered why I had let myself fall into such despair. Retreating into sleep seemed the solution for me, but Dr C insisted that I talk with him. Making an effort to sit and listen to him felt as difficult as shifting a mountain.

'You have been with us now for almost three weeks,' said Dr C. I didn't feel like replying. Dr C repeated what he had said. I wanted to close my eyes. What will my children think about me leaving them for three weeks, I thought. I cried into my arms trying to avoid the psychiatrist's eyes. 'I need to leave. I don't like the pills you give me.'

He replied, 'If you broke your arm I would put it in a sling so it could heal. The medication helps your depression.'

'What is the matter with me? I have everything I ever wanted.'

'You are clinically depressed,' he replied.

'Are you telling me I had a nervous breakdown or something like that?'

'Yes. There are issues we have to work through together. I can help you, Angie. Let me help you.'

I began to cry. Dr C went into some long parable about how my mind must have been overloaded for a long time, so when the automobile accident happened it spilled over like an overflowing bucket of water. I tried to take in what he meant.

'Only rich Americans get nervous breakdowns,' I said, 'not Irish people.'

'I'm aware that you have an Irish temperament and it differs from an American temperament. I want to help you. We will talk together. We will start with your childhood.'

Once again he reminded me I could talk to him about anything that bothered me, as he was a psychiatrist, a physician. 'Be easier to put me head in the oven,' I said. 'That's the first time you have smiled,' he said.

'He's a strange duck,' I thought on my way back to my ward. I pondered the idea of having had a full mind like a bucket of water that could not take in another drop. In a nutshell didn't he mean I'd lost me marbles?

I wondered what Ma and Da and my three brothers back in Irishtown would think of their daughter and sister succumbing to a nervous breakdown in America. Ma would blame herself for it happening. Blame it on me going to America. She'd want to fly to my side. How could I write a letter home about such a shameful thing? I'd lost my backbone and let everyone down. I'd lost the starch out of me shirt. Become a washout. I closed my eyes in despair. From out of nowhere I felt my mother's arms encircle me.

I told Eddie what Doctor C had said about me having a breakdown. He explained that he and the doctor had had a talk. He assured me that everything would be fine, that my sons loved me and were anxious for me to come home. He handed me a letter from my brother Bob in Ireland.

> *Dear Angeline, Eddie and the boys,*
> *Well it is a while since I got a letter from you. The last letter you*
> *sent went to Iran instead of Ireland someone got bad*
> *eyesight.Noel had too much to drink and fell off a motorcycle*
> *and had to go to the hospital. He got his x-rays taken at the*
> *Meath Hospital. There is a lot of trouble going on up in Belfast*
> *that could spill over into Dublin. Most of the trouble is caused*
> *by the UVF gang up there. Members of the I.R.A are being put*
> *in prison all over the place. Well the warm weather is on the*
> *way. The Terns are in they are a small seagull and they only*
> *come when the small Herrings arrive in the River they are in*
> *very early this year. If the small Herrings are in, the Mackerel*
> *follow them. I will be able to do a bit of fishing until called back*
> *on the boat.*
> *Love Bob.*
> *P.S. Give the boys a dig for me.*

Ed told me our cat, Frances, had had five kittens and the boys wanted to keep them. I told him it would be fine with me if the boys wanted to keep all the kittens if they promised to take good care of the mother cat and the babies. Eddie agreed. He asked me how I got along with Dr C. 'He asks a lot of question and I don't feel like talking mush. The questions about me growing up in Ireland jaded me brain. I heard some of the patients say that Dr C is a Mormon, a Jack Mormon, whatever that is.'

Eddie laughed.

'They feed us like lumberjacks here,' I noted to Ed, looking at my dinner tray that had just arrived. I offered him half of the large meal. Between bites Eddie told me that NASA expected to land a man on the moon by the end of the week. Neil Armstrong would be the first man to walk on the moon. Ed talked as if it were not a big earth-shattering event, but something expected from American scientists. After he left for home, I wondered what people around the world thought about putting a man on the moon, having a mortal walk across the face of such a sacred thing. I thought of all the names I'd heard over the years for describing the moon in the night sky: Lady Moon, Old Man in the Moon, Harvest Moon, Hunter's Moon, Lover's Moon, Silver Moon, and God's Moon. I'd read a poem about the Moon to my children written by the poet Amy Lowell called 'The Crescent Moon.' I had read it so many times to my kids that I could recite it in my mind:

> Slipping softly through the sky,
> Little horned, happy moon,
> Can you hear me up so high?
> Will you come down soon?
>
> On my nursery window-sill
> Will you stay your steady flight?
> And then float away with me
> Through the summer night?
>
> Brushing over tops of trees,
> Playing hide and seek with stars,
> Peeping up through shiny clouds
> At Jupiter or Mars.
>
> I shall fill my lap with roses
> Gathered in the Milky Way,
> All to carry home to mother.
> Oh! What will she say!
>
> Little rocking, smiling moon,
> Do you hear me shout—Ahoy!
> Just a little nearer, moon,
> To please a little boy.

I dreamed of a man landing on the moon with a feeling of apprehension. In my dream, he cut ridges into the face of the moon causing rivulets of blood to trickle down onto the earth like teardrops. I knew July 20, 1969, the day of the moon landing would be linked in my mind with being in a madhouse.

More and more I began to take an interest in what took place in my surroundings in the psychiatric ward.

Dr C, with the assistance of two orderlies, brought a young man into the room across the hall from mine. News got around that the new patient had been a Mormon missionary in some Central American country. He was put into the hospital because he had suffered a breakdown, so the scuttlebutt went. Later on in the week the Mormon appeared in the hallway dressed in black trousers and a white shirt, in his stocking feet. He made laps up and down the corridor while holding his shoes in his hands in front of him. The poor eejit, I thought on seeing him. Mad as a hatter, God bless the mark.

While sitting in my usual spot by the window in the lounge watching the antics of the pet turtles in the wooden box on the coffee table, I saw the missionary peeping into the lounge. I liked picking up one of the small turtles and feeling how lively it was in my hand, so full of life. The pet turtles were a form of therapy for patients. The small creatures felt like they had more life in their elfin bodies than I had. I liked to see them scamper on my hand and play with them on the table.

I had one of the turtles in the palm of my hand when the missionary patient walked into the lounge with a shoe in each hand. He looked at me then noticed the wooden box that acted as home for the pet turtles. Without a word, he put his shoes on the table and shoved turtles into their toes. Before I could say a word he went off to pace the hallway with the pets in the shoes. 'What a mutton head,' I muttered. I was still at my perch by the window when the Mormon kidnapper came back into the lounge with the shoes now dipped downwards to keep the turtles from getting out. Muttonhead gave me a sharp look and sat down, putting his brogues on his lap. Seeing him roused me out of my dreamy state. 'Are those baby turtles still in your shoes?' I asked him sharply. 'Put those innocent turtles back in their box this minute.' He didn't blink an eye. Instead he made a face at me — he stuck his tongue out like a gargoyle. I heard my voice shriek like a street fighter at the cheek of him making a face at me and still holding the pets as prisoners.

'Everything fine over there with you folks?' rang out the voice of the nurse on duty. 'He's stuffed two baby turtles in his shoes and won't put them back in their box even thought I asked him to,' I called out to her.

'Is that true, Jon?' she asked Mutton. He stayed mute. 'Let me have your shoes, Jon,' said the nurse like a mother. The bugger put the shoes behind his back. 'Jon,' repeated the nurse, 'let me explain to you . . . ' She took the shoes from him and released one crunched turtle that appeared half dead. The mite in the toe of the other shoe had given up the ghost, poor little thing. Jon got out of the chair and began his pacing in the corridor. Seeing him pace day after day made me have pity on him. I started to compare my lot with his, thinking, 'A man complained of having no shoes until he saw one who had no feet.' In my estimation, the missionary had lost all his marbles, I still had some.

Dr C sent one of the nurses to my room to get me to come to group therapy sessions he held in the lounge. Who wanted to be 'Queen for a Day' spilling her guts like the television show? I had refused to attend the group therapy but I knew the nurse wanted me to go in order to get Dr C off her back so I went for her sake.

Dr C sat on a chair in the middle of a circle of patients. He nodded for me to take a seat and join the circle of loony people. 'Glad you decided to join us,' he said. Holding pad and pen in hand, he began the session.

'Why would Barbara want to kill herself by taking an overdose of pills?' He expected us to come up with some insights. Jesus, how did I end up in such a group? I asked myself. Some people in the group offered some explanations. Next question: Nancy recently moved to Idaho Falls from New York to be with her husband who is part of the nuclear programme at the site. She overdosed on pills after her husband left for his job at the site, why? 'Why me arse,' I wanted to say but lacked the energy to raise my hand. And so it went for an hour. How could such attractive young women be so unhappy, I wondered. How could they be so blind? I began to attend the therapy sessions in what felt like a semi-conscious state, thanks to large dozes of Thorazine. 'If you are not from around here and you are not LDS you find yourself isolated,' explained someone at one session, 'that's why she cut her wrists.' Peggy began to cry because she too had cut her wrists. 'What a cold-hearted fucking bastard that doctor is,' I said to myself still finding it hard to offer any lip service. Listening to the women talk about wanting to die and trying to die made me wonder about myself. Why would I want to sleep the sleep of the dead, at twenty-seven years old? After one of the sessions, I remarked to a nurse on the floor, that Dr C had no heart. 'His intent is to find ways to give patients some insights into their own problems by listening to what other patients are going through.'

Until taking part in the group, I would never have known of the unhappiness some wives and mothers held inside. Jon the missionary started to sit in on the group therapy sessions with shoes still in hand. Dr C told the group about Jon and why he got depressed. Jon and some other Mormon missionaries went on a mission to some town in Mexico. After they tried to convert some people, the villagers attacked them with sticks and threw rocks at them. The police were called in to rescue Jon and the other missionaries. They were called back to their headquarters in Salt Lake City which ended Jon's mission for the church. Jon kept his head down while Dr C talked about him. Dr C told us that Jon blamed himself for everyone having failed the mission. Who could not feel pity for the poor bugger believing he could convert a whole village into the Church of the Latter Day Saints when he couldn't put his shoes on? I felt like saying 'It's a bloody good thing he and the other missionaries never went to Ireland to try and convert some people I knew in Irishtown or Ringsend. They would have been pelted with bricks and mortar, cabbages, turnips, and volleys of empty porter bottles.' No-one in the group spoke up about what might be ailing Jon, maybe because they shared his religion. As did another poor soul picked on by Dr C who had joined in the therapy sessions.

Edna sat in with the group, having spent over a week in her room rocking in a chair. I noticed her one morning, the aged full-figured farm-woman, as she was led out of her room for some medical tests. She continued to refuse to talk with anyone, including the psychiatrists. Edna's husband brought her to the hospital because of her ongoing fits of anger and refusal to talk to him. The couple farmed in Shelly, Idaho, famous for russet potatoes. According to the doctor, Edna's husband said his wife's problem began on Thanksgiving when all of their extended family on both sides showed up at the farmhouse for the annual Thanksgiving feast (or 'pig out' as Edna grunted aloud to the group). Her husband Wilder shot a pair of wild turkeys on land around the farm in Shelly and took them back to Edna to pluck, clean and stuff. When the clan seated themselves around the large dining-room table waiting for Edna to feed them, trouble began. Edna swayed back and forth as she struggled into the dining room bearing the platter with the roasted stuffed wild turkeys. She eyed all of the relatives sitting around the table with their mouths open waiting for her to serve them dinner. To their surprise, Edna flung the platter with the turkeys against the wall of the dining room and screamed, 'You all go to hell and be damned!' Edna ran from the farmhouse and out across the farmland belting low-flying magpies to the left and right with her ample elbows as Wilder hurried after her.

'Any comments?' Dr C asked the group after we heard about Edna's descent into depression. Barbara spoke up, rearranging the drip in her arm. 'Edna must try so hard to please everyone and it's still not enough.'

'Could you be a little like Edna?' asked the psychiatrist. Barbara looked surprised by the question.

I spoke up for the first time and said, 'I think Barbara tries to make everyone happy, always looking beautiful for her husband, and doing whatever she is expected to do for the Mormon church.'

'I see,' said Dr C, 'and Edna?'

'That husband of hers should have plucked and cleaned his own turkeys.' I should have kept my gob shut because the next person offered up for 'Show and Tell' became yours truly.

'Angie is originally from Ireland. She is married to an engineer at the site and has three elementary-age sons who love her. She had persistent thoughts about leaping from some high place to the ground below, ' said the doctor to the group.

I waited for someone in the group to make a comment.

'It's hard coming from another country,' said Barbara as a way of explanation.

'She misses her old life,' said another genius.

'If she jumps from a high building she will be killed and her husband and children will be left alone,' sniffed Nancy.

I tried to close my ears and eyes to the goings-on around me.

'Maybe she's a hippie and smokes pot,' shouted out the lone male voice in the group. The voice belong to the eejit Jon.

After the session, Dr C told me he would like to see me in his office later on in the afternoon to talk about things.

'Nothing to talk about.'

'We will see when you get there, OK?'

The word 'backwash' flowed into my mind and I envisioned how the incoming tide and the outgoing tide created all sorts of rubbish along the strand. Memories were the backwash in one's mind that ebbed and flowed and went nowhere.

Dr C kept his office dimly lit. He always sat in a swivel chair near the edge of his desk. 'What is the most important thing on your mind now?'

'I'm an Irish woman, the mother of three children and it's my job to care for the family come hell or high water. I'm a washout.' The doctor told me that he had observed how my children acted towards me when they came to see me. 'They love you very much. I'm in a position to know such things. Little Eddie, only four years old, and Robert and Stephen are still very young to be without a mother. You made the right choice to come into the hospital for care.'

He asked me to explain some Irish customs that were different from customs in the United States. I replied that I did not want to play quiz games, although such games were now the rage on television.

'I would like you to describe one custom for now.'

'An important custom is not to bring disgrace on the family such as a wife, sister, or mother having a nervous breakdown and ending up in a psychiatric ward.'

'I see,' he replied jotting my response down in his writing pad. 'Have you ever written to your parents about having difficulties while living in this country?'

'Of course not. Irish emigrants only write happy letters to the folks back home.'

'I see.'

I wondered if he did. 'Hour is up,' I reminded him looking at my watch.

'See you, Angie,' he said. I muttered back, 'Maybe yes maybe no, maybe certainly so.'

'Ever wanted to become a writer?' he asked.

'You ever wanted to dig ditches?' I replied, feeling drained as a ditch.

Back in my room, for some reason I felt a bit lighter in spirit. Maybe God led me to Idaho Falls so I might talk with Doctor C about things that might upset some people. As much as I resisted the idea of being a patient in a psychiatric ward, I began to feel some hope. Could talking with the doctor help the awful feeling of gloom? Doctor C told Ed that he felt I had issues that needed to be discussed with him about growing up in Ireland. What issues? I wondered, telling myself that growing up in Dublin in the 1940s and 50s had to be hell on earth not just for me but also for thousands of other poor people in the Republic of Ireland. Why go mad now in the arms of grand luxury compared with the past? I felt like a person who had survived a horrible war—the sense of being disconnected, the sense of being tattered and torn in spite of having so many blessings.

I tried to describe some of my Dublin childhood memories for the psychiatrist. Dr C listened attentively as he wrote some of my comments down on his writing pad. I told him some details about my parents and three brothers. I described how the six of us lived in one rented room in a dilapidated tenement building in O'Brien's Place. I told him that my father served as a soldier during this time, only getting a pittance from the government to feed and house his family. 'When he went soldiering, Ma begged and borrowed to keep us from dying young. We never had enough food to eat. Always hungry. Our room resembled a stable—no running water, electric light, no indoor plumbing, no heat unless we had money to buy turf or coal. Dampness ran down the four walls like raindrops. At night the rats ran wild. Rats lived in the walls and under the floorboards. Their squeaks as they scurried about made my head blaze. My mother held my hand throughout the night assuring me that God and his Holy Mother kept watch over us. The six of us slept in the one bed. My mother tried to lull us to sleep by telling us stories.'

I stopped. The doctor asked me to continue.

'As I'm telling you all of this it is all real again. It makes me feel sick and fearful.'

'Have some of this water,' he offered.

'I remember my father leaving us again to go on manoeuvres around the Irish countryside. I feel the cold of our room, I can smell the human bodies buried under a pile of rags, hear my infant brother whining for food as my mother tries to breast-feed him. She always looks like a desperate animal caught in a floodlight. If I had to go number one or number two, my mother would go with me to the stinking outhouses in the back of the tenement. The fear of falling down in the dark or stepping on rats caused me to cry. And the awful sounds of poor sick children and adults who coughed up blobs of green and yellow phlegm in the building. The desperate mothers and fathers and old-age pensioners trying to survive on half nothing. I wished often that God would lower a basket for us all to jump in and pull it up to heaven.'

'I see, 'said Dr C. 'How are you feeling?'

'Could I hold onto your hand? I feel like it's getting dark.'

He must have held my hand for a long time. We stayed in silence.

I vaguely recall the nurse leading me back to my room and tucking me into bed. I began to feel my mother's love enfolding me, her daughter, and I fell into sleep.

'Hi! You the gal from the Old Country?' asked the attractive young woman looking at Barbara who was sitting on the bed raking her red-curled hairpiece with a long bobby pin. 'Me? I'm from Ririe near the Snake River where we like to fish and hunt. Better shot with a gun than any one of my five brothers. Angie is in the next bed. She's the one from the Old Country.'

The young woman came over to my bed, cocked her head sideways like a bird, and said 'Dr C prescribed a massage for you. I'm going to massage your whole body. Hi! I'm Pearl and I'm a physical therapist.' She told me to put on a bathrobe over my pajamas and follow her to the nurse's station. 'Got to sign you out first before we can go,' she said. The idea of having to have someone sign me out to go down stairs to physical therapy annoyed me. I came into the damn hospital of my own accord and I should be able to leave of my own accord. 'Am I in the United States or the Soviet Union?' I asked myself.

'Stay close by me now,' ordered Pearl after signing me out. We got on the elevator to the bottom floor. On arriving at her work station Pearl told me to take off my pyjamas and put on a hospital gown. I followed her orders like a dumb beast expecting to be skinned alive. I undressed, put on the robe and lay on the table. Pearl slipped a warm sheet over my body, and began to hum as she fixed and fiddled with a bevy of bottled lotions. I whiffed the smell of roses and lavender. 'Love this lotion,' Pearl declared shaking the bottle like a boozy hussy craving a martini. She went to work on my body like a longhaul truck mechanic.

She massaged one foot then the other, one leg and the other, one arm and the other, before slavering my every finger and thumb. She turned my head back and forth as if trying to remove it, palmed my forehead with perfumed hands. Rubbed my ears red. Lengthened my neck by stretching it upwards and forward, and then went to work on the rest of my body with firm and powerful hands. I could feel her kneading all the grayness out of my body. She hummed all the while she worked. By the time she had finished, I felt renewed and fresh and ready to meet the day.

'I got my training in Utah,' she told me. 'I'm Mormon,' she laughed. 'We're all over the place here. My boyfriend, Chad, and me are planning to be married this fall in the LDS Temple, right here in Idaho Falls. It's so special.' Lucky she had not massaged my mouth or else I would not have been able to respond to her. The LDS Temple, tiered like a white frosted wedding cake, stood facing the banks of the Snake River. Only Mormons were allowed into the building.

Pearl busted out, to my surprise, 'Mom had me out of wedlock, took off somewhere. My aunt and uncle raised me like one of their own kids. Paid for my education. Now I'm getting married. My boyfriend completed his two-year mission last Christmas.'

I offered her congratulations on her up-coming marriage. She cocked her head sideways like a bird again, and said, 'Ever eat white angel food cake? That's the kind of wedding cake I'll have — with raspberry sauce.' She took my hands and jerked me up into a sitting position. 'All done. Git goin' now. Come to our wedding reception in September. Send you an invitation. Be too, too much fun.' My whole body tingled with vigour. I felt rosy, happy, and revived.

Back in my room, the ward nurse filled me in about a newly admitted patient. 'Kay,' she said, 'is an artist and will be with us for a while. Why don't you go have a visit with her.' Kay sat on the sofa in the lounge looking at some fashion magazine. I could tell right away she was a site wife not a Mormon mom. I went over and said 'Hi', and she invited me to sit down opposite her in one of the soft chairs.

'How long have you been here and why are you in here? Are you Mormon?' I shook my head, and she seemed relieved. I told her that my husband worked at the site. 'Physicist, nuclear engineer, researcher?'

'Research engineer,' I replied.

'My husband, Mr Big Shot, is a project manager out there. He talked me into coming here to "dry out" as he puts it. Tells me I drink too much in front of his associates. Well, I smoke too. Wonder if they will let me smoke cigarettes in here?' She went back to reading the magazine and I strolled over to the picture window to look downwards at the midget-sized humans zigzagging about on the sidewalk.

Dr C wanted to know how I got along with my father. I thought, oh here we go he wants to play Dr Freud. Practically everyone's heard of the crazy Dr Freud even back in Ireland where I grew up. When I though of Da, me auld fella, my head split into shades of darkness and light. I only wanted to feel love for him.

'Tell me, what kind of man is he?'

Images of being back in the room in O'Brien's Place began to flood into me. Da coming home on leave from the army wearing his bottle-green wool uniform, looking very young. How I felt shy around him after he had been gone for some time. He always brought home cans of food that he had saved for us to eat from his military rations. When he went away once, he left his overcoat with us to use as a blanket on our bed of straw. My mother hummed a lot when he came home, even when the cupboard remained bare. He seemed to love her, too, always wanting to steer her onto the bed and she saying, 'Ah, stop that with the children in front of you.' He had a great love for Ireland even though low-ranking soldiers like him lived in poverty.

'When I talk about him a terrible feeling of love streams back.'

'What do you mean when you say a terrible feeling of love streams back? Let's wait until the next session to talk about him, Angie.'

Eddie told me that he had written a long letter to my mother and father explaining that I had a bit of a problem and needed some rest, and that's why they hadn't received any mail from me.

He said, 'I guess I carried an over positive picture of life in Ireland for a lot of families living there.'

I nodded, adding, 'Everyone loves the Ireland of dreams. What I loved about it most were all the old people living among us, especially the grannies with their stories, sorrows and chimes.'

Kay, the artist, surprised me when she came to my room. She looked upset and asked if we could have a cup of coffee together in the lounge. We went to the lounge and the nurse gave us each a cup and a smile. It amazed me once more how kind and considerate the nurses and orderlies were to the patients.

Kay explained that she had been an inpatient now for over a week and her husband had not bothered to come and see her. 'He's probably on a super-duper project,' I suggested.

'Bull! He's keeping it a secret I'm here. He's probably paying the hospital bill out of our savings account instead of submitting the medical bill through our company insurance plan.'

I inquired if she had any relatives nearby. Her only son lived in Seattle, and her relatives all lived back east. 'A son should not have to know his mother is being treated for alcoholism. He's a lot like his dad,' she said. I told her that I didn't want any of my family knowing that I'd gone crazy either.

'Don't mention to anyone that I'm in a psychiatric ward,' I begged my husband.

'Reassure yourself, Angie; you are not the only one who suffers from depression. Most people will understand that.' But he still looked stunned about me being in such a setting.

There were often sad and odd acting people strolling along the mean streets of Dublin in the 1950s; they were not expected by the larger crowd to act like the rest. Over here, I thought, such grim-faced and oddly behaved people were more likely to be shunned because they negated the image of American bliss. Being a success-ful citizen in America required acting chipper twenty-four hours a day, seven days a week, year round. Being happy apparently meant that the country was exceptional, successful, and superior. Keeping up appearances had, for me, become a real endurance test over the years: Mrs Happy Wife, Mrs Happy Mom, Mrs Happy Neighbour, grateful, smiling emigrant, happy newscaster to the Old Country, and eager cheerful civic participant. Not being able to fill, or even want-ing to fill, each happy slot brought numbness to my mind, making it slow down—like a snail barely moving on the outer edge of a brick wall.

I received a letter from Bob.

Dear Angeline, Eddie, & boys,

Well it is a while since we had a letter from you. Everything is grand here me ma is fine she was at Bingo last night. She won two pounds so that was a good start.

It's five o-clock on a Friday evening and I'm watching the guys on the Moon on television. It is on all day. They are going for a walk now. You are probably watching it yourself.

We could not phone you with the Post Office strike on in England all the calls to America have been stopped for the last 3 weeks. As soon as the strike is over we will get a load of newspa-

*pers and send them over to Eddie. I hope the boys are keeping
quiet give them a good dig for me. Tell Eddie I was asking for
him.*

*The weather here is lovely and mild the evenings are getting
bright again. Well I better finish for now I will write again soon.*
Bob xxxx

Bob's devotion to keeping contact with me over the years proved a
wonderful bond between a brother and sister. We'd had an arm's length
relationship in our childhood because of the close space we shared in
the small cramped room we were raised in. Like other families living
in such close and crowed quarters, sisters and brothers rarely touched
each other physically or got too close emotionally. Because of the thousands of miles that separated us now, and the distance in time gone
past, Bob and I had a closer and warmer understanding between us
than before. His xxx's at the end of all his letters showed it.

'Let's see where we left off last time,' said the doctor as I sat restless on
a chair in his office. He started off by itemizing my areas of improvement: more lively, more contact with other patients, eating well, not
crying as much, more positive outlook on things. He issued me a pass
to go home for the weekend and spend time with my family. I'd been in
the hospital almost a month. The thought of going home for the weekend pleased me. I didn't like the idea that I needed a pass to get out,
because I'd volunteered to come in for treatment. But it would be great
to get out of the institution and away from so much human fragility. I
left for home with Eddie on Friday evening and had to be back in the
brig on Sunday evening.

The boys were waiting in the station wagon for me. We hugged
and kissed each other as their dad drove us home. Eddie had bunches
of fresh flowers all over the house. He'd gone to the store and got
everything we needed. It felt strange to be out of the hospital and home
again. I asked the boys what they wanted me to cook? 'Chocolate cup
cakes and spaghetti and meatballs. Dad doesn't cook us any. He makes
macaroni and cheese or frozen fish dinners.' After dinner and catching up on everything that had happened, the boys took their shower. I
gave little Eddie his bath and shampooed his head of blond hair until
it spun as lovely as silver light. Steve hugged me as if never wanting to
let me go. Robert, eldest of the three, grinned as I hugged and kissed
him like there were no tomorrow.

That night Eddie and I made love like old times and fell sleep in each other's arms. But I still found myself having to fight off depression in spite of the fact that my family meant everything to me. I began to believe depression had a life of its own and I wanted it to play out, and get out of my existence.

At my next session with Dr C, he inquired how the weekend had gone. I told him 'great'. He asked me if Eddie and I had made love. 'None of your business,' I replied, knowing he could read between the lines to find out what took place between the sheets. Dr C referred to the notes from my last session. 'Let's see, you were telling me about your father, how you felt shy when he came home on leave from the army.'

'My mother got a letter from some official in the Irish army to inform her that Da had been put into the army hospital in Phoenix Park, Dublin. My mother took me along with her to find out about Da. She went in to see him and came out and told me a doctor told her that Da had been hospitalized for mental exhaustion, and would remain in the hospital for a while. Ma repeated this, as if to herself. She'd never heard of anyone being put into a hospital for mental exhaustion. They let me in to see him one Sunday afternoon. He lay propped up in bed dressed in blue and white pajamas. He looked like he had the red measles. He seemed feverish, and acted nervous. I thought his jitters and nervous condition resulted from him not having any liquor to drink in the hospital. The army quietly discarded him after he left the hospital, and he came home to join us in the small room. Da, sick and now unemployed, caused havoc. The army washed their hands of Da even with all his years of honourable service to Ireland. The government issued him a monthly army pension of about five dollars for a family of six to live on, and he in a terrible and strange state of illness. Dr C I need to stop. I feel sick and my head is swirling in dark clouds.'

'OK.'

'Is it all right to hold your hand for a minute?'

'Yes. You are experiencing feelings of acute anxiety. Take a deep breath.'

At the next session Dr C said 'Let's continue from last time.'

'Do I have to? Let's just talk about the weather.' I told him that bringing up memories from the past made me feel upset, but I knew that for a long time my thoughts had needed weeding out. 'As a child I had to live half in the world and half out of the world in order to exist,' I told him. 'When the army discharged Da and he came home to live with us, he remained sick. Not a penny came through the door to help my mother pay for food, rent or clothing, so she had to beg and borrow from the neighbours to keep us from starving. Da felt the pain of not being able to provide for us. What good were four children who needed to be fed? What good is there in living or letting live children who are constantly hungry and little to feed them? I knew Da singed his soul with such thoughts.

'When my mother left to forage for bread, and my three brothers were gone on their foraging, I stayed alone with my Da. Sometimes he went into a rage with me and would beat me on the buttocks until he left welts. When I hesitated to stay alone with him, my mother knew something must be amiss. I showed her my buttocks outlined with his finger marks in purple. She told him that if he ever laid another hand on me she'd cut his heart in two. I had all this love for Da and complicated feelings about him. He muttered to me the last time I stayed alone with him that we would all be better off dead, and that maybe he should get a hatchet somewhere. Although I was about seven years old at the time, what he said filled me with fear. I'd heard stories of mayhem and murder from growing up in the tenements.

> *Lizzie Borden took an axe*
> *And gave her mother forty whacks*
> *When she saw what she had done*
> *She gave her father forty-one.*

I wondered if Lizzie's spirit had taken over Daddy. I hid my fear.'

The session ended with me getting nauseated and upchucking into Dr C's wastepaper basket as he kindly handed me tissues. Dr C remarked that the lack of social services for needy families in both Ireland and Idaho were a disgrace. The Saint Vincent de Paul, supposedly the charity wing of the Catholic Church, wouldn't give our family so much as a dry biscuit when asked, so help me God. Why didn't Ma marry Roy Rogers the singing cowboy instead of this husband, I thought more than once, and then felt guilty about me auld father, sick as a dog, sitting under a cover of rags in the family bed.

One day Dr C came into my room and told me that I'd be going home by the end of the week. I'd been in the hospital for almost two months.

I knew that in spite of being away from my husband and children I had done the right thing in admitting myself and finding medical help for my frightening depression. Dr C would see me on an outpatient basis. Eddie and the boys were delighted that we'd all be together as a family. I knew the woman going back into the household had changed.

I left the hospital with a sack of anti-depressant pills. Barbara and Kay also went home. We promised to keep in touch but didn't. I guess a reunion of former mental patients lacked glamour. Back to the powder puff and lipstick and trying to put on a happy face. As hard as I tried the feeling of grayness continued. I kept busy with the children, making their favourite food, cleaning the house, and being a good wife to my husband. I kept asking myself: isn't there more to life?

On August 29, 1969 there came a phone call to tell me that Da had died. 'He died peacefully in his sleep, love,' said my mother. 'He didn't suffer, thank God. Off like a baby. How are you doing, love? What is it Eddie's trying to tell us in his letters about you being upset? Y'r daddy always loved you no matter his condition.'

'I know, Ma. I loved him not with just half a heart but my whole heart.'

'Ah, he knew that, love. Didn't you send him all them detective murder stories he loved, smuggled in with the other stuff in the parcels over the years? The auld drink killed him. He couldn't stop, Angeline. Took him over, it did. I'll miss him terrible. Ah don't cry and upset y'rself. Don't bother to come home for the funeral. Don't leave the little boys. Come when you can all come for a holiday. I'll put a spray of flowers on his coffin in your name, Eddie's name and his American grandchildren: Robert, Stephen, and little Eddie. He loved you, always know that.'

Hanging up the phone, I turned to Eddie and burst out crying. 'That's one of the terrible parts of being an immigrant, being so far away when someone in the family dies. I've always dreaded the day I'd get a phone call, like now, telling me either Ma or Da had died.'

'Does she need any financial help?' asked Eddie. 'We can send her a cheque to help with the funeral expenses.'

I gathered my boys in my arms and told them their grandfather in Dublin City had died, that he had loved each of them and would continue to love them. On seeing me cry, they cried for a grandfather far away in a place called Ireland. I had the consolation of knowing that Da would not be buried in a pauper's pit with unknown companions as other members of my family had been. Thanks to coming to America and finding employment, I'd been able to send some money home earmarked for a family plot in Dean's Grange Cemetery on the outskirts of Dublin. The private plot allowed Da to be buried with all the honours due an Irish army soldier. The tricolour flag of Ireland would be draped on his coffin, rifle shots fired overhead in a salute, and the remains lowered into a sliver of native soil purchased with American dollars. Had the burial plot not been paid for in advance, Da, like other impoverished soldiers of the Irish state, would be ditched as a pauper without a single bugle blow.

I asked my mother to plant red geraniums on top of the grave after it settled; red geraniums were Da's favourite flowers. 'They'd flourish in a whiskey bottle.' Bob called to say he had a leave from the boat to take care of my mother and arrange the funeral. Ma held a wake for Da that lasted a day and a half. Neighbours in George Reynolds flats and old neighbours from O'Brien's Place were at the wake. My mother wrote, 'He had a grand sendoff.' Da had had little fear of death; he told me, 'It banished all sadness away.' My love for Da, mingled with joy, anger and sadness, didn't fade. Ma would miss him a lot; drunk or sober she cared deeply about him.

I continued to see Dr C once or twice a month depending on how he felt about my condition. My depression hung on like a bad flu. I took care of the children and their needs, but other than that, sleep wrapped me in its wings like an albatross endlessly drifting over the same ocean. The medication did little to lift the depression and often I felt the tiny pills were worthless pebbles against the boulder in my brain. The doctor suggested that a trip back to Ireland to see my family might shift things. Eddie, bless every bone in his body, got a leave of absence of three months from work. We sold the big house and put the furniture in storage. Robert, Steve and Eddie Jr were ready for an adventure. We would stay with my mother, as she insisted. Bob would be at sea most of the time. My younger brother Noely remained at home. Bob wrote that Noely drank like a fish. Still in his early twenties, he'd drink any kind of alcohol that would snuff his senses. Eddie and I thought we might be able to help him get off the sauce.

My mother and my brothers Bob and Frank met the five of us at Dublin airport surrounded by luggage. Frank told us he had parked his work lorry outside the airport and he would load the kids, all of us, plus the suitcases, in the lorry, and drive the lot to George Reynolds flats. We squeezed into the cab of the lorry and the luggage and Bob and the three boys sat in the back of the truck happy as the day.

Frank drove like a demon across a Dublin recently drenched from a shower, the sun above fidgeting in and out of the cumulus clouds. The red-painted doorways of houses and storefronts looked festive, as did the buckets of flowers, sacks of spuds, and all the green vegetables stacked for display alongside of the shops. My heart filled with delight at the sight of home. I knew Da would not be at the flat to greet me; he'd become part of Dublin in a different way now. Over bumps and cobblestones and keeping one eye on the road in front of him, Frank waved his hand out the window to show us all the new building going up in the city. He told us that his boss, a small Dublin building contractor, had got jobs tearing down the old places so that others could build the new places. 'The face of Dublin is changing, Angeline.'

'Are you getting rich from all the building jobs?' I asked

'Ah no, but I own me pick and shovel now. The boss, auld Ferguson, paid for them. Auld bastard. Ah, still, he's not the worst to work for. There's worse blackguards out there raking it in.' Eddie tried to catch the meaning of Frank's remarks, but appeared puzzled or else we were too scrunched up in the cab of the lorry for his ears to pick up words. Frank drove like he owned the road. He complained about slowcoach drivers on the road. 'Auld rich ones from the country and outside of the country are the ones gaining from all the building going on. Puttin` up the price of everything: Even the feckin' pint's gone up.

'Feckin' price of bread and coal gone up too, but wages hasn't,' joined in my mother.

'We're getting more like America, Eddie,' Frank yelled across to him. 'We'll be all Yanks.'

The back and forth of bantering remarks sounded wondrously familiar to me. Eddie looked a bit stunned at Frank's driving. He drove the old truck in and out of traffic like he was threading a needle, missing an oncoming double-decker bus by a hair's breadth. 'I've been driving since the age of fifteen,' he assured Eddie. 'Never had a crash. I know Dublin like the back of me hand, right, Ma?'

'Look out for them two young wans on the bike!' she screeched out, demanding that Frank keep his eyes peeled in front. 'Eddie's gone a bit pale,' she remarked.

There were more cars on the streets of the city than bikes. The switch from bikes to cars must mean some in the city were making money. There appeared to be a new vibrancy everywhere I looked. Frank went into low gear crossing Butt Bridge, increased speed heading for Ringsend and on to Irishtown, and then he made a turn and drove into the courtyard of George Reynolds flats. Bob and the three boys were red faced and smiling as they got out of the back of the lorry. 'Me son's a grand safe driver,' Ma said to Eddie. As soon as Frank parked the lorry, kids in the flats flocked over and asked. 'Mrs Kearns, Bobbler, who's moving in with ye?'

'Me daughter, her husband and my three grandsons,' Ma told the kids. 'The three of them will be out playing with the rest of ye when they get a bit of rest.' We hauled the suitcases up the three flights of stone stairs, greeting old and new neighbours on the way up. Bridie had the front door wide open and greeted us with open arms. Noel, my youngest brother, was nowhere in sight.

The smell of Irish stew streamed through the doorway as did coal dust and Brasso polish for door handles and letterboxes. The flat seemed smaller than I recalled. With us all inside, we were packed. Frank and Bridie introduced us to their five growing children, who acted as shy as their three cousins from America. Before you could say 'Bob's y'r uncle', Ma had us all sitting down for dinner. She put the large pot of stew on the table and ladled it out on an assortment of plates, some I recalled from years gone by, and others made of plastic. She passed around slices of fresh cut bread stacked with butter. Frank and Bob opened bottles of Guinness setting the bottles on top of the table. Bob offered a Guinness to Eddie who looked at his watch and said, 'Bit early for me to drink beer.'

'Too bad,' said Frank, 'y're going to need a good gargle living with this lot for a while.' Ma told him to shush. We talked about Da. I missed him bitterly and had he been with us drunk to the gills, it would have been better than any crock of gold. The Irish and American cousins toured the flat, ran out the door and down the stairs to play with the other children below. My two lovely nieces stayed close by. Angeline, aged nine, looked like her mother, and Sylvia, aged eight, looked more like her da. My mother said we all looked alike. Frank took off for work. He remarked that auld Ferguson would short shift his wages if he didn't get back to tearing and knocking down some building along the Grand Canal.

Bridie had her hands full rearing five children. She took it in her stride, saying, 'Having five or six children in Ireland is normal. After the next one though, Frank is going to sleep outside or wear a suit of armour.' Bob took off to do a bit of fishing. He promised to bring back a sack of flounders for tea. 'You remember how to fillet a flounder?' he asked me 'I remember. If you catch any I'll do the gutting.' We walked Bridie and the five kids to the bus stop. They lived at Basin Street Flats, off James's Street. Their two-room flat, owned by Dublin Corporation public housing association, had long since grown too small for the family. Bridie mentioned they might put in for a transfer in the hope of exchanging the flat for a house in Ballyfermot with more room for a growing family.

Eddie and I and the three boys slept in one of the bedrooms, the boys in one bed and Eddie and I in Da's age-old wooden crate of a bed. Ma had outfitted both beds with new bedding except for our mattress. It felt strange to sleep in Da's old bed, the bed he died in, but with Eddie beside me nothing seemed amiss. My first night home, I slept like a baby. Next morning, though, Eddie complained of being itchy, and pointed to his leg covered with tiny 'red hopper' bites. I explained that red hoppers were like American fleas. He said he'd never had a flea bite him in America and such things occurred in flophouses not in family homes. I asked Ma if we could do anything about the hoppers. She got DDT powder from the chemist's shop and sprinkled it like salt over the mattress; it killed the little buggers outright, as if she had dropped an atomic bomb.

Eddie and the boys took off that morning for Sandymount Strand with Bob. He wanted to show them the place he loved most in the world, the Shelly Banks out by Poolbeg lighthouse. While they were gone, my mother asked me how I felt and if the depression still bothered me. I showed her my paper bag filled with bottles of Thorazine and some other kind of anti-depressant drugs Dr C gave me for the trip home. 'I've put on forty pounds, Ma. The doctor blames it on the pills but he wants me to take them.' 'Don't worry about putting on a bit of weight, love, consider it more Irish love.'

Then she said, 'There's a lot of young mothers in this country suffering with nerves. Some have moved back home with their mothers in the flats. The only way, love, is to fight the depression best you can.'

'I try, Ma, it's not that easy. It's a terrible feeling that comes on out of nowhere.'

'Is there anything, any single one thing that is really bothering you?'

'No, Ma. Maybe it's an ungrateful bitch I am and that's the whole of it.'

'Ah, go on; don't talk like that. Nerves are apart from a person feeling grateful or ungrateful. You're here with me now and you'll be fine.'

'All I seem to want to do is stare into space and it makes me afraid. Eddie is so good to me and the boys.'

My mother went to the window to look out to see if Noel was anywhere in sight. He'd been gone two days. He took off occasionally, she said, to stay with his chums. He'd been disappointed in love. A couple of years ago, his girlfriend refused to marry him because of his drinking and it caused him to guzzle the bottle more than ever.

I asked my mother how she felt about Da being gone. Her lovely violet blue eyes misted. I knew that she'd had terrible times with Da along with her golden thoughts of their early life together. She received a widow's pension from the Irish government; without that little bit of help she would be broke. Bob paid the rent out of his pay and helped out as much as he could. Noely offered sweet nothing.

As if on cue the front door opened, and in walked Noely. He came over and gave me a hug, asked where Eddie and the boys were, and went into the bathroom to shave and clean up. He looked like he'd slept on the streets. I couldn't help but think of him as a small boy, lovely as an apple, and into every devilment he could muster. When he came back for a mug of tea, Noely asked if Eddie'd brought over a fistful of dollars. 'Probably nailed to his arse,' he said. Ma told me not to pay attention to what he said. 'Why have you come over for three whole months?' he inquired. 'Isn't the great big yonder all it's cracked up to be? You missed Da's funeral.'

'She didn't feel up to the mark,' said Ma, annoyed at the tone of his voice. Noel acted like he disliked everyone. 'Have you any of that mouthwash they use in America?' he asked me. 'Eddie brought some; it's in the bedroom. Why do you want mouthwash?' 'Got alcohol in it. I drink anything to get drunk, me skin and blister.'

'Drink y'r tea, Noely,' said Ma. 'Drink's an Irish scourge; young fellas like Noel would simmer in it if they could,' she said. Noel shrugged his shoulders, found a cigarette butt deep in his pocket, lit the butt, inhaled and said, 'Life's a fucking bastard. Where's Eddie with a few dollars for his Irish brother-in-law, Noely Kearns Esq.?'

Mother of God, I thought, what will Eddie think of Noel and the way he acts and intends to act? He might want us to find an apartment of our own so the boys would be apart from Noel. Noel intended to act the hooligan. At twenty-five, Noel acted like a reckless and rudderless man without any employment prospects except for scraps here and there.

Eddie told me that he had made a visit to the United States embassy to let the embassy know we, an American family, would be living in the city for at least three months. Staff at the embassy gave him a short list of private schools in which to enroll our children. They told him not to enroll the boys in the national schools, as they were inferior and were mainly for the working class who were content with religious instruction. The national schools, he was told, were allowed to use corporal punishment on the children. Robert and Stephen had made fast friends with the kids in George Reynolds, and wanted to go to the same school, the Star of the Sea National School in Sandymount. So we enrolled them at the Star of the Sea. The three boys were having the time of their lives. They loved the freedom children had in the flats. Unlike the States, where parents watched their kids like hawks, the kids around us had the freedom to play with anyone they wanted, to go places together, and make do with whatever they had. The three American kids became well known around the neighbourhood, and for a while became as wild and free as their friends.

Ma thought it would be a good idea for Robert and Stephen to make their Confirmation. I talked with one of the teachers and he told me the two could make their Confirmation while in school. The two boys were put into the Confirmation class to begin intense religious instruction. Robert and Stephen started to get upset when others in their class, non-Americans, were slapped on the hands with a strap or cane for not having memorised their Catechism. One afternoon, Rob arrived home to the flat in a flood of tears at having his hands caned purple by a visiting teacher who expected him to name every Irish saint that ever lived. Seeing my child cry because of a cruel teacher made a flood of memories rush back from my own experiences of being a child in an Irish school.

The United States may not be a Land of Saints and Scholars, but it won hands down in how it treated young people in the public schools. Corporal punishment would not be tolerated. A fog of unreason still overshadowed public education in Ireland. I soaked Robert's hands under the cold tap water and my heart hurt for the young in Ireland and caused me to wonder why such cruelty got such a foothold in the land of affection.

Noely's drinking binges upset Eddie. Being a non-drinker, Ed tried to counsel him about its dangers, but Noely continued to get drunk, his ear cocked for every christening party, wedding reception and wake within walking distance of Ringsend and Irishtown. Ed volunteered to accompany Noely to discuss the drinking problem with medical experts, and said he would pay for the treatment. Noel played along with his Yankee brother-in-law on the first visit to the doctor. He told Ed from then on he'd take the bull by the horns on his own, thanking him with a benign grin as if butter wouldn't melt in his mouth. He told Eddie he needed to see the doctor three times a week and hated to ask for the bloody bus fare both ways in order to get to the clinic. Ed responded by giving him money for the bus fares in advance and told Noely that idle hands added to all drinking addiction. I could detect my brother heating up under the collar at the Protestant dressing down. Noel had been unable or unwilling to explain why he and his mates lacked an education that Eddie took for granted as a result of growing up in the United States.

My depression lifted in spite of everything else happening around me. I noticed Eddie seemed to be anxious about being away from his job and from Idaho. He started to become upset by the school situation, and the intense focus put on religion instead of other important things. He kept busy visiting the museums, historical sites, and taking the boys on trips round the city, but he felt his children were missing out on a great deal by not being at school back in the States. They were starting to behave and talk like Dubliners — giving me guff picked up on the streets. Their dad cringed at being told, 'Hold y'r water. Gimme money to git inta the dance in Pearse Street. Dad, that fucker called us mutton-headed Americans.' Sometimes, my patient husband looked like he might have the urge to fall into a sonorous sleep and dream of the leafy abodes of his childhood, or, God forbid, Boot Hill. He gave up trying to reform Noel after finding out that he had rummaged through our personal belongings and had made off with stuff to sell or exchange for drink. He even nicked my bottle of

Thorazine pills. We might never have known what had happened to the tranquilizers had my mother not bumped into one of the neighbours in George Reynolds.

The neighbour told her that she had heard from a bus conductor that Noel Kearns and his mates had boarded a double-decker bus to Bray for a day excursion. When the bus arrived at the terminus in Bray, the conductor called out for everyone to get out, it being the end of the line. Noely and the pals remained in their seats upstairs. The conductor went upstairs to tell them to 'get the feck off the bus,' but found them slacked out. 'Drunk,' he thought, 'at this time of the morning.' No amount of shouting or shaking got any one to open an eyelid. 'Never heard such snoring,' remarked the conductor. The driver and the conductor decided to leave the lot upstairs asleep until the return trip back to the city centre. When they finally opened their eyes, one of the boyos yammered in amazement, 'Jaysus Christ, Noely, them American tablets'd knock out a bleedin' carthorse!'

I tried not to laugh when my mother ended the story. I assured her that Noely probably felt awful now for what he did, selling my son's favourite toys and items of my fancy underwear. I told Eddie what Noel had done. He said it wasn't worth the fuss of making an issue of it on account of my mother, who blamed herself for everything that happened in the universe.

The weeks passed too quickly in the company of my mother and our neighbours, Mrs Harris and Jenny from down the balcony. The three older women lifted my spirits with their stories, encouraging comments and funny quips. They also filled me in on all the neighbours — who'd left the flats to go over the sea, who'd got married, who'd had bushels of babies and who'd been buried under the sod. Those who had to leave Ireland to find work always sent money home to their mothers back in George Reynolds. Mrs Harris said the postman could tell from the weight of the letter which ones had money either from England or America.

Robert, Stephen and Eddie Jr were having the time of their lives visiting their granny. They loved the liveliness and camaraderie of Irishtown and made friends with other children their age living in the flats. They did not like the school, so they learned how to 'mitch' for other activities, especially the two older boys. The two spent afternoons on the Sandymount dumpsite with their friends. They saw how homeless men lived in old junked automobiles on the dump, and others in makeshift shacks made out of driftwood. The men who lived on the wasteland had no time for trivial games with kids, and cursed them if they came near their territory. The boys also got acquainted with the rats that nested in the dirt and rubble around Dublin city and dumped on the site. Older boys brought along air rifles to kill the rats, and acted like cowboys on the open ranges of the American West. Rob and Steve never had so much fun and excitement in their lives as this time in Dublin. They still talk about how they learned to jump on a moving double-decker bus, and how to jump off the moving bus without paying the fare. Steve got a part-time job helping out Harry the coalman, who delivered coal to the flats in George Reynolds. Steve helped carry up the coal for Harry and got to ride all over Ringsend and Irishtown with Harry and his helper. He arrived back at my mother's flat dusted with coal dust and reeking of cigarettes, causing his father's eyebrows to rise. Eddie, our five-year-old, also took to life in the flats like fish take to water. He fell in love with the sweetest little Irish miss from another block of flats. The two young playmates went everywhere together and were constantly eating ice cream or candy.

My mother loved having us with her. She and Eddie got along fine and she cooked him an Irish breakfast of eggs, sausages, black and white pudding and fried bread every morning which he ate with relish. Bob brought the boys some little trinkets when he came home from the sea. The children loved him. Bob and I liked to talk politics to-

George Reynolds flats, Irishtown, Dublin

gether. We talked about the politics of Ireland; tried to figure out why so many young people willingly left home to find work elsewhere, and why they did not stay and demand the government do something to bring good jobs to Ireland. Bob thought if the six counties in the North united with the South things would get better for everyone in Ireland. He viewed the partition of the country as being a bad thing for everyone, as did others. He enjoyed playing the record album I brought him from the States. 'Easter Monday, 1916: Songs of the IRA' with Dominic Behan.

Eddie's mother wrote to her son to find out when we were going to return to America and get resettled in the States. Time had moved forward too quickly, and the three months of work leave without pay had almost come to an end. Eddie had inquired at several places if they had any work available for research space engineers. 'Sorry' went the refrain. Finding employment for Eddie in my country of birth proved impossible.

I felt like a different person living in Dublin with my family and old familiar neighbours. The melancholy that had enfolded me subsided. I cut back on the anti-depressant pills, and dropped the forty pounds of weight I'd gained in the States. Idaho Falls seemed like the last place in the universe I should return to, to raise my children and grow old, but I'd made my bed when marrying Eddie who unselfishly did everything to make our family happy. He told me that we had to go back to the United States where he had a good job and could earn a living. He missed the land of his birth and wished to return. Robert also seemed to be getting homesick . A studious young boy, he missed going to his old school in Idaho Falls. And so it was time to pack and part from my family and the city I loved so well. It felt bitter to leave my mother, Bob, bad Noely, Frank, Bridie and my nieces and nephews we'd all come to know and love.

The boys and their friends said good-bye, promising to write to each other as long as they lived. Harry the coalman gave Steve a handful of copper coins for being his helper, and told my son that he would always have a job with him.

Before leaving, my mother reminded me that everyone's mind needed a rest from worry and having a good laugh proved to be the best medicine of all. 'You got too serious,' she said. 'Sure, Angeline, we'd never have survived without a laugh; how did you ever forget that? Being serious all the time, worse than a bullet in the heart.' I tried to explain to her that life in the United States had a very sober quality, especially where I lived in Idaho Falls, with its heavy population of Mormons. 'Well, love, without a bit of humour is life worth living? If poor people in Ireland didn't have a sense of humour or a joke to tell, we would have died off. Remember Granny Martin and Granny Carey telling us jokes so sharp they'd bite? Both dead now, but the stories they told soaked many the pair of tattered knickers.'

I'd begun to realise that some Americans' expectations of immigrants felt like a straitjacket. Part of what got me down in Idaho Falls had been the forced patriotism and Americanism imposed on newcomers: binding immigrants up in the flag as if it were a winding sheet instead of a free-flowing emblem. Furthermore, I began to question the folderol of being the perfect wife, the all-giving mom, the happy shopper, and the empty-headed corporate spouse. Taken altogether, such requirements would plough even Wonder Women under the sod.

I knew baggage remained from the past that I needed to air with Dr C. Being back in Dublin, especially being with my mother, restored some flint to my musket. Before returning to the States, I told Eddie that I would not go back to live in a house in suburbia cut off from life, no matter how big or fancy the house might be. I'd had my fill of home ownership and isolation wrapped up at the pinnacle of the American dream, along with den mothers constantly tailoring the behaviour of newcomers. I wished to be surrounded by a variety of people who did not hold just one model for living.

Turning points

On returning to Idaho Falls our family moved into a newly-built condominium complex within walking distance of shops and the elementary school. The three boys were enrolled in school and after a few
weeks, they settled in. An interesting mix of people lived in the condominiums — many were site families. There were lots of children of
various ages for our boys to play with. The condo also had a swim-
ming-pool that became the gathering place for the neighbours during the hot dry summer months.

My neighbours next door were immigrants from Toronto, Canada.
The husband had a Ph.D. in nuclear science and worked for one of
the corporations at the site. Carol, the wife, had worked for a while
back east at a private elementary school before meeting her husband
and moving to Idaho Falls. The couple had two small children, and
one on the way. Carol told me when I met her for the first time, that
she had had Henry Kissinger's two children in her class, and got to
meet Kissinger at parents' day at the school. She said, 'He thought
his kids were brilliant. They were ordinary, and plain looking like
their dad.' She preferred to live in the condo instead of suburbia because she liked to see lots of people coming and going. Her husband,
like the rest of the site workers, took off for work early in the morning and returned at six in the evening. Having other women in the
same boat close by offered the opportunity to have more friendships
and more coffee klatches.

Carol noticed that I never sat in the sun while out at the pool. I
told her that I'd had a nervous breakdown, and still needed to take
anti-depressant pills, which would cause me to get serious sunburn
if I got out of the shade. She told me that a sister of hers in Canada
also suffered from depression. She confessed that she had bouts of
depression whenever she thought of being separated from her family back in Canada. 'America's different,' she exclaimed. 'Feel that
way too?' she asked.

'Can't quite put my finger on that difference, after all these years,'
I replied.

'Let's face it, we're foreigners,' said Carol.

'Our children won't feel that way,' I replied adding 'I like the American West. Something about the West catches my breath and stirs my heart without any effort from my brain.'

She nodded her head in agreement.

My feelings of sometimes being 'out of it' persisted. I went back to see Dr C. I was now seeing him once a month. I wanted to stop taking the pills as they made me drowsy and my life seemed to be sliding on ice. 'Depression is an illness,' he said, and kept me on the pills. I used to enjoy making love a lot before the depression, now I didn't have the energy required to giggle and jostle; it seemed too much. Eddie tried to understand, but he loved me, and wanted to express it physically. I knew my getting better would be a struggle. It seemed so tempting at times to quietly slip into oblivion. I fought back every day to get out of the chrysalis of despair. Getting letters from Ireland still lifted my spirit. Sadly, no more letters from Da, packed with yarns and the latest news. His absence felt heavy on my heart, as I knew it did for my mother. One letter from her read:

> *Dear love, I got your letter today . . . There's terrible trouble going on in the north. There is a boycott of all things in the supermarket that is made in England all places in Grafton Street that had England goods were blown up. The IRA will never give up they will fight till last. I am glad you are keeping well and Eddie and my three loves. I didn't get your parcel yet. Mrs. Harris is in the hospital. I feel well my self TG [Thank God]. I went out to your da's grave yesterday. Billy Cummins brought me out in his car. He has a little boy. This is all for now.*
> *Ma xxs, Bob xxs, Noel xx. God Bless youse all.*

Sometimes it took a while to decipher my mother's writing. Her letters meant more to me than the Holy Grail.

Among the neighbours in the condo, two of my favourite people were Sally and Sid. They swam in the pool all summer. Sally became known for the wonderful Bloody Marys she made by the pitcherful. Sid had worked at the nuclear site since the early 1950s. In 1955, an experimental breeder reactor came perilously close to a meltdown during a test; the accident was attributed to operator failure. Sid and a handful of other workers risked their lives to get the men out of the contaminated workspace. The whole event of the accidental meltdown became a hush-hush matter. Sal worried about Sid's expo-sure to radiation from the accident. She feared that he might get cancer. He was eventually diagnosed with a rare blood disease that killed him. Others involved in the rescue died from cancer. While sitting and chatting by the pool, neighbours commented on this or that person they knew who had worked at the site being diagnosed with cancer, and having to quit working. The dreaded disease seemed common as flu in Idaho Falls. Although the topic of cancer came up often in con-versation, everyone knew that underneath any concern lurked an un-spoken commandment: Don't bite the hand that feeds you. Don't talk bad about the site.

At one of the company dinner parties, I met a couple, Dot and Pete, who originally came from California. They had ancestors who had emigrated from someplace in Ireland to work in the gold mines of Northern California. In the course of conversation, they revealed they were Democrats, a small minority in Idaho, especially in Idaho Falls. Dot and Pete wanted to know if I would like to be involved and help out in the McGovern/Shriver 1972 Presidential campaign.

'Be a tough nut to crack, getting folks to vote for the McGovern/ Shriver ticket,' Pete told me.

'Who are they running against?' I asked.

'Nixon and Agnew.' I volunteered to pass out brochures for the Democratic nominees in the neighborhood.

'Be prepared for insults,' warned Dot.

Eddie thought my getting involved with something outside the house would be good for me. He told me he planned to vote for Nixon over McGovern. He'd never vote Democrat, I knew, as long as his arse faced the ground.

Most of the people I gave the McGovern/Shriver '72 handouts to rolled the flyers into a tight-fisted ball and pitched the material into the nearest trash container. Some rolled their eyes upwards upon being asked to vote the ticket, but one bearded guy invited me into his apartment to smoke a joint. Nixon took the state of Idaho by a landslide.

Helping with the campaign gave me a lot of energy. Getting out and talking to different people from all walks of life had been inter-esting. I patted myself on the back for getting involved in something I believed in, regardless of how others felt — glory be to God, I'd acted and felt like a somebody. The Chairman of the Democratic Party in Idaho Falls took the time to write me a letter of appreciation, the first of its kind I'd ever received:

> *Dear Angie, Thanks for all your help during the McGovern Campaign typing, passing out brochures, helping at the Mall. Without such efforts as yours our Campaign would not have been possible. Indeed, despite its lack of success the McGovern Campaign was truly a people's campaign—supported and carried out by people just like us all across the country—and this may be the greatest significance for the political future of America.*
>
> *I enjoyed meeting and working with you and hope you will remain interested in the Democratic Party in Idaho. Thanks again, Dick Hobbins*

Dr C thought it a good thing that I had been involved with the political campaign. He wanted me to return to telling him about growing up in Ireland. He thought my feelings of anxiety and depression originated then. 'How long have you been married and how many children do your have?' I asked the psychiatrist. I also asked him, 'Would you have treated me and continue to see me without medical insurance?' He replied that he'd married a high school sweetheart, had six kids, and he would have seen me as a patient with or without insurance.

'You have six kids?' I said with surprise.

'They keep my wife busy; she wanted a large family.'

'Is she a Mormon?'

'Yes. Anything else you want to ask me before we continue?'

'No! Do you like me?'

'Yes.'

'Am I crazy?'

'No.'

'Have you ever thought that you were crazy?'

'Sometimes I wonder,' he laughed.

'Sometimes your eyes look blue to me.'

'Really?' he replied. 'They are blue.'

'What are you writing down now?'

'Just notes to remind myself.'

'I inscribed in my head ever since I was a small girl. No need for notes.'

'Where were we? Oh yes, we were talking about your early memories.'

'Let's go out and have a cup of coffee together.'

He smiled and said, 'Let's continue.'

'I don't want to talk any more to another Yank.'

'Is that what I am to you?'

'Yes, no and certainly so. That's a childhood rhyme.'

'Don't keep pushing back the memories that cause you to be anxious and depressed.'

'I'm not doing that.'

'You are, Angie. So, tell me, are you and Eddie making love?'

'None of your beeswax. I'd never ask you such a raw question.'

'I'm a psychiatrist and I need to ask my patients all kinds of questions.'

I told him that I had nightmares, still, of picking cinders on the dumps to sell to other poor people for fuel. The stench from rooting through mounds of garbage of every kind still clung to me. It took all day to fill a gunnysack full of cinders. Silently I asked God above, as I rooted through the garbage, not to let a rat bite my fingers. The thought of a fat black rat, big as a cat, with fanged teeth snapping into my finger caused me mind to scream inside my head, and bolts of thunder to fill my ears. Sometimes, when I reached down to pick up a cinder from the garbage I felt a strong hand covering mine like a soft glove. God knew that if a rat latched on to one of my fingers, I would have flung myself down the mountain of garbage to the sea below, and busted my head open with a sharp rock.

One afternoon, one of the small boys who also rooted on the dumpsite for a living spiked up a bundle of wrapped newspaper. Bingo-Bongo was the name the kids called him. He undid the layers of newspapers and tea towels to discover the tiny, mummified baby. The ashen infant looked and smelled like dried flowers found in an old book.

'I kept thinking — why didn't I find the best thing ever found on the dump, instead of Bingo-Bongo?'

'What would you have done?' said the doctor, seemingly from miles away.

'I'd have put the little mummified infant under a pane of glass over a shoebox. I would have made a lovely place for it — like the Seven Dwarfs did for Snow White in the Hollywood film.'

'I see,' said Dr C. 'What did you do after working on the dump? Were there any child labour laws in your country?'

'A girl or boy had to be fourteen years old in order to be hired in a factory. I got a job as a factory girl just before my fourteenth birthday. They let some of us in under the counter.'

Eddie picked me up from the doctor's appointment. I told him that talking about stuff with Dr C made my head feel light, but it made me feel much better afterwards, as if rising out of a shit hole to seek fresh air. He didn't flinch at me saying a bad word. I wondered why so many people got wound up over off-colour words instead of more important issues.

My niece and namesake, Angeline, wrote to bring me up on the latest news from her home front.

> *Dear Aunt Angeline, Hope you are all well as we are here. I just came home from my granny, she was in town in the morning time and she got her Christmas decorations and goods. She is always talking about you. I am working in a pub in James Street doing cleaning and serving the drink for an hour or so. I think of you often aunt Angeline and Eddie, as you were both very good to me when you were over here. I am doing my Christmas exams in school at the moment. After that we are getting our holidays from school. I hope you all have a very happy holiday and a prosperous New Year. That's all for now. God Bless. Xxxxx, Angeline*

Having a fourteen-year-old girl in to clean and pull pints in a pub in James Street, Dublin, to earn extra money for her family spoke to me of how the children of the poor were still treated like chattel. Likewise, children who lived in poverty in Idaho Falls, in the richest country on the planet, were also treated like chattel. The promises of equality and justice for all in the Emerald Isle, as in the Land of the Free, remained promises betrayed.

I became involved with a kindergarten project through people I'd met in the Democratic Party. The husband, Sky Bradley, worked as a lawyer for the Idaho National Energy Laboratory. His wife, Cam, had a degree in elementary education. The couple had three darling sons under the age of nine. The Bradleys, instead of moving into a fancy home in one of the posh suburbs, bought a 'fixer-upper' in Happyville, where poverty reigned. During this period, the State of Idaho would not appropriate funds for public kindergartens for the children of Idaho. If parents could not afford to send their offspring to private kindergarten, they stayed at home. Cam and other concerned women in Idaho had volunteered to set up kindergarten classes around the state, free for children who could not afford to pay. The teachers and their assistants would receive no pay for their work. Cam asked me if I would be her assistant in a class she had started out of her home in Happyville. Fees collected from parents who could afford to pay went for materials used in the classes and snacks for the children.

I discussed the matter with Dr C and he encouraged me to get involved. It would be a year-long commitment. Eddie and my three boys were glad to see me excited about working with Cam and helping to run the kindergarten. My depression had improved over the years, but there were times when it would hit me. Regardless of my own feelings, the commitment to Cam and the children would be my priority.

Happyville, an 80-acre area west of Interstate 15 between Broadway and Pancheri, within walking distance of where I lived on South Skyline Drive in Idaho Falls, got its name from the Happy brothers who built several houses in the place. The street signs were nailed to tree limbs, or bare boards here and there. It looked like the march of progress had left the area behind long ago, although about seventy families lived there. On first sight, you might picture Happyville in its heyday as a boisterous mining camp. But when I first encountered the place it felt as if the families in Happyville had fallen into a deep sleep, or that they'd given up on the American dream. The Bradleys' house was on a half-acre. Cam planted a garden, the children tended caged rabbits, and a woebegone, aged donkey shuffled around in the clumps of sage and brushwood. Compared to the rebuilt Bradley house, the other abodes were like lean-to-shelters on the verge of toppling over. Sky told me that there were definite health hazards in the area. Many of the residents needed to haul water to their homes by hand. Septic tanks and cesspools would overflow during the summer. The city of Idaho Falls had refused to extend water and sewage to the area, located on the desert crust. Sky had a plan to rally the people of Happyville to get the city of Idaho Falls to extend water and sewer lines to the place.

Ten children registered in Cam's public kindergarten classes plus two of her own children. The classes met Monday through Thursday, from 9.30 am to 1 pm. Cam assigned me various tasks, including reading stories to the children and keeping an eye on her youngest child, three-year-old Chad, while she worked with the older children. I helped with art and craft projects, and with preparing snacks for the children. The school sessions flew by, especially when I was not struggling to keep depression at bay.

One small, thin, quiet girl named Hope got my attention. The child, at age six, did not chatter away as one would expect at that age. 'She grunts to express herself,' said Cam. Her parents had cut themselves off from other people, and their children seldom went out to play with other children. Happyville contained several families like that, people who were isolated or believed they would not be accepted by others either inside or outside of Happyville. Cam worked diligently with Hope to bring her out of isolation. Hope's family lived on half-nothing, like a lot of families I grew up with in the Dublin tenements.

I tried to be extra helpful to Hope. I took care of her occasionally when she did not want to participate with Cam and the other children. One day we went outside where I picked up two small sticks, handed one to Hope, then knelt on the ground and began to dig up pieces of coloured glass and shards of pottery that had been long buried in the hard desert dirt under our feet. Hope followed my example and began to dig up gems on her own. We put our collection in a glass jar. She began to describe her discoveries for me:

'Look a bu on. Look a twen on. A brn on. A ed on. A urple on.'

She loved to go outside with me and collect colourful household tidbits left over from a pioneer past that littered the ground in Happyville. At the end of the school year, Hope stood before the other children with her prized collection of glass and pottery bits and pieces. She retrieved different tidbits from the jar and held them in her hand for the other children to see, proudly noting as she did so: 'Look a blue one. Look a green one. Look a brown one, a red one, and pretty purple.'

Cam spent endless hours teaching Hope phonics, showing her flash cards and teaching her how to write her name. Hope and the other children who enrolled in Cam's volunteer public kindergarten class would be off to a successful start in first grade. On learning about the successful outcome of the volunteer public kindergartens operated around the state, the Idaho legislature were convinced that the state should at last finance public kindergarten for all the children of Idaho. Governor Cecil Andrus sent every citizen who worked with the volunteer kindergarten programme a diploma proclaiming each an official 'Honored Citizen of the State Idaho.' The year I spent as Cam's assistant and the wonderful children enrolled in the classes brought waves of sunshine into my life, giving me more courage to pursue my future. Happyville, Idaho remained a special place to me, poverty be damned.

My mother died on August 9, 1974. I got the call late at night from my brother Bob in Dublin. I knew before I'd picked up the phone that she'd walked through Heaven's Gate. On hearing of my mother's death, I could not cry, or discuss it, or even write about it. Only memory sufficed. Memories of her trickled in, and then flooded my mind. I paddled in the memories, floated in the memories, swam in the memories, but I did not drown. One image that lingered is of her and me standing together on the footpath waiting for the funeral of Big Jim Larkin to pass by. It snowed that day in Dublin like never before. My mother held me close to her to keep me warm. I looked up at her as thick snow petals the size of pennies fell. The oncoming flakes covered her black wavy hair, giving her the look of a Spanish dancer, although the dire poverty we lived in was apparent in every pore of her body. Had I a gun that day, although a mere child, I would have robbed the Bank of Ireland to buy food for her and ease the daily suffering of her mind.

Now out of the blue, I recalled a part from one of her letters that urged me to pray a prayer to Mary and Jesus that guaranteed every fallen soul a place in Heaven. 'In the time it takes to boil a three-minute egg, souls will be saved,' she had written. 'Such is the power of saying the names of Jesus and Mary. It's all in God's love.' Eddie later commented on me muttering to myself on more than one occasion. The silent muttering went: 'Jesus, Mary I love you, save the souls.' I knew Ma had gone to Heaven before her head hit the floor.

My sister-in-law, Bridie wrote me a letter filling me in on the details of her death.

> *Dear Angeline, I'm sorry I did not write you when your Mother died. But I could not bring myself to write. I just could not believe she was dead. I used to think I heard her at the door and when I went out to the shops I used to think I seen her coming to meet me. She was so good to me since I married that she was like my own mother. I was down with her the day before she told me she had a pain in her left arm. I asked her would I go to the*

doctor with her. No she said I'm going back to the Hospital in the morning to see the doctor, which she did. It seemed the doctor told her to rest. She died 2 hours after seeing the doctor. But I think she is happy now with your father. But I still think she is around us all the time. I often think of you how you must miss her. She loved you so much so she'll be very close to you always. Well, goodbye for now, All my love Bridie xxxx

My mother tried to understand the larger picture of life instead of condensing it to a snapshot. She tried to teach me that, but in spite of my love for her, there were parts of my thinking that differed. My brother Bob took care of the funeral arrangements. My mother would be buried with Da, whom she loved in spite of everything. I did not go back for the funeral. Eddie said my mother would understand. He did not want me to make the long journey back to Dublin alone; neither did Dr C. Eddie could not accompany me because of work demands, and our three growing boys needed one parent nearby in case of an emergency. In my heart of hearts a fear arose that returning to Ireland to bury my mother, and the overwhelming emotions that would entail, might make me fall completely apart and leave my children stranded.

I knew Bob and Noel would find life terrible lonely without Ma as would their old mutt, Darkie the dog. It would not be the same without our mother bustling about the place. Bob wrote to tell me that she got a great send off; old neighbours from O'Brien's Place and friends and neighbours living in George Reynolds flats came to her wake and toasted her royally with straight shots of Paddy Power's whiskey. The staff in Ed's office at the site sent me a beautiful bouquet of red roses. Americans continued to surprise the hell out of me.

More than ever, I realized that my emigration from Ireland was permanent. My children were American children. With their grandparents in Ireland dead, visits back to the Old Country would never be the same. My sons spoke with a distinctive US accent like their father, devoid of any shading of Irish. We celebrated Saint Patrick's Day, but other than that the boys showed little interest in anything Irish. When I knitted each one a woolly Aran sweater to wear for going fishing, they looked at me with a twinge of pain on their faces. Each tugged at the turtle necks as though they were cast out of cement instead of knitted from imported Irish wool guaranteed sheared from the rumps of sturdy sheep that foraged in sunshine and rain among gorse and heather in the wilds of Connemara. By the time the three boys finished elementary school, they were addicted to American football, baseball, basketball, speedway racing, monster movies, and far-out space shows on television, not to mention earsplitting rock music.

We loved to take trips to Mud Lake, a place not far from Idaho Falls. Migrant birds flocked to the lake, and many made it their home for the summer. The boys liked to fish for carp in the lake while Eddie and I tried to identify the hordes of visiting birds nesting in the bushes, in clumps of willow and aspen, or nesting on the lake.

While trying to identify a flying flock of birds overhead, I saw the sky as being vivid blue; not only that, but everything around me seemed more vivid that before. A feeling of pure horror and fear washed over me. I didn't know what was happening. I thought that I had lost my mind. I began to panic. Eddie noticed me staggering about, and asked if anything was the matter. I couldn't answer. I couldn't open my mouth. My face felt paralysed. He got Rob, Steve, and Eddie Jr back in the station wagon and we headed home.

He called Dr C and told him that something was wrong with me, and that I could not talk. Dr C met us at the emergency room in the hospital where he examined me to make sure I hadn't had a stroke. He tried to talk to me, but I couldn't reply. He gave me a pencil and paper and asked me to write down what had happened. I wrote that the world was suddenly in colour, and I didn't know what had happened. He assured Eddie that I had not had a stroke or a brain seizure, but that I was in shock. He wanted me to check into hospital but I refused. He gave me an injection, arranged for me to see him the following morning in his office, and sent me home with medication.

Eddie assured our children that their mom would be fine. I could not talk to them because my mouth remained numb. I asked God to please help me, and in asking for God's help, the terrible memory that I had locked out of my mind tried to come back. My tongue began to protrude out of my mouth. I had to hide the horror of what seemed to be happening from my children's eyes. I went to the bedroom and Eddie gave me some of the sedative medication ordered by the doctor to make me sleep until morning.

I don't recall going to Dr C's office. I still could not talk; my mouth remained numb. The doctor told me that I was in a state of shock and not to be afraid. We could work through whatever was happening. I went to see Dr C daily for the next week without being able to say a word. 'We can work through the traumatic event in your past that has brought this on,' he assured me. At that stage, I did not know whether to believe him or not. I had been seeing him every two months since the breakdown, now almost six years in the past. He held my hand for reassurance. He tried to explain about 'repression and displacement, and how the human mind tries to defend itself in times of perceived or threatened danger.' I remained mute. I ate baby food until the numbness went away. Being assured by the doctor that I would be OK helped me to keep going. My children were wonderful to me, but did not understand the condition their mother was in. A new medication, some powerful anti-anxiety pills, lessened my dread, and with the help of Dr C, I confronted the past horror that now split me apart.

As the dreaded scene in Baggot Street Hospital, Dublin, came back; I could not sit in the chair facing Dr C. I paced around the office, sat down, got up, grabbed his hand, wailed for my mother, threw up, and wished my mind would shrivel and die.

I related what had happened as if it were taking place at that very moment. My mother took me to Baggot Street Hospital because I got very sick and could hardly breathe. Ma bundled me up in an old blanket, and we inched our way up to the hospital; I felt very ill, and had to stop and rest often along the way to catch my breath. We waited until a doctor had time or the inclination to take a look at me. We sat on hard wooden benches where other charity patients waited; some had been there from early morning, and now late evening had come. A nurse came and took me into a small curtained cubicle where, after a long time, a doctor came in and examined my chest with a stethoscope. He told Ma I needed to be admitted into a ward. The doctor wrapped me up in a red woolly blanket and carried me in his arms to the hospital lift and up to the ward. The only light in the ward sat on the nurse's desk.

The nurse pointed to an empty bed in the dim light and the doctor put me into the crib-like bed and covered me up. I begged my mother not to leave me there; I'd never spent a night away from her, and I was frightened to be among strangers. The nurse told my mother to go. I could not see any of the other patients sleeping in their beds because of the darkness.

As the night wore on, and morning light began to enter the ward through the windows, I heard stirrings in the bed next to mine. I waited a while before opening my eyes to look around. I saw the child in the bed next to me. She did not look like any child I had seen before; she could have been straight from a nightmare. She stood up in the bed shaking the rails. She didn't speak, but began to grunt like an animal. I turned my face away, but felt compelled to look back when a terrible smell of shit filled the space. I looked at the girl child standing up in the crib and saw her bright eyes looking at me, big as saucers and her wet pink tongue sprouting out her mouth. She looked at me as she licked shit from her hands. She smeared it over her face, hair and white night dress. She looked like someone out of Hell. I couldn't move my eyes away from her. I felt my mouth going numb with horror.

As the ward got brighter from morning light, I saw the other children. They all looked like her. There were no children in the place who looked like me. I thought that I must be dead, and God had sent me down to Hell. Fear and shock took me over. I felt my whole face, even my eyes, going numb. I had to struggle to keep from sticking out my tongue like the others around me. I truly believed that I had died and gone to Hell for being a sinner. I felt myself crying in my mind to think that God had sent me to Hell, when I thought he loved me. All the faces looking towards me from the other beds were the faces of drooling gargoyles, the faces of demons described by the nuns at school.

While I talked to Dr C about what had happened, sepia images of the children and the hospital ward filled my mind. It felt like the unreeling of a horror movie. The doctor asked me to continue telling what had happened in Baggot Street Hospital.

I saw the nurse come into the room and stop at each bed. She acted as if everything were normal; she didn't seem to notice that the occupants of those beds were demons from Hell. I couldn't seem to make sense out of anything or understand what had happened to me. The nurse must not be able to see the real faces on the children, I reasoned, or she would have reacted in horror. She came over to my side of the room, rushed up to the devil-child in the bed next to me and shouted 'Ann Mullen!' which must have been the devil-girl's name. Next, a ward maid brought me a bowl of porridge and a mug of milk for breakfast. I took the spoon in my hand and tried to eat the porridge.

The thing in the next bed was still covered in shit. Her smell was overwhelming. My mouth remained shut. It felt like someone had wired it shut. The ward-maid came back, noticed that the food remained untouched and scolded me for wasting good food.

I lay in bed, unable to stir or open my mouth to say a word. Another nurse came in holding a washbasin and a long pair of gleaming silver scissors. She told me to sit up in bed. She began to cut off chunks of my hair. She cut and cut till all my hair lay in the basin like scythed hay. After she left, I reached my hands to my head and drew them back in anguish, feeling the stiff, clipped stubble on my head, no longer now than that of my brothers. She returned with a basin of water, and without a murmur began to wash my body as if it were a disgusting sight. When she got to my feet, she stopped and berated me for being a big girl—a girl eight or nine—with dirty feet. Her words filled me with blazing shame. Had I been able to talk, I would have told her that I didn't have any shoes to wear to keep my feet off the dirty ground. In her eyes, she saw another scruffy, dirty, Dublin child, not worthy of her compassion or respect.

I pleaded with God, my heavenly father, to take me out of this terrible place. He never came. I thought if God existed, he would rescue me. When God did not rescue me, I realised there was no God. There wasn't any God. Someone had made it up. There wasn't one. They had lied.

When my mother came to see me she acted as though I were the same girl she'd left in the hospital earlier on. She did not see anything out of the ordinary. She looked around the place, at the girl in the bed next to mine, and made the sign of the cross. The nurses kept telling me to eat, but I kept choking on the food. I found it impossible to swallow. Then a voice came into my mind and told me to make my 'real self' go away—told me to 'fade away'; it said the 'me' in colours had to go away forever, and that only a me in grey could live. It said, 'Angeline in colour wants to die. Send her away. Make her disappear. If you don't make Angeline in colour fade away, you won't be able to live.'

In order to stop the voice in my head, I began to say my prayers and recite arithmetic tables, sing songs and hymns backwards and forwards, over and over again. If I didn't keep it up, the demanding voice returned. I hoped to drift away and die.

'Is that why you refused to eat?' interjected Dr C.

'Yes. I can smell the watery potato soup they gave me.'

One night, I told Dr C, someone woke me up and lifted me out of bed. A young nurse held me in her arms. She rocked me back and forth. 'You must eat something,' she told me. She said, `I'm going to stay with you until you eat something. I will take care of you. You must eat; if you don't, in the morning the doctor is going to put a rubber tube down your throat to feed you. It will hurt you. Please, for me, eat.'

She began to put a spoon of food into my mouth. I had no feeling in the lower part of my face. I began to vomit up salty water. She cleaned off my face with a washrag. She told me to lie back down and she'd return soon. She returned, and this time she whispered my name. She lifted me up in the bed holding me in her arms. She said to me, 'You're a lovely child. Do you know you are a lovely child?' She whispered in my ear. 'I went to one of the private wards and stole some lovely tasting food for you. I'll feed it to you with my fingers.' She pried apart my sore, dry lips and inserted tiny pieces of chicken with her fingers. I tried to swallow the food but could not. I vomited. She cleaned out my mouth with her fingers. She tried again, and bit-ter, salty water spouted out. She told me to rest. She began to brush my shaved head gently with her hand. She tried to feed me again, using her fingers to pry apart my lips. She squashed a sweet berry inside my mouth and its juice began to trickle down the back of my throat. I tasted its sweetness and swallowed. She did the same again with another berry, and another berry. She told me to rest. She lifted me once more into a sitting position in the bed, keeping her arms around me. She put a tiny bit of chicken meat in my mouth, and I began to chew it. I began to feel hungry. The nurse kept saying to me 'Oh, good! Oh, good.' Before leaving, she told me that she would tell the doctor right way in the morning that I'd eaten food, at last. I closed my eyes thinking Jesus still cared about me. He must have sent the lovely nurse to care for me.

'Then what happened?' inquired Dr C.

'I'm very tired. I've never felt so tired.'

'All right. We will resume where we left off tomorrow.'

Eddie had waited down in the foyer for me. He wanted to know why my session with the doctor had lasted three hours. I didn't pos-sess enough energy to reply; instead I reached for his hand and locked onto it like a lost and bewildered child.

The next day Dr C greeted me with a smile. He read his notes from the pad and said, 'You began to eat food again. Then what happened?'

'I hate to go back again in my memory to that awful place. It all becomes real again for me.'

'I know. You had no choice but to disassociate yourself from what happened in that hospital.' I didn't get his meaning of disassociate, but I told him some more about the hospital.

'When I was allowed to get out of bed, I recall walking around the ward. I noticed a nurse letting some of the kids out to play on an outside balcony. I went onto the balcony and the world outside looked so beautiful and I could smell the fresh air. The sky overhead seemed so blue, blue like a glass marble. All the colours looked astonishing outside after being in the ward. The wrought-iron balcony reached high over my head. I looked through the railings down to the street and saw the people were passing by. From the height of the balcony, the people below looked small. As I stood looking through the railing, I saw birds flying upwards to the balcony. One bird flew close to me. I started to call out to the birds flying by, asking them to carry me away from the awful place I was in. The birds told me, "You're too heavy. You have to stay where you are." Then the stern voice sounded in my head again, and told me to climb up to the top of the balcony and jump over. "It won't hurt," the voice said. It got more demanding, and kept shouting "Jump over! Jump over!" I began to climb up the railing to reach the top of the balcony. The iron grille work that surrounded the balcony stuck into my bare feet. I continued to climb. Each inch I made upwards by sticking my toes into the grille work hurt more and more, and it became harder to climb upwards. A nurse shouted at me from inside the ward to come inside immediately. I began to rage at myself for not being able to heave my body over the balcony and get away. Before I obeyed the nurse's order to come back inside the ward, I looked once through the grille work and told myself that because the outside world looked and felt so beautiful with its colours of blues and greens, I never wanted to see it again. I hated it! I hated all the colours; especially I hated the blue of the sky. While in bed that night, the voice came back, sounding more reasonable. It told me I could never live in colour again, only in gray. It said, "Angeline who loves colours can't live anymore. Send her away. Send her away. If Angeline in colour is not sent away, you, the Angeline in gray won't be able to hold on anymore."

'I don't remember leaving the hospital. Now I'm back home in O'Brien's Place looking at gray birds pecking on the ground outside of our room in the lane. All the birds were dull and gray, the colour of rats, instead of familiar robins, sparrows, and finches that alighted in O'Brien's Place. The gray birds kept trying to fly up into the air, but kept falling back down to the ground. I told the birds, in my mind, that they were stupid little birds with broken beaks and broken wings, and that I hated them, and would never give them any more breadcrumbs. One of the birds looked at me and said, "We're all broken just like you." I never ever wanted to remember all of this.'

'I understand how you must feel,' said Dr C. 'Only someone very strong could have survived the experience,' he added, getting out of his chair to give me a bear hug.

Dr C wanted to know if my parents noticed my depression when I returned home from the hospital. 'I remember staring into the flames of the fire and into the flame of the candle, not wanting to talk to anyone, not even my mother. She began chiding me a bit for not responding, or talking to her and Da. "What's happened to our gabbygut?" Da told me stories from his childhood, sang old ditties, and challenged me with boyhood riddles until he got hoarse as a horse with a dose of bronchitis. He drew back the gray curtain in my mind allowing in strips of blue.'

'I'd like you to draw a picture for me with crayons.' said Dr C. 'Draw a picture of before and after, of how the outside world looks to you now.'

I did as he requested. He seemed astonished and sad. He asked me if I'd like a cup of coffee

'I thought Mormons didn't drink coffee.'

'I'm a Jack Mormon, remember?'

'You're a nice Mormon. Funny, I hardly noticed how you looked until recently.'

'How do I look?'

'Bit of a smasher.'

He handed me the cup of coffee. I could fall in love with this big fella. Later when I met with the doctor, I reminded him how long I'd been coming to him for counselling. 'You needed me,' he said. 'For a while I thought you would have to have shock treatments to lift your depression. You may not recall it now, but you were seriously depressed.'

'Well, I feel reckless now. I'd run off with you this minute if you asked me.'

He laughed out loud then commented: 'Both of us have families that depend on us. Your feeling of recklessness is expected after dealing with so much repression.'

'Is that medical talk?'

He laughed. 'Maybe.'

'Would you run off with me if you could?'

He rearranged himself on the chair. He often rearranged his body when put on the spot. 'I can't run away with anyone. That's not to say I could not be tempted. I have patients who depend on me like your family depends on you.'

'Do you love me?'

'There is more than one kind of love. With all we have been through together, yes, I feel something special for you.'

'Do you love me?'

'Yes, in a special way.'

'Is it in a romantic way?' I asked.

'That's one way to love a person, but there are other ways.'

'Do you think I'm attractive?'

'Very attractive. Your husband is aware of that, especially now when you smile more often.'

'So you don't want to head off to the woods with me, like two frogs on a lily pond?'

'I like the way you put it, but I can't. You and I have responsibilities towards others.' In order to change the heavy mood, he reminded me about transference — he'd explained it earlier on in my treatment. 'I know now the heart is capable of loving more than one person. You can name it whatever you like.' His pleasant face aimed towards less expression and more the Buddha image. I had angry feelings towards him at the idea of being brushed off.

'I guess you don't want me then?'

'I will always consider you to be a special person in my life.'

'Blue blazes to that,' I replied, miffed. We were both relieved when the session came to an end.

'Are you going to charge me ninety dollars for this chitchat?' I asked him on the way out. 'Only if you care to pay it. Keep in mind you are angry at me now, but later on you will know I did the right thing for you.'

In a softer tone, I bid him good afternoon. I still felt reckless, wanting to do something out of the ordinary, something unpredictable, something mouth watering, and head-spinning. I told myself to put such idiotic ideas out of my mind, and be thankful for all the love I already had. But some wild little bitch still hid in my shell.

An unexpected package from a dear, loved neighbour in George Reynolds flats came in the mail:

> *Dear Angeline,*
> *I was looking at photos of your family they are young men now*
> *they look a lot like you. You did not change much you are still*
> *very good looking well Angeline all my family are married*
> *except 2 Angeline and Robert can you believe that they are now*
> *19 and 15. I sometimes get very lonely and sad I would love to*
> *see you come home soon I have 15 grandchildren now.*
> *Well Angeline we did have some good times we knew how to*
> *laugh at anything we were very happy even though we were*
> *poor. I miss your mother my best friend I miss her. I could tell*
> *her anything. You can always stay with me if you come home I*
> *can put you up in the front bedroom. If you have anything in*
> *the way of clothes if you have any clothes belonging to yourself*
> *or Eddie you don't want I would be grateful. Your friend Jenny*
> *PS it's a Brigid cross.*

Jenny's letter brought back a barrow load of funny and sad memories. Everyone in the flats loved her, especially my mother and myself. I looked at the Saint Brigid's cross woven out of rushes, and wondered why she had sent it. A lifelong Protestant, Jenny never allowed herself to be converted to the Catholic faith in spite of extreme pressure from others. She loved everyone and made no distinctions about religion. She knew my second name was Brigid and heard my mother refer to me as Brigid many times. Some information came with the odd shaped cross. A pamphlet described how the owner of such a holy relic, and their animals, would be protected from natural calamities—from fire, storms, lightning, illnesses relating to childbirth, and it would also counter the state of barrenness.

The pamphlet informed me that Saint Brigid came from Faughard in the northeast corner of County Louth, Ireland. She consecrated her virginity to Christ, founded a convent, and erected a chapel. She also plucked out her eye to avoid being recognized and pursued by a determined suitor. I hung the cross on the wall, contemplating Saint Brigid gouging out her eye to keep a wolf at bay, losing half her vision in doing so. Young girls back in Ireland are taught to admire such sacrifice. Saint Patrick plucked a mere shamrock and became the focus of worldwide celebrations and oceans of green beer on March 17, although in Idaho Falls St Patrick's Day got celebrated with Wild West rodeos, parades, and championship dog shows. This line of reasoning, comparing the two saints, reflected my increasing ability — or confidence — to put two and two together for myself.

The owner of a local bowling alley, the Skylane, got my name from a mother of a child attending the public kindergarten Cam and I supervised. He phoned me and asked me if I would like to start and oversee a toddler's nursery school at the bowling alley. The women bowlers wanted a nursery for their pre-school age children. I would work three mornings a week, taking care of the little kids, doing art projects with them, and keeping them out of their mothers' way while the moms bowled. I almost champed at the bit, delighted at the offer to take care of little kids and do art projects with them. I would get a hundred dollars a month. I talked about the offer with Eddie, who worried that I would not be completely at the disposal of our three now-teenage sons, who were starting to need more supervision. I reminded him that working would be good for me, and that the bowling alley was in walking distance and our kids already went there to bowl, with or without our permission. I also told him that being a housewife did not suit me any more. Going out to lunch with site wives or neighbouring women was tiresome. I liked the challenge of creating a nice little niche for the children at Skylane Bowling Alley while their mothers flung balls down the laneways. Though I did not have to go out and earn a living like less fortunate immigrants, having my own bit of income mattered to me. My intent on coming to America had been to engage with it, not to take advantage of anyone, nor to sit on my bum.

My nursery class at the bowling alley became quite popular with mothers. More and more young mothers, mostly farm wives who'd heard of the nursery class, joined up for the winter leagues to get out of the house and leave the care of their young children with me for a couple of hours. The farm wives bowled like demons. They threw the bowling balls down the alley like cannonballs aimed at an enemy. That Christmas season, the farmers' wives pitched in to give me a Christmas gift for taking care of their children. I ended up with enough Avon products to last three years.

The job at the nursery class provided me with a small income. I put most of it aside for our sons' education, but I also kept a little in 'me auld tobacco box' as my mother, years ago, had advised me to do. The idea had occurred to me that maybe down the road a little cash would be handy to further my own education.

Being involved with the nursery class and the delightful children was like a tonic for me, although after three hours with ten or so little ones, I gladly handed them back to their mothers. My visits to Dr C became less frequent. I took the anti-depressant medication at a much lower dose. Getting out and doing something outside of myself helped a great deal, as had moving out of suburban isolation into the condominium with its mixture of people, nearby shops, and kids coming and going.

Eddie and the boys loved to swim in the pool with the rest of the residents. Most of the married men who lived in the condominiums worked at the atomic site. They looked forward, after their long bus ride home in the hot weather, to swimming with their wives and children in the pool. Some joked that if any body of water in Idaho Falls contained traces of plutonium; it would be the condo pool. We laughed in meek agreement, realizing a possible reality.

Rob, Steve and Eddie Jr swam in the pool the whole summer long with their friends. The boys were growing up. I would get calls from Skyline High School at least once a week asking why either Rob or Steve, especially Steve, had not shown up for school that morning. 'I sent them off,' I'd tell the school clerk on the telephone, wondering where the divil the boys were. They were told from kindergarten about the importance of education, and how lucky they were to be living in a country that provided public education up to the age of eighteen. I also reminded them that children back in Ireland still had to work as errand runners, newsboys, and scavengers to make money to help out their families. And what a wonderful thing America offered by giving everyone a chance to succeed, regardless of their past history, noting at the same time that black children still had a hard row to hoe in getting a decent education in the Land of Opportunity, and why that had to change. In spite of the lectures, the calls kept coming, inquiring where my darlin` sons were.

'Better not be off somewhere smoking dope,' said their school counsellor.

'My sons would never do that.'

In conversations with my two older sons and their friends over plates of sandwiches in the kitchen, I heard about the problems many faced while attending Skyline High School. Mormon teachers were said to have no interest in dealing with students outside of their religious point of view. According to the boys, Latter Day Saints' kids got preference, as did the jocks, or students enrolled in the Reserve Officers Training Corps programmes. The rest, according to what I heard, were dismissed as 'hippies' or 'weirdos.'

'We're treated like shit by some teachers, counsellors, and the school cops,' complained my sons and their friends. Their complaints were upsetting to hear. I believed all students merited respect and equal treatment, regardless of their religious beliefs, or whatever groups they belonged to. I talked to Eddie about what the boys had said, and their sense of being cast aside in school. Eddie and I met with some of the school counsellors and teachers to discuss the situation, and to make them aware that our sons and their friends were unhappy about what went on in the school. A few teachers shrugged their shoulders in response to our concerns; others were sympathetic; some denied that problems existed at Skyline High. Unfortunately, what happened to Cookie Collins showed tragically that problems did exist at the school.

Cookie's family had moved from California to Idaho Falls so the boys would have more open space. The Collins, Irish-American Catholics, were a close-knit family. Mr Collins started a pet food factory in Idaho Falls. I met Mrs Collins through her son, Cookie, a close friend of my son Steve. Cookie's older brothers played football for Skyline High and they acquired a reputation for playing a big part in winning the games for their school. Cookie had other interests besides football. He often came to our place with Steve to eat lunch. I liked having him come, as he'd eat anything I put on the table, not grumbling about the same old thing like some others I won't mention. Cookie looked like a poet. He wore his hair long, as did the other kids; he liked to listen to music, and talk about books. This being the late 1970s, having long hair meant a lot to the boys' self image. Cookie, under pressure, got involved in football, and expectations were that he would be a great player like his brothers. But the football jocks insisted that Cookie cut off his long curly locks in order to play the game. As they saw it: no sissy looking hair. Cookie refused. So some of the jocks attacked him, knocked him to the ground, and forcibly cut off his hair with scissors, and then shaved his head with a battery-operated shaver. The devastated, now bald-headed Cookie went home on his lunch hour, took a gun out of the closet and fired a bullet into his heart.

When Steve came home after learning that Cookie had killed himself, he and I cried and cried at the loss of a close friend and a wonderful lad. The jocks got away with what they did to Cookie. 'Too bad it happened,' was the story of the day. Cookie's parents and brothers were brokenhearted. The family had a Mass for their son at Holy Rosary Catholic Church in Idaho Falls where many pretty girls cried their eyes out at the loss of such a charming young man.

Another sad occurrence happened in the neighbourhood when two brothers shot their father in the head as he slept on the sofa. The two boys attended the same school as my sons. The older of the two boys was accused of pulling the trigger. He seemed to be a quiet and polite young person. Rumour had it that the whole family were fearful of displeasing the father who ruled the roost. The father insisted the boys do as he bid. He would not allow the teenage boys to dress or wear their hair as fashion dictated. Instead he shaved their heads like a set of billiard balls. It was said that the dad also behaved in a heavy-handed way towards their mother. To make a long story short, the boys shot the man, took the body in a truck, and left it near a ghost town far away from Idaho Falls. The next spring a hungry bear uncovered the body, leaving the head intact with bullet holes letting in the light of day. A sheriff traced the killing back to the sons, and they were arrested and sent to a juvenile detention centre.

Idaho Falls was a harsh place for young people who resisted the black-and-white conformity promoted by the city fathers. Especially hurt were boys in their teens who could not be forced to fit a mould.

Fears about kids smoking marihuana gripped us all. I'd never seen a pot plant. Rob and Steve had their own bedrooms where they kept their own stuff, and listened to rock music. Like most teenage boys, they kept their bedroom doors locked. 'Keep Out' signs were posted on their doors, not to be ignored. I respected their wishes, but, when one of the boys forgot or did not bother to lock the door to his bedroom, I took it as a chance to clean up the room. I opened the bedroom closet and discovered a beautiful, green-fringed plant growing in a pail underneath a string of grow lights.

I thought my sons were wonderful. Imagine them growing such a lovely plant to give me, probably for my birthday. I'd discount all the bad things adults were saying about the younger generation after seeing this vision of nature in the closet, almost palm tree size. Seeing such a sight would gladden the heart of any American mother. My sons must have been thinking of Jack and the Beanstalk and those magic beans when they planted the tree in the closet. I filled the teapot with fresh water and gingerly sprinkled the plant as tenderly as sprinkling powder on a baby's bum. When Eddie came home from work, I told him about the boys' hidden treasure. He gave me a serious look, rushed down the stairs to the bedroom, opened the closet door and began to uproot the majestic plant from the pot. I let out a cry of protest at the sight of something so lovely being ripped to shreds. 'It's marihuana, ' said my husband.

'Marihuana?' I repeated, remembering all the dangerous effects of the drug I'd read about in the newspaper. Jack and the Beanstalk me eye, I thought. Still, tearing the lovely plant up by the roots seemed overkill.

A turning point in my life occurred on March 20, 1979, with the nuclear near-meltdown at Three Mile Island in Harrisburg, Pennsylvania. The local news in Idaho Falls and the national news on television showed viewers the alarming possibility of a man-made disaster. The nuclear reactor at Three Mile Island overheated, releasing radioactive gas. Thousands of residents living in the area fled to emergency shelters. President Jimmy Carter went to Harrisburg to see the consequences for himself. The meltdown was described as the worst nuclear disaster in US history.

When discussing the fiasco no one wanted to ask the scary question whether such a thing could happen at the Idaho nuclear testing site. On hearing a young woman who worked with my husband say she might be sent back to Three Mile Island as part of a cleanup crew, I told her she might want to reconsider. She had recently married and wanted to have children. 'Any exposure to radioactive gas would be unhealthy for a potential mother,' I told her. The shit hit the fan. One of the big bosses overheard me. Eddie got tagged and brought into the office the next day. He 'needed to re-educate me about nuclear issues,' according to his supervisor at the site. Eddie felt and looked embarrassed at having to discuss the incident with me. 'Shit, shite and cauliflowers!' I hissed on hearing the dictate. 'I live in the United States of America, not Éireann go Brágh. I've no intention of buttoning my lip.' Instead of being 're-educated', I decided to read up on nuclear issues regarding its health risks. Ed, wisely, let the incident slip away like the morning dew.

I viewed myself as an ordinary woman who wanted to know more about the goings-on at the nuclear site, aware also of what might happen to felines seeking out information not meant for their eyes. Although I had little formal education it did not prevent me from learning on my own and keeping an eye on events of the day. I began to read pamphlets, news accounts, and newspaper articles on life at the Idaho National Laboratories scattered across the south Idaho desert.

Using my mind in this new way, outside of the usual domestic issues, made me consider going back to school, knowing I'd have to start at the bottom of the scale. I read in the local newspaper that free adult basic education classes were being offered at the YMCA in downtown Idaho Falls. Upon registration, each individual would be given an assessment to determine his or her educational level. Dropouts and others who needed to improve their educational level were invited to attend classes taught by professional public school teachers. I read and reread the notice, hemming and hawing whether or not I should take advantage of the learning opportunity. False pride stood in the way. I'd have to shift my image from corporate wife to uneducated immigrant, who needed to start at the bottom of the educational ladder. I thought about my brother's children and countless others back on the foggy little island who would have to leave school and begin to make a living at the young age of fourteen. In the face of those others trying to make the most of their meagre choices my struggle with false pride seemed stupid. When I discussed going back to school with Eddie and Ed Jr, they thought it a good idea, but a little bit odd. Robert and Stephen, now at university, liked the idea. Eddie gladly offered to cover any expenses needed for me to go back to school. He proved once again that old adage: 'Love is not afraid of giving too much.'

I talked the idea over with Dr C. I still saw him occasionally to make sure my depression would not overwhelm me again. He encouraged me; he told me to write a book about my life. 'It would help other people who read it,' he said sincerely.

'Maybe some day,' I replied, 'but it will be down the road a way.'

Back to school

Only a scattering of students showed up for the basic education classes at the YMCA. A woman from Taiwan and myself were the only adults enrolled in the basic English, writing and arithmetic classes taught by Nancy, our teacher. A class in English as a second language had six genteel looking Japanese ladies, all beautifully and fashionably dressed. Their nuclear scientist husbands had been working at the Idaho atomic site for a year or more under a US government exchange programme. The English classes had been created for the visiting wives. Sue, originally from Taiwan, came to Idaho Falls when she married her American husband, now a machinist for the Navy at the atomic site. The couple had three small children. Sue explained to Nancy that she needed to improve her English because she wanted to become an air stewardess. She'd seen the glamorous images of the stewardess in magazines and yearned to work for Pan American Airways. By marrying an American and coming to America, she thought becoming a stewardess would be a piece of cake. Two weeks into the classes though, Sue had to drop out because she couldn't find an affordable babysitter. Nancy felt very sorry about losing her other student. She also lamented the fact that so few were taking the free classes. She knew that there were a number of people, young and old, who could benefit from them.

I became the focus of her excellent teaching and she became my role model. With her assistance and knowledge, I got through elementary lessons, secondary school materials, and on my way to a high school education in three months. In the meantime, being a student, having such a wonderful teacher, and occasionally listening to the instructor teaching English basics to the Japanese ladies, added great interest to my life. Nancy had her feet planted firmly on democratic ground, unlike the instructor who taught the Japanese visitors. Nancy and I would listen in on her instruction. Her English lessons included teaching the Japanese women tips on going shopping for clothing. 'Ladies, repeat after me: Ralph Lauren. Ralph Lauren,' she articulated over and over like a drill instructor. 'Walf Lauren, Walf Lauren,' repeated the ladies. After fifteen minutes of getting nowhere teaching the foreign students how to talk like a lifelong American English teacher, the instructor gave up: 'Tea time.'

The Japanese students brought all kinds of goodies to share. Their families back in Japan sent edible delights not available in Idaho Falls. The gracious women placed a cloth on the table and set out delicate cookies, colourful candies, crackers and squares of dark green seaweed. Nancy and I were beckoned to join the tea party by one of the ladies. Her beautiful manicured fingernails were polished a cherry red that matched the tint of her lip colour.

The English as a second language teacher did not seem pleased that we had joined in the party. She reminded all of us that her husband, naval commander so and so, at the Navy site in the desert had been stationed in Japan and travelled extensively in the Orient. I wondered if the word Orient meant Japan in a foreign language. The refreshments offered to us were scrumptious — except for the seaweed squares. I bit into one, and it reminded me of the time I'd tried to eat a sod of turf as a child to quench hunger pains in my belly.

My teacher Nancy told me our class would be the last held at the YMCA because of low attendance. She would be transferred to the relatively new Vocational and Technical Training campus on the other side of Idaho Falls. Come September, I would have to finish my high-school equivalency classes there. I would have to pay tuition fees, so thank goodness for the bit of green put aside from my work in the bowling alley nursery. I didn't relish the idea of Eddie footing the bill for my education when he had his plate full covering university fees for Rob and Steve. Eddie Jr would be next in line.

September rolled around fast, and Vo-Tech beckoned. I knew the students who went to the technical school were mostly teenagers who wanted to specialize in mechanical training or to master other skills not offered in the regular high school. I'd be the age of the students' parents. Would they resent having an older person taking classes with them? Thankfully, Nancy would be there. All of the classes offered by the technical school were crowded. Thirty students were enrolled in my class, and much to my pleasant surprise some were older adults who were returning to school after being in the US military or were changing jobs. The younger students in the class had dropped out of high school and now hoped to get an equivalence certificate to get into the technical classes offered on campus.

Sadly, of the thirty enrolled in our class, only ten graduated from the programme. It took a lot of hard work and study for me to get the certificate; being out of school since the age of twelve made it harder than for some. Eddie celebrated my getting the high-school certificate by giving me, would you believe it, a bottle of Irish whiskey, red roses, and a cake lavished with cream. Upon graduation, my instructor, friend, and mentor Nancy encouraged me to apply to get into Idaho State University in Pocatello, Idaho. I hesitated, feeling unqualified but she insisted. I filled out an application, not expecting to receive a reply. Only when I got a letter of acceptance to attend the university in Pocatello did I realize the magnitude of this step—a girl from the gutter becoming a woman about to enter a place of higher learning.

Eddie drove me down to Pocatello to register at the university. He thought it a great opportunity even though we would see less of each other than ever before. I purchased my bus pass from Idaho Falls to Pocatello a distance of fifty miles each way. I'd travel five hundred miles a week on the bus. The bus left Idaho Falls at 6.30 in the morning and arrived back at 6.30 in the evening, so it became early to bed and early to rise. The night before going to classes at the university felt like Christmas Eve. I tried to imagine what surprises waited in store for a thirty-nine-year-old housewife entering a university.

After breakfast the following morning I heaved my book bag onto my shoulder, kissed Eddie goodbye, said, 'See you later' to my youngest son, who still scratched his head at the idea of me going off to the university. I headed out into the breaking September morning in the direction of the parking lot to catch the bus for Pocatello.

I joined a group of people, looking half dazed, waited for the chartered bus for Idaho State University, in Pocatello. The morning air felt chilly as we waited for our transportation to arrive. As soon as we were seated in the bus, the majority of the passengers hunkered down in the seats and went to sleep until we arrived at our destination. Kevin, the bus driver, aware of his sleeping passengers, kept his radio on low as he drove down the freeway like a bat out of hell covering the fifty-mile stretch in an hour. 'Poky,' he shouted out over the heads of the sleepers, coming to a standstill. 'See ye all at five sharp this evening. Be on time or walk back to Idaho Falls, yak, yak, yak.'

I took the campus map out of my pocket when we arrived at the university to find the building where my first class would be. The title of the class, 'Introduction to Sociology', sounded interesting, but I had no idea of its content. In my excitement I got a bit confused and went into the English department, my heart rocking in my chest like a rocket struggling to get off its base. 'Excuse me, please,' I said to the first person I saw in the building, 'Is this where sociology classes are held?'

The tall serious man looked at me and at the map shaking in my hand and said, 'I am Professor So-and-so — do I look like a sociologist?'

'I don't know — I've never seen one. I'm a new student to the university.'

'You certainly took a long time to get here. You must be twice the age of our regular freshmen. The sociology department is in the next building.'

'Thank you,' I said adding, 'I'm aware of being an older student and not a pup like yourself, Mr Professor whoever the hell ye are.'

I found my class in sociology and listened with four ears as the professor, originally from Iran, taught the class in his difficult English.

During the semester my professor made it plain how much he despised the middle class in the United States and listed how they curtailed social justice at every turn. I concurred, especially after studying Karl Marx and his critique of capitalism. Marx's stuff made my head spin. Now I understood why the poor were poor and the rich got richer and made damn sure they stayed that way by any means possible. I could not wait to share such mind-blowing information with my husband. I wondered why he never spoke of the writing of Karl Marx — surely he studied him at the university. The only Marx he'd mentioned up to now were the loony Marx Brothers of movie fame. I'd become a revolutionary on the side of the proletariat, no doubt about it, until the topic of 'patriarchy' got discussed in class. Hearing about the male system of power and domination over women gave me fits. Patriarchy seemed more evil than unrestrained capitalism and its exploitation of the masses. Male domination of women justified by them having a willie instead of a ball of yarn left me speechless.

Our professor's lectures on the 'Protestant Work Ethic' decreased my desire to become a wealthy woman, considering how much work it required. Dr S stopped me on the way out of class and wanted to know if I liked my class in sociology? He detected my faded 'Irish brogue,' as he put it. He seemed surprised that an Irish immigrant lived in remote Idaho Falls instead of the more populated areas like Boston or New York. 'We're both immigrants,' he said. He asked if I were going to the social in the afternoon put on by Iranian students. Other students from my class would be there.

I'd followed the Iranian Revolution of 1979, on American television. Ayatollah Khomeini and his followers overthrew the US-backed Shah. The United States government did not like the change of events — not one little bit. I recalled how angry the followers of the Ayatollah were as they set fire to the flag of the United States in street demonstrations in Iran as a protest for the United States backing of the Shah whom they claimed was a dictator. The Iranian students putting on the social at the student centre had come to the US when the Shah got booted. The Ayatollah Khomeini must be an Iranian-style pope, I thought to myself, the way his followers kissed the ground he walked on. All I really knew of the Middle East came from stories written about Ali Baba and the Forty Thieves. I admired the adventures of Ali Baba as much as I liked the adventures of Fionn Mac Cumhail.

Lively Middle Eastern music played in the background as the Iranian students handed us small cups of dark black tea, sweet as honey. They also offered honey-dripped cookies that melted in the mouth, along with dates, figs and nuts. The young Iranian men and women spoke English clear as a bell. Over coffee one of the women told me she planned on graduating with a degree in biology. I found out that the female students roomed together in a boarding house in Pocatello. Fatima giggled as she explained how their brothers and cousins watched the girls' every move. 'They don't want us to marry American men. They want us to marry Iranian men just like them.' I learned that the parents of the students had fled for their lives after the fall of the Shah, and that's what had brought them to the United States. The parents lived in California not in Pocatello. Upon graduation the Iranian students planned to find jobs in California close to where their relatives lived.

I drank cup after cup of the dark sweet tea, savouring each mouthful and happy to be in the company of the young people. I noticed a young female student from my English class sitting and laughing with an Iranian student, a look-a-like of the young Elvis Presley in *Jail-*

house Rock, pout-mouth and all. The blonde American girl and the Iranian double for Elvis Presley appeared to relish each other, causing curious glances in their direction from some of the other Iranian men and women in the room.

Before leaving the party, the student from my English class and her Iranian escort came over to say 'Hi' to me. The young Iranian man noticed the Aran sweater over my shoulders for the trip home on the bus. He pointed to it, saying, 'Irish? I know a little history about Ireland.'

'I've been away a long time now,' I told him.

'Ireland and England don't like each other, isn't that so?'

'Yes,' I replied, feeling faint stirrings of Irish nationalism. Before I could blink, I blurted out, 'If you want to know, I detest Margaret Thatcher.'

'Are you a supporter of the IRA?' he asked, surprised at my candour.

'I don't like Thatcher.'

He sat down opposite me, sipping strong black tea while his friend acted bored.

'Some of the student revolutionaries who opposed the Shah in the Islamic revolution in 1979, sympathized with Bobby Sands' hunger strike action to end British rule in Northern Ireland.' This information astonished me. I'd heard and read about the IRA hunger strikers in the Maze Prison in Belfast. Thatcher let Bobby Sands and the other IRA political prisoners die. 'My brother wrote me about what happened,' I told Mohammed. He said that students who opposed the Shah all sympathized with Bobby Sands. They had Winston Churchill Street in Tehran, where the British embassy is located, re-named Bobby Sands Street. 'That kind of information never made it into the US news as far as I know,' I replied. I told Mohammed it surprised me anyone in Iran would have the slightest interest in what took place in Northern Ireland.

The Iranian students' social had been an interesting and pleasant experience. I would likely bump into some of the students on campus; hopefully, they would say hello to a woman the same age as their own moms.

My brain constantly churned from being exposed to the theories of Emile Durkheim, Max Weber, Karl Marx, George Herbert Mead, Charles Horton Cooley, Sigmund Freud, and to feminism, patriarchy, and above all else, to insights into the working of capitalism as an economic system. Ever since early childhood my mind had tried to grasp the gap between the rich and the poor. I knew that living in poverty had nothing to do with being lazy, being ugly, being dull minded, or having low morals. Studying the writings of Karl Marx awoke my mind like never before. I wished my parents had had a chance to read what Marx wrote. They would come to see that they were not to blame for our family living in poverty. They did the best they could under extreme circumstances, as did others struggling for a bite to eat.

I finished my first semester at the university and felt forever changed by the experience. Professor S inspired me to consider sociology as a major. I looked forward to spending more time with Eddie discussing ideas that I encountered at the university — over mugs of tea, he still declined alcohol. Robert and Stephen were coming home from the university to spend Christmas with us, and Eddie, still in high school, would be glad to have more of my attention. I also planned to see Dr C to reassure myself that my depression remained in check.

Returning to school had given me confidence and a new perspective on the world. I did not want such changes falling asunder. I thanked God for having given me a wonderful husband who supported me. Yet I found myself struggling with unspoken thoughts: did I want to resettle in the domestic nest, and let the rest of the world go by? I berated myself for such selfish musings. At the age of forty, I still wanted to see if I could accomplish anything on my own.

I let my family know over the Christmas holiday that I took my education more seriously than ever and planned to get a bachelor's degree in sociology, even if I died in the attempt. Eddie and the boys were taken aback by my look of determination. 'Is this our Irish mother/wife?' begged the surprised looks spreading over each countenance. 'I'm a co-ed for God's sake,' I joked, adding, 'a re-entry woman, a non-traditional student and a sweatshop warrior. How's that?'

'Grrrreat,' came the unified response.

'I made you guys spaghetti and meatballs. Set the table and let's have a beer. Up the rebels.'

My husband gave me a faint smile and the sweetest kiss. 'I love your cooking, Angie. Albertson's supermarket take-out meals don't measure up to your home prepared food.' 'Their roasted chicken is not bad,' I replied, hinting he'd consume a flock of the birds when I returned to the university in Pocatello for the spring semester and recommenced my hundred-mile round trip bus journey each day.

By the time the bus pulled into Idaho Falls from Pocatello in late evening, I didn't care whether I nibbled on chicken-wings or the carcass of a mouse as long as it tasted salty. Going back and forth between home and the university each week, and studying on the weekends, left little time for husband and wife stuff. Instead of cracking the bedsprings, I had to crack the textbooks.

When I asked Ed if he thought Freud had it right about the 'unconscious' and the 'tip of the iceberg' thing, he responded by asking me to go for German applesauce pancakes at our favourite restaurant. Because of having to concentrate hard at my studies, I turned down most of his invitations, feeling like a bitch for ignoring him as never before even in stressful times. Had I had more of a background in formal education, it might have been easier.

Trying to brighten things up, I informed Eddie and Eddie JR that I had signed up for a class in social problems and one in abnormal psychology. I promised to discuss both classes as the semester progressed, hoping to re-embrace the pair, conscious of having derailed our home life. Neither one should be expected to share in my derring-do or giddy-up feelings about venturing beyond the garden gate.

I met Kara on the bus at the beginning of the new semester. She and I were the same age. The minute Kara stepped on the bus, eyes turned in her direction. She looked like a fashion model in some magazine instead of a woman on her way to classes at Idaho State University in Pocatello. She looked down the length of the bus for a seat. The young men moved over towards the far side of their seats making a space for her to sit down. She saw me sitting by myself and came down the aisle and sat down beside me. She shifted her book bag from her shoulder and tucked it under the seat. She smiled and said, 'Hi, I'm Kara.' I introduced myself to her, glad that I'd have someone to talk with on the long and tedious bus ride to Pocatello. Kara began to fill me in on her life.

Her husband, a Navy commander, had been transferred to Idaho Falls where he worked at the Idaho National Laboratory advanced test reactor, which ran experiments for the US Navy. She hated Idaho Falls. Her husband either worked all day out in the Idaho desert at the nuclear site or went back to Washington DC. The couple had two children, a girl and a boy. 'I'm a Navy site wife. Even worse, I am a commander's wife. He has a doctorate in nuclear physics,' Kara said.

'My husband also works at the site,' I told her. 'I'd rather be a non-traditional student, a re-entry woman, a displaced homemaker than a corporate site wife,' I blurted.

Kara gave me an earful about her personal life while we were riding back and forth on the bus. Some Americans were like that, they didn't really know you from Adam, but spilled the beans anyhow. Kara told me that she had a bachelor's degree from some women's college in Virginia. 'More like a finishing school,' were her words. Her parents saved and scrimped to send her to the rich college in the hope that she would meet and marry a Navy officer.

'Our college was just across the state line from Annapolis, Maryland. The cadets were invited by our sorority to socials and dances. That's how I met my husband. The college educated me to be a good naval officer's wife.' Her husband went on to command his own ship out of San Diego, California. 'It was such an honour for our family. The whole crew adopted our family as their own.' She paused a while before commenting, 'Now we have been stationed at the armpit of the universe for going on two years.'

'I guess Idaho Falls isn't like San Diego?'

She gave me a hound dog's look. 'I'm getting a Master's degree in Speech Pathology. This is my third semester.'

I wondered if her Navy commander husband knew how much she hated living in Idaho Falls. Obviously, she'd been the belle of the ball before coming to live in the Eastern Idaho desert.

I lowered my head against the headrest on the back of the seat and wondered 'Are there happy people anymore?'

Before our bus reached the parking lot in Pocatello, Kara leaned over towards me and whispered with a giggle in her voice, 'I'm having affairs with two professors on campus: one prefers anal sex and the other is a cuddly teddy bear.' My head sprang forward like a spring on a mousetrap.

'You're joking! You would never dare do such a thing. I know we just met, but you don't look like a person who would do such a thing.'

'Time to get wise, marble eyes.'

'What would your husband, the commander and nuclear physicist, say if he found out?'

'He has lady friends back in Washington DC he spends time with when he's back in the nation's capital on business.'

'The dirty bamboozler,' I exclaimed, wondering how he could do such a thing.

'We've grown apart. I want a life of my own other than being a Navy site wife, 'Kara declared. 'Have you ever had an affair?' she asked me.

'Of course not. And I've been married for twenty years.'

'You don't know what you're missing. You're probably Catholic, am I right?'

'Yep.'

The bus pulled into the parking lot. 'Let's go to the student lounge for coffee,' invited Kara. She nibbled on dry toast and sipped black coffee while I dug into a plate of scrambled eggs, greasy bacon, and marmalade toast. I gulped down large draughts of coffee as Kara talked about meeting her two 'boyfriends' in their hideouts after her classes for fun. 'You have sex with three men,' I burst out, 'and you're still standing?' She laughed and started to correct a part of my speech. 'You pronounce the word "three" as "tree". Like a tree that grows in the forest. It's "three", not "tree". Watch how I place my tongue and lips while I say "three".' 'Tree,' I repeated unable to make the 'th' sound she insisted upon.

'I think you have a speech impediment, 'Kara concluded.

'It's probably leftover Dublin sounds, not a speech whatever you call it,' I answered, feeling irritated by her smart alick assurance.

'I need to read a few chapters in my abnormal psychology book before class,' I said to the adulteress.

'See you later,' she smiled, waltzing on air instead of dragging her butt in a sling as penance for unholy trysts. Feeling virtuous, I opened the heavy psychology textbook that claimed to explain what made people tick. I wanted to gain insights into my own moods and the moods of others. An odd thing about living in the United States, it seems to me, is how some outrageous people are treated well while others are stamped as being mentally ill. Movie stars, celebrities and politicians are allowed to be as wild as monkeys in a zoo. Hippies, on the other hand, are called 'crazies' because they oppose war and violence. Who is crazy and who is not is the question of the day. I hoped my upcoming class in 'abnormal psychology' would furnish the answer.

There were over a hundred students in the class. I got a seat in front so I could see and hear better than back in the last row. A middle-aged woman walked to the podium carrying a fistful of papers and introduced herself. She had a head as wide as her shoulders, an indication of brilliance according to Irish legend. The professor explained to the class that she got into psychology in order to understand her own family problems. Briskly she jotted down three major psychotic disorders. She sounded out each psychotic term as if measuring a person for a strait-jacket.

Honest to God, the very sound of the words shocked the nervous system. Had my psychiatrist, Dr C, applied any one of the deadly psychotic terms to me when I sought help for depression, I would still be exiled in a fog. I recalled some facts learned in my sociology class from the previous semester dealing with the concept of power and how it is used in society. Those in positions of power and authority get to label and stigmatize others of lower rank. Who got sifted and sorted in society depended on peacocks not street sparrows.

There and then, I decided that sociology would be my major, not psychology. Calling people names for whatever reason did little good. I thought of raising my hand to make this point, but the earnest expression on the professor's face stalled my hand in midair.

After class, I skidded down the hill to the sociology department to my class in 'social problems'. I noticed a mix of students in the class. Most of them looked more scraggy than neat and tidy. I, on the other hand, had on my slim black skirt, green cashmere sweater and matching black fitted jacket, heels and pantyhose. The ones sitting up front sprawled this way and that among the seats waiting impatiently for the professor. My nose picked up the odour of pungent weeds coming from the front of the classroom. 'That's the smell of marijuana,' I thought, recalling my teenage sons and their friends' brief encounter with the 'evil foliage'. Two guys outfitted in Fidel Castro type uniforms with bushy beards were impatient, having to wait for the professor.

'Where the fuck is Blain?' spat out the blond guy, scrunching his face into a Halloween mask. The dark-haired grizzly turned around in his desk to gauge my response upon hearing the F word uttered out loud by his buddy.

I quietly looked towards the blackboard at the front of the room, keenly aware of feeling out of place in a roomful of students ten years my junior. I began to nibble the top of my pencil amid the increasing tension of waiting for the professor to show his or her self to the class.

A blond blue-eyed beachcomber type of a person entered our class, folder in hand. He looked sheepishly around the room, smiling at everyone and no-one in particular. 'I'd a hard time getting up this morning. Needed a couple of pots of coffee, 'he said by way of excuse for being four minutes late.

'Yeah, we know, 'called out the two Fidel Castro look-a-likes.

'You two guys back in my class for another semester? 'joked the professor.

'What kind of a bloody class is this going to be?' I thought. 'Maybe I'll switch back to psychology.'

As if reading my mind, the instructor looked straight at me as if I might be a mirage or an organizational spy. I returned his look without a flinch. He talked about what he proposed to cover for the semester. 'The ruling class in American society are responsible for social problems, not people on the bottom of the social hierarchy. We will examine "social stratification" and the effect stratification has upon your life chances.'

'Shit, here we go again. Say it like it is, brother,' rang out the pair of Castro fashion plates at the front of the class.

'Took us two years in 'Nam before we figured how this country is run,' remarked the blond guy.

'I have great trust in our American government,' said a young woman in the back. 'I don't see or live in a social hierarchy,' she argued. And the give and take about the issues continued back and forth like a game of ping-pong.

This sociology professor had the style of a Mike Jagger, jutting and prancing back and forth across the classroom in his tight blue jeans. He wore a blue floral long-sleeved shirt, the tail tucked into his pants. His curly blond hair made him resemble 'Little Boy Blue.' He'd been around the block a few times, I estimated. Probably drank and smoked pot like a heathen. He smiled a lot at the students. He really liked engaging the class in discussion and did not put anyone off if they agreed or disagreed with his views.

Our eyes met briefly across the room. He had no fear about criticizing the powerful in society. 'What kind of an American is this?' I wondered, not having been out of Idaho in years. He came originally from California which in my mind represented the land of milk and honey, rock n' roll, convertibles, movie stars, individual liberty, good

*Dr Michael Blain, sociology professor, speaking at
an anti-war demonstration at Idaho State
University 1981.*

pot and, currently, 'too many damn defense contractors'.

One student asked him what he thought of the current president, Ronald Reagan, and his wife Nancy. 'Reagan represents the rich and the corporate elite.' It didn't seem that his class in social problems would cause students to doze off, whether they agreed with him or not.

After class, I went to the student union hoping to run into Kara. I'd tell her about Blain and his war howl against the power elite in American society. 'Kelly the boy from Killane' came to mind on listening to his lectures blasting the high and mighty.

> *Tell me who is that giant with gold curling hair*
> *He who rides at the head of your band?*
> *Seven feet in his height with some inches to spare*
> *And he looks like a king in command.*

Two weeks into the semester, I came down with a terrible case of the shingles. While recovering, I pondered on the changes going on in my life. Concerns about domesticity gave way to erotic musings. Were the painkillers causing brain fever? Why else would a forty-year-old female start to wonder about sexual development for the first time since leaving the Old Sod at the age of eighteen?

My upper legs looked like two red spotted salmon as a result of the shingles. The doctor inquired if I were experiencing much stress in my life? 'Stress can cause shingles,' he said. 'It's a bad dose,' I replied, 'but it's not caused by stress. I'm a relaxed person,' I lied.

Ed took over the household chores after work and did the cooking. No wife ever had such a loving and generous husband. Both our sons were able to attend the university because of his hard work, and our youngest boy would be joining them soon. Our family never lacked for anything because of him. Why was the sand shifting under my feet? Why this desire to move on?

My views of life and society had always been a bit different from my husband's. Now, mine were becoming more radical, more critical of what went on in society. Ed didn't complain about my changing views. He obviously thought it a passing fancy. He loved me. I could be an axe murderer and he'd remain loyal.

It took over two weeks for the shingles to subside. I could hardly wait to get back to my classes and re-engage in all the social and political debates. Dr Blain seemed pleased that I had returned. On the way in the door he exclaimed, 'I thought you dropped the class. Glad you're back. I missed you.'

'I'd shingles.'

'Shingles? Hope my lectures didn't cause them.'

'Not likely.'

The following Thursday a guest lecturer came to our class in social problems to discuss Native American problems. Our guest speaker, Dolores, identified herself as being from the Shoshone-Bannock Indian Reservation at Fort Hall, Idaho not far from Pocatello. The social problem that concerned her related to the contamination of the Snake River aquifer which ran through the reservation and was the sole source of clean water for the tribe.

Radiation waste from the Rocky Flats nuclear testing centre in Colorado got brought to the Idaho site for reprocessing. The waste leeched radiation into the ground that ended up in the Snake River aquifer. She also noted problems with the chemical processing plant at the desert site. She described the scientists and engineers who worked at the nuclear reactor site as 'white ghosts'.

As a parting shot, she told the class that some 'newcomers' who found employment at the nuclear site became 'arrow and pot-hunters' on weekends when they trespassed on Indian land and dug up artifacts for personal souvenirs. Dolores invited students in the class to ask questions or make comments regarding her presentation.

The pair of Vietnam vets told Dolores they were not surprised that the 'big shots' out at the site were concealing the fact that radiation was getting into the Snake River aquifer. They told her how the US government was using the air force to dump 'Agent Orange' over the Vietnamese countryside. 'Like Gold Medal flour falling every fucking where. Tons of the chicken shit!' I felt a need to add to the mix by telling the class how my husband had been told by the big boss to re-educate me about raising the issues of radiation and the safety of nuclear plants. 'The shit hit the fan,' I burst out before sealing my mouth.

The professor cast green-blue eyes in my direction while Dolores inquired, 'Do I discern that you have an accent?'

'I used to be Irish, ' I replied, feeling my face crimson. She looked at me in a serious way that made me say with humility, 'I'm an Irish blow-in.'

Dolores thanked our instructor for allowing her to address the class on issues concerning Native Americans. Only one other class on campus had allowed her to do so. This was because, as Blain informed the class, the administration at Idaho State University worked hand in glove with the Idaho National Engineering Laboratory. They got rewarded with cash grants to the university. 'The administration is not likely to publicly disagree with anything that goes on at the site in the desert.'

Dolores' discussion about the plight of Native Americans touched my heart. In some ways the Native Americans were treated much as the Irish were under British colonial rule. Anyone tampering with the source of life, the water supply, were barefaced crooks and grave robbers, it seemed to me, and deserved to be haunted by the spirits they disturbed.

On the way out after class an attractive younger woman remarked to all within earshot: 'Blain's a left wing radical, communist, and woman chaser.' I'd gathered from what he said in class that he wasn't in league with the Idaho Republicans who wanted the country to be a fortress, and toe-danced along with the Reagan Administration's denouncement of the Soviet Union as 'The Evil Empire and Godless Society. ' The Republicans viewed the INEL as a site for freedom. Exposing innocent US citizens to radiation by air or by drinking water seemed only a minor infringement.

Going back to Idaho Falls after a long day at the university became more of a strain. In spite of loving my family, I felt my life drifting elsewhere — more towards being a student at the university than a homebound woman. It became harder to shift states of mind. I refused to play the corporate site wife who had to clam up when it came to the nuclear industry. I made an appointment with Dr C as I had done for the last ten years to talk about issues on my mind.

Dr C listened with interest as I told him about my classes at the university. How sociology held my interest. Why I found 'abnormal psychology' to be a bit of a joke. He asked me if I were feeling anxious and depressed.

'Yes, now and then. But so are a lot of other people that I've met through my classes.'

'I see.'

'I think the world of you for helping me get better,' I reminded him.

'I could have lost you,' he reminded me. 'How are you and Ed getting along? He's a great guy and cares for you a great deal.'

'I know.'

'Anything wrong?'

'Oh! Sometimes I've a yearning to leave this history behind and scram.'

He smiled benignly. 'Don't we all. Taking your antidepressant pills regular?'

'Yup.'

'Anxious about anything?'

'Nooo. I suppose you want me to take these pills for ever. Continue therapy forever?'

'If you feel the need to.'

'I'm marooned.'

'Pardon?'

'Nothing. Being silly. What if I move to Pocatello?'

'Is Ed willing? Have you discussed it with him?'

'I'm the one with itchy feet.'

'Don't do anything rash. Call me if you make any decisions.'

'I will and I won't.'

'What does that mean, Angie? You will and you won't. How are your sons doing at the university?'

'Great.' I said. 'I like sociology. Are you aware the capitalist are primarily interested in making surplus profit above everything else? Socialism, on the other hand, is concerned with providing the necessities of life for all of the people.'

'Who is teaching your class in sociology?'

'A guy from California. Told the class he's a confirmed liberal.' Until then, I didn't have words to describe my political outlook. 'I'm a liberal too,' I told the doctor. 'I'm also anti-nuclear. I'm going to join a group on campus called Nuclear Counterbalance — my sociology professor suggested it.'

Dr C had little to say about what I intended to do. Instead he slatted his fingers together into a steeple as if contemplating a response. He gave me a look of disbelief.

'I want to be part of the anti-war movement. I think President Reagan and the Soviet Union might come to blows and have a nuclear war.'

The doctor fashioned his mouth to a tight ring and rocked back and forth in his chair, his fingers still fixed in a pyramid. He and I were painfully aware that our long relationship had ended. I'd set sail on a new course in life.

One day, my sociology professor asked me out for a beer and we talked about art and politics for hours not realizing the time was flying by. I knew he'd picked up potential girlfriends in his classrooms, or so the gossip said. He told me that he had recently ended an affair with a female professor on campus. In spite of my growing attraction to him, I saw him as a dirty dog for cheating on his wife. He told me that he and his spouse had an 'open marriage', whatever that meant. I began to avoid him after class. But in class our eyes continued to focus on each other. 'He's a sexy sinner,' I thought, and I didn't want to get caught up in his sinful ways. However, he was the only professor who publicly spoke out about social injustice, the futility of war, the ongoing danger of a potential nuclear showdown between the East and the West, and a host of other social issues that needed to be attended to.

I attended the die-in on the quad organized by Blain and other members of Nuclear Counterbalance on campus. The lovely Idaho spring afternoon made me conscious of the delights of being alive on a lovely planet. A siren gave off a mock warning that a nuclear war had started. One by one students fell on the grass as if dead or dying. I dropped face down on the grass. Blain appeared out of nowhere and dropped down on the lawn beside me. 'If this was the real thing we'd be dead in seconds. What would be your last wish?' We looked into each other's eyes, and he drew me close and kissed me. 'I love you,' he said. 'Don't be ridiculous,' I replied.

I made the most painful decision of my life when I moved out of my home in Idaho Falls to a rented room in Pocatello. I had ended my marriage of over twenty years. The sermon in stone, 'till death do us part', crumbled. I didn't go because of lack of love or respect for my husband of twenty years. I just wanted to move forward on my immigrant journey — and discover what the feck else might be around the corner.